D1593403

Out of the Silence

Quaker Perspectives on Pastoral Care and Counseling

Out of the Silence

Quaker Perspectives on Pastoral Care and Counseling

Edited by

J. Bill Ratliff

Pendle Hill Publications
Wallingford, Pennsylvania 19086

VNYS BX 7745
.O88 2001 c.1
KGQ020Z-2005

Copyright © 2001 by Pendle Hill

All rights reserved
For information, please address Pendle Hill Publications
Wallingford, Pennsylvania 19086-6099
1-800-742-3150

Library of Congress Cataloging-in-Publication Data

Out of the Silence: Quaker perspectives on pastoral care and
counseling/edited by J. Bill Ratliff.
     p. cm.
     Includes bibliographical references.
     ISBN 0-87574-939-9
  1.   Pastoral theology–Society of Friends. 2. Pastoral
     counseling. I. Ratliff, J. Bill (John Bill), 1939-   .
BX7745 .O88 2001
253'.088'286--dc21
     2001036912

TABLE OF CONTENTS

QUAKER PERSPECTIVES

REFLECTIONS ON PRACTICE

STORIES OUT OF THE SILENCE

Acknowledgments

Practitioners of pastoral care and counseling tend to do little writing for publication, due to the press of other duties. The annual conference *Quakers in Pastoral Care and Counseling* has provided the ongoing support, without which this book would not have been written. Our deep appreciation goes to family and friends who have supported each writer to put her/his thoughts on paper. Persons at work have, for the most part, also supported our doing this and, in some cases, helped us find the time to write.

A special word of thanks goes to the Earlham School of Religion, which has supported *Quakers in Pastoral Care and Counseling* through the years with staff assistance and support for the editor. Phyllis Wetherell has provided staff support and effective assistance with this book, for which I am deeply grateful. Also, thanks to Paul Dodds for helping with research for some footnotes and to all those who read various drafts of parts of the book.

List of Contributors

Jane Brown - *Chair of Human Development, McGregor of Antioch University, Yellow Springs, OH*

Muriel (Mickey) Edgerton - *Hospice Pastoral Counselor, Holy Redeemer Home Health Agency, Philadelphia, PA*

Ingrid Fabianson - *Social Worker in a Substance Abuse Treatment Center and Chaplain in Psychriatic Hospital, Richmond, IN*

Maureen Graham - *Mental Health Specialist for Jackson County, Medford, OR; small pastoral counseling practice in Ashland, OR*

Worth G. S. Hartman - *Chaplain, Hendicks Community Hospital, Danville, IN*

List of Contributors (continued)

Felicity Kelcourse - *Assistant Professor of Pastoral Care and Counseling, Director of Training for Pastoral Psychotherapy, Christian Theological Seminary, Indianapolis, IN*

M. Susanne Kromberg - *Chaplain, Stevens Hospital, Edmonds, WA*

Keith R. Maddock - *Graduate of Toronto School of Theology, former youth minister living in Toronto, Ontario, Canada*

Judith A. Owens - *Assistant Director, Penn Council for Relationships, Voorhees, NJ*

J. Bill Ratliff - *Professor of Pastoral Care and Counseling, Earlham School of Religion, Richmond, IN*

Marthajane Robinson- *Private practice, Philadelphia, PA*

Daniel O. Snyder - *Teacher, Pendle Hill: Quaker Center for Study and Contemplation, Wallingford, PA*

Deborah E. Suess - *Pastor of West Branch Friends Church, West Branch, IA*

William P. Taber - *Recorded Minister of Ohio Yearly Meeting, Conservative, retired teacher of Quakerism and Spirituality at Pendle Hill, Wallingford, PA*

Carolyn Wilbur Treadway - *Pastoral Counselor in solo practice, Connections Counseling and Resource Center, Normal, IL*

INTRODUCTION

Bill Ratliff

The idea for this book began in the early 1990s, shortly after the beginning of the annual *Gathering for Quakers in Pastoral Care and Counseling,* which attracts Friends in the helping professions from across the country. A number of us at that Gathering felt that Quakers who were in the broad area of the helping professions, and more specifically practicing in the discipline of pastoral care and counseling, had something in particular to contribute to the discipline and to our Quaker communities. We are glad now to offer this book as the fruit of our work together.

The Religious Society of Friends has been concerned, from its inception, with the way religious faith is lived in daily life. Friends have also historically nurtured close-knit communities, more set apart from the world at some times than is true in the present. Both of these factors have produced a caring for others that has been strong and deep and consistent with Quaker beliefs and practice. As a result, pastoral care has been a central part of the life of the Quaker community.

The rise of interest in spirituality among the helping professions makes this a good time for Quaker practitioners to join in the public discussion. We want to communicate with all practitioners who are interested in how their religious faith informs their practice. We hope to stimulate and to support those persons who work as caregivers: pastors and other leaders of faith communities, chaplains, pastoral counselors, members of Oversight Committees in Quaker Meetings and members of pastoral care teams/boards in other faith groups, seminary teachers and students, as well as mental health counselors, psychologists, social workers, and psychiatrists.

For those unfamiliar with the Religious Society of Friends, this brief overview summarizes basic beliefs and practices. Wilmer Cooper's *A Living Faith*[1] offers a comprehensive discussion.

Following are some of the basic beliefs and practices:

1. Direct access to God. Beginning with Fox's experience, Quakers believe that everyone has access to God, without the need for any intermediary. Indeed, there is "that of God" in every person, as Fox put it.[2] This belief results in elevating the inner experience of the person, along with testing that experience in community.

2. Worship. In Fox's time, worship began with people gathering in one place and waiting upon God. Silence prevailed until a person was given a message. Since everyone had access to God, any person could rise and speak, as she or he received a message from God. Every person is a minister. The universal ministry, in which everyone was a minister, was distinguished from specialized ministry, which recognized particular gifts.[3] Later, people were called to specific pastoral roles on the American frontier in the middle to late nineteenth century. More pastoral Friends exist in the world today than do "unprogrammed" Friends, the name used for those who primarily worship out of the silence.

   Because Quakers meet together for worship, the groups were originally called meetings, rather than churches. Today, some pastoral Friends use the word "church." A pastoral Meeting for Worship will include many of the elements used in any other Protestant worship service, with two exceptions: a significant period of silence will occur either before or after the sermon and sometimes in both places; and the presiding minister listens to the Spirit during the worship service and may alter her or his sermon or lay it aside, as the Spirit directs.

3. Business Procedures. A business session is called a meeting for business and sometimes is called a meeting for worship for business, to underscore the central place of worship in the conduct

of business. Each business session begins and ends with worship. Because everyone has access to the truth, then everyone must be listened to, in making decisions. The Spirit of God leads to unity, Quakers believe, as each person seeks to know the truth. The clerk of the meeting prayerfully listens to what is being said, while also listening to the Spirit. The clerk will articulate the sense of the meeting on a particular issue under consideration, which does not have to reflect unanimity or even majority sentiment. The persons attending will then discern if the clerk's statement indeed does seem to reflect the sense of the meeting as the Spirit directs. If a person cannot be in unity with the sense of the meeting, there are two options: she or he may wish to be recorded in the minutes as standing aside, so that the meeting can move forward. On the other hand, if the matter is serious enough, the person may find it necessary to "stand in the way" of the decision. This action does not often occur and is treated very seriously when it does. The meeting then has to labor with that person or the issue, until clarity is found. No action is taken on the issue under discussion while this laboring goes on.

4. Testimonies. The inner experience manifests itself outwardly in daily living. "Let your lives speak" is an often-quoted phrase among Quakers. Formal theology has been suspect as separated from life. Quakerism is a way of life rather than a set of beliefs. The focus is on: To what does a person's life testify? What are called "testimonies" have served as guides for the ethical life for Quakers. While additional ones could be listed, Wilmer Cooper suggests the following basic social testimonies today:

> Integrity - Honesty lies at the heart of Quakerism. As Cooper states, "It is a testimony rooted in the Quaker respect for truthfulness."[4]

> Simplicity - Simplicity in lifestyle is the aim, although it is not as severe today among most Quakers as it has been in

some times in history. The historic black clothing without ornamentation comes out of this testimony. Today simplicity more often refers to being good stewards of all that we have, while being sensitive to the needs of others.[5]

Peace - This may be the best known of the testimonies. The Mennonites and Church of the Brethren also share this ethic.[6] Peace does not mean simply the absence of war, but includes active justice-making and conflict mediation, which take away the occasion for war.

Equality - This testimony builds on the basic belief that everyone has access to God, and that access is equal. From the beginning, women were treated equally with men, although that was not true later on and even today, in some places. Concern for Native Americans, the imprisoned, the enslaved, the insane and the poor also grew out of this testimony.[7]

This book considers the ways in which these beliefs and practices have influenced the pastoral care and pastoral counseling that Quakers have provided. Certain themes emerge all of which are not exclusive to Quakers, of course.

First is a basic respect for others, a respect which comes from the heart of God. If everyone has access to God, then everyone, including those who are currently receiving care, has access to truth. Persons are listened to, then, not just to find out where they are and what they need, although those areas are important. They are listened to because they bear potential revelations of God for themselves and others. The caring relationship can be revelatory for both care giver and care receiver. A basic sacramental quality exists in life and in relationships, and especially in caring relationships. This theme shines in almost every chapter, although it may not be directly stated.

Second, because Quakers are not bound to a liturgical tradition, but instead to an inner, spiritual experience, they are free to be flexible and adaptable in ministry situations. The central concern is to discern how God's Spirit may be directing the care giver at any given moment. As a result, Quakers who have never preached in their life or administered Holy Communion may do so as chaplains in institutions. Others may decide that they can do one or the other, or perhaps neither, with integrity. The issue is to preserve integrity, whether the outward act is performed or not.

Third, Quaker pastoral care follows the leading of the Holy Spirit. While Quakers are now trained in seminaries, in Clinical Pastoral Education, and in pastoral counseling training programs, these skills and abilities will be used in the service of God's leading them in a specific situation. Quakers pay attention to their spiritual attunement before, during, and after a pastoral care encounter. As anyone knows who provides pastoral care, great courage is often required and great discernment as to what to say or not to say. For the Quaker in pastoral care situations, courage and discernment come from a spiritual center informed by technical training.

Fourth, Quaker pastoral care providers do not rest easy with power and hierarchy, especially when injustice is perceived. Quakers providing pastoral care are concerned not only with the persons but also with the systemic and organizational problems that have contributed to individual problems. This concern of Quakers means that they often question authority and need to be convinced personally concerning an issue, rather than taking it on the word of a teacher or supervisor. The questioning has caused some problems for Quaker students in Clinical Pastoral Education (CPE), for example. Unfortunately, some supervisors with CPE have interpreted some Quakers' difficulties with CPE as having to do solely with personality issues and have not been willing to look at cultural and religious differences, or consider legitimate critiques of the CPE program or the institution. Depending upon the context and their own openness, supervisors may see Quaker CPE students either as irksome trouble-makers or as creative leaven in the loaf.

Fifth, pastoral care belongs to the whole community. Because every Quaker is a minister, every person has the responsibility and possibility of providing care for others. In practice, Quaker communities recognize that some are gifted in caring and there are often committees of overseers that attend to the personal and psychological needs of the community. Even in pastoral Meetings, however, the work of the pastor does not take away the responsibility of everyone to provide pastoral care. For this reason, Quakers have been slow to accept pastoral care and counseling as a professional discipline. With the difficult experiences of Quakers in their own faith communities and in their own lives, they have become more open to care from persons who are professionally trained.

Finally, many personal stories fill the chapters in this book. The focus of Quakerism on the inner experience and the focus of pastoral care on the relational experience with the care receiver come together in the telling of stories. Reflection on experience, which is at the heart of modern pastoral care, and reflection on experience, which is also at the heart of Quakerism, join easily. Quakerism diverges only when it is more concerned with the faithfulness of listening to God in the experience.

The book is divided into three sections. In the first section, the chapters focus on Quaker perspectives of faith and practice which inform pastoral care and counseling. Maureen Graham, after a thorough description of Quaker faith, looks at the theme of respect for "that of God" through three lenses: centered presence, relational engagement, and prophetic witness. Bill Taber describes his understanding of how to adapt an early Quaker worship practice called an "opportunity" for use in pastoral care settings. Felicity Kelcourse discusses the subtleties of discernment. Bill Ratliff puts both concern for discernment and respect for that of God to the test of use in cross-cultural settings. Finally, Deborah Suess and Ingrid Fabianson look at two very context-specific ministry situations that call on Quakers to trust continuing revelation:

1) programmed meeting for worship and 2) the Alcoholics Anonymous program.

In the second section, authors focus on practical experiences in their professional and religious work. Judith Owens weaves a sacred thread between her personal inner life spiritually and her skilled training in listening as a therapist. Keith Maddock considers children in the faith community as givers and receivers of pastoral care. Daniel Snyder wrestles with the challenge to hold domestic violence offenders accountable at the same time one sees "that of God" in them. Carolyn Treadway gives nuanced details about the process of transformation in love that clients experience. Marthajane Robinson explores the meaning of healing especially with the therapeutic use of touch in finding the balance between spiritual listening and technical training. Susanne Kromberg details some of the systemic and theoretical problems Quakers face in training programs.

In the third and final section of this book, three chapters focus primarily on the telling of stories. Jane Brown looks at "that of God" in the caregiver, the care receiver, and in the relationship. Worth Hartman recounts a story in his personal life and a story in his role as a hospital chaplain, and reflects on these stories. Muriel (Mickey) Edgerton then gives us four stories from her work as a hospice pastoral counselor, all of which demonstrate God's healing work.

The mystery of God's healing work is profound. Friends often turn to a teaching of George Fox for guidance in the way of life that trusts that mystery and gives rise to healing.

> Friends, in the power of life and wisdom, and in the dread of the Lord God of life, and heaven, and earth, dwell, that in the wisdom of God over all ye may be preserved, and be a terror to all the adversaries of God, and a dread, answering that of God in them all, spreading the Truth abroad, awakening the witness, Confounding deceit, gathering up out of transgression into the life, the covenant of

life and peace with God. . . . Bring all into the worship of God. . . . So the ministers of the Spirit must minister to the spirit that is transgressed and in prison, which hath been in captivity up to every one; whereby with the same spirit people must be led out of captivity up to God, the Father of spirits, and do service to him and have unity with him, with the Scriptures and one with another. And this is the word of the Lord God to you all, and a charge to you all in the presence of the living God, be patterns, be examples in all countries, places, islands, nations, wherever you come; that your carriage and life may preach among all sorts of people, and to them. Then you will come to walk cheerfully over the world, answering that of God in every one; whereby in them ye may be a blessing, and make the witness of God in them bless you.

When we center our lives in worship, we are empowered to recognize Truth, awaken people's witness to it and bring broken spirits out of captivity into unity with God. Our lives are to be lived sacramentally in order to preach of the life and wisdom that comes from worship. And thus, we will know blessing and cheer, answering that of God in every one. In healing work these teachings take on particular power as the authors in this anthology know well. We hope these chapters will encourage all ministers of pastoral care and counseling especially by calling to the powerful intersection of spiritual life and healing. We pray that all of us will increasingly find ways to embody the love of God in our daily life and ministry.

Notes

1. Wilmer Cooper, *A Living Faith* (Richmond, IN: Friends United Press, 1990).

2. *Journal of George Fox*, edited by John L. Nickalls (London: Religious Society of Friends, 1975), 263.

3. Dean Freiday, ed., *Barclay's Apology in Modern English* (Philadelphia, PA: Friends Book Store, 1967), 214f.

4. Cooper, *A Living Faith*, 104.

5. Cooper, *A Living Faith*, 105f.

6. Cooper, *A Living Faith*, 106-109.

7. Cooper, *A Living Faith*, 109-111.

Quaker Perspectives

The Importunate Friend

The Parable of the Importunate Friend.

WHICH of you ſhall have a friend, and ſhall go unto him at midnight, and ſay unto him, Friend, lend me three loaves;

For a friend of mine in his journey is come to me, and I have nothing to ſet before him?

And he from within ſhall anſwer and ſay, Trouble me not: the door is now ſhut, and my children are with me in bed; I cannot riſe and give thee.

I ſay unto you, Though he will not riſe and give him, becauſe he is his friend, yet becauſe of his importunity he will riſe and give him as many as he needeth.

And I ſay unto you, Aſk, and it ſhall be given you; ſeek, and ye ſhall find; knock, and it ſhall be opened unto you.

For every one that aſketh receiveth; and he that ſeeketh findeth; and to him that knocketh it ſhall be opened.

Luke, Chap. xi.

v. vx.

I. Quaker Ministry and Pastoral Care:
Centered Presence, Relational Engagement, Prophetic Witness

Maureen Graham

I N RECENT YEARS more and more Friends have been drawn to the ministries of pastoral care, chaplaincy, and counseling. Some of us have come to this work informally, some through secular training programs in counseling and psychology, and others through structured programs of clinical pastoral training. Those of us who have taken the latter path have met peers and supervisors who challenge us to speak about our work as pastoral care givers from the perspective of our Quaker faith.

We have searched ourselves to put into words, in our theological reflection papers and pastoral identity statements, how our spirituality becomes real in our practice of care and counseling. We have worked to identify in the language of our Quaker faith the theological issues and spiritual needs raised by our clients and patients as they struggle with pain and loss. Since Friends have traditionally resisted formulating doctrines and theological statements, we have been forced to articulate the knowledge that we have come to "experimentally." We practice a profound and practical spirituality which has shaped our own lives and which pervades our work of pastoral care. The voices we have found speak in this book.

My task in this chapter is to outline some general themes which are central to Quaker spirituality and which inform

Friends' understanding of ministry in general and the specialized ministries of chaplaincy, pastoral care, and counseling in particular. I hope that identifying these themes will help us to ground our pastoral practice in the rich soil of our corporate spirituality. While I speak from the perspective of a Friend nurtured by the unprogrammed form of worship, I believe that all Friends will relate to the themes identified. Beyond Friends' circles, I hope that this chapter will demonstrate how a Quaker approach to ministry can offer a unique perspective for theological reflection on the practice of pastoral care and counseling.

Quaker faith and practice are essentially experiential and based on an understanding of the active work of the Spirit within and between individuals. This "active work of the Spirit" is understood in a very literal sense; through our words and actions, the minutiae of our everyday lives, the Spirit is incarnate among us. The Spirit is present and active at all times, accessible to our awareness, prompting us toward inner change and outer action. Because of its active, experiential grounding, a Quaker perspective on pastoral care is less tied to the scriptural, theological, and ecclesiastical traditions of the institutional church than more traditional formulations. A Quaker perspective on pastoral care, as seen through the symbols of differing faith perspectives, can speak to the ecumenical, cultural, and clinical diversity which is present within today's pastoral care movement.

A Quaker Understanding of Ministry

What do Friends have to say about the truth they have found in their spiritual experience which forms the ground for their pastoral caring and ministry?

Typically, when Friends use the word "ministry" they are referring to the words that are spoken during meeting for worship, or vocal ministry. For Friends, therefore, ministry is defined first and foremost as an activity, rather than a profession, role, or function. It is an activity of the Spirit which takes place in a gathered space of worship. Meeting for Worship itself stands at the heart of Quaker spirituality. Here we experience the reality of the Spirit's presence in our lives. In meeting for worship, Friends open themselves to the presence of a living God felt in the depths of our inward experience as a sustaining, guiding, and transforming power. Its power lies in the inner transformation that happens slowly and surely within the gathered stillness and the rhythm of speaking and silence. It is an intimate meeting with the mystery of life and love revealed as truth in the depths of our souls.

Worship is a dynamic process of awareness, clarity, and expression. Some of its components are the following: the practice of waiting in the silence; centering ourselves in a place of stillness; opening to the deepening awareness of the thoughts, feelings, and promptings in the depths of ourselves; openness to the words of others; increased clarity about ourselves and our connection to others; a sense of guidance and direction; and the prompting toward action and expression. The whole process forms a mode of spiritual practice which heightens our sensitivity to the movement of the Spirit within ourselves, within others, and in the gathered group. Meeting for Worship is a discipline and an art. The continuing process of spiritual formation through which we find ourselves transformed over years compels us toward lives of greater faithfulness, compassion, humility, and loving engagement with the world.

Some branches of Friends today follow a more traditional Protestant form of worship. This "programmed" approach often includes periods of "open worship" where spoken ministry may be offered by anyone present. Despite differences in form, the spiritual basis of programmed worship remains rooted in the direct experience of God's presence in the gathered group. The purpose of the programmed, as well as open worship, is to enable people to reach that place of stillness within themselves where they encounter God and can feel the Spirit's movement in their lives.

Within Meeting for Worship, the experience of vocal ministry is an experience of being touched by a power greater than oneself. Over time we feel shaped and formed by the interweaving of speaking and silence, and our capacity for centering and listening increases. As we become more familiar with worship we learn how to discern what needs to be said, what is not meant to be shared, and when we should speak. Vocal ministry is an experience and expression of the kind of life to which Friends aspire—a life lived in receptive listening and responsive action to the Spirit of God known as a sustaining and guiding presence in our own hearts and in a gathered community. Vocal ministry, grounded in the discipline of waiting and discernment, acts as a model for a more general understanding of ministry among Friends.

Thus, from a Quaker perspective, ministry arises from an encounter with the Spirit where we find ourselves addressed, challenged, and led to specific actions. Such ministry requires a life of discernment and faithfulness; a commitment to the discipline of centering, stillness, and listening; a willingness to speak and act as moved by the Spirit; and a willingness to be formed and shaped through active engagement with others and the world.

The Ministry of Pastoral Care

When I meet with a person, a couple, or a family, in need or pain, I consider this meeting a special form of meeting for worship, a meeting where we gather to focus on the needs of the person or family and seek to discern the healing and guiding movement of the Spirit. Such a meeting is sacred. It is a place of meeting—of encounter—with ourselves, with each other, and with God. It is a place where we may be surprised by God, where we may be confronted by painful realities, where we may find a deep sense of relational connection and where we may discover healing, new life, and empowerment.

These journal reflections embody some of the experiences from which I draw to articulate an understanding of the ministry of pastoral care.

I sit across from you as your tears fall and cries of pain and longing grope their way into words. I listen. I cast into the depths of myself for words which do not come. I wait. I open my heart. I feel my longing to take this pain away. I breathe. I reach out spirit hands to hold you gently as you cry. I pray. That I will stay present. That your heart will be soothed. That love and life will prevail. We struggle on.

In this dialogue of soul and soul, this place of meeting where we reach for the light and moisture and tenderness that will nurture life, I wonder. What is this sacred task— this communion of blood and tears become warm and living flesh? A sacrament. A testimony to a faith beyond knowing made present in our midst.[1]

In this sense, we can say that pastoral care is sacramental. Pastoral care affirms the presence and power of the sacred in the everyday realities of our lives and struggles, and it affirms our capacity to experience that power and presence. Proclaiming the presence of a life-giving, healing power at the heart of life, it calls all present into the experience of the transforming power at the heart of our lives.

Within the sacred meeting of pastoral care, the ministry of the pastoral care giver has several dimensions which I have named *centered presence, relational engagement,* and *prophetic witness.*

Centered Presence

When I meet with others in pastoral caring, I aim to provide a centered and centering presence. I aim to be aware of my own thoughts and feelings, to listen deeply, and to discern the movement of the Spirit within myself, among others present, and in our interactions. Through centered presence the pastoral caregiver accompanies others in the search for healing and guidance. The pastoral care giver can act as a midwife, opening up places of pain and woundedness, encouraging, facilitating, and naming where life and power are moving within, helping to discern the movement of the Spirit and the opening for new life in the events and relationships of others' lives.

The pastoral care giver facilitates others' awareness of *their* inner reality and of the healing, guiding presence that can be found at the center of their lives. Psychological healing and growth depend on attention to one's present experiencing, the integration of split-off and repressed aspects of the self, the discovery of one's capacity for integrated action, and the ability to use our creative power. Quaker spirituality fosters such psychological awareness when used in the practice of pastoral care.

To offer pastoral care from the perspective of centered presence is challenging and humbling. To facilitate others in their own process of inner discernment and decision-making, the care giver has to pay attention to his or her own experiencing. We must open ourselves to the deep places within us, become aware of our own inner spaces of feelings, thoughts, desires, and listen deeply from those spaces. We are asked to live in the life and power of the Spirit, to listen, to speak, and to act from that place of life and power. This kind of pastoral care requires that we commit ourselves to a continual discipline of stillness, centering, and discernment.

Relational Engagement

In addition to offering a centered and centering presence as we meet with others in sacred space, the ministry of pastoral care also involves encounter, engagement, and dialogue. Friends speak of "meeting one another in that which is eternal," "speaking to the conditions of others," or "answering that of God" in others. Such speaking and answering is rooted in that deep, centered place where we are addressed by the Spirit and are open to the words of God spoken to our hearts through others. When we are engaged in pastoral care, both our words and our silence can be acts of ministry. We speak to the condition of others in relationship when we speak from a deeply centered place and allow ourselves to be addressed and moved by their words; honor silence and stillness; and engage in a dialogue of speaking and answering to that of God.

Pastoral care giving is a form of relational engagement where individuals meet with one another in a shared relationship in the service of support, healing, and growth. The capacity to enter fully into this relationship, to engage with others with empathy and mutuality so that one allows oneself to be moved, changed, delighted or saddened is essential to the process of psychological and spiritual transformation. As a pastoral care giver I offer not just a supportive or guiding presence but also the willingness to engage with another, to allow my own humanness to meet the humanness of another. I must be willing to participate, to feel deeply, to make mistakes, to risk connection, to experiment with what it means to speak to and answer that of God in myself and in others. I must be willing to love.

Not much is said about love and the practice of pastoral care partly because of the need for clear boundaries between personal and professional relationships. From the perspective of ministry, however, love has been seen as the place from which Friends respond to others in need. In John Woolman's ministry to Native Americans, "love was the first motion."[2] Margaret Fell spoke of early Friends' commitment to "no other cause but love."[3] When our encounters with others in a pastoral care relationship reach that place where we meet each other as human beings, then we know ourselves to be of equal worth and value to those with whom we work. We respect others' humanity and wisdom, and we open ourselves to be moved by their pain and struggle. Our caring is a particular form of loving, one through which healing can occur.

Pastoral care is about loving—about entering a relationship with another, a connectedness through which the Spirit can speak and move. To enter this kind of relationship is risky. It requires living on the edges of our own comfort, meeting others in their pain, despair or joy; being clear about our limits and ethical boundaries, yet trusting in the movement of the Spirit within each of us and in our relationship. When we meet with another and are deeply in touch with both our own humanity and theirs and open to the movement within and between us, emotion and pain can be expressed and received. The bonds of self-hate, shame, guilt and fear are loosened through the experience of empathic connection, and self-clarity emerges from mutual dialogue. Through such relational engagement, the presence of God can bring healing, acceptance, and empowerment.

As pastoral care givers, we are called to risk entering more honestly and more compassionately into relationship and dialogue with others. As we learn to do this, we become tenders of souls and hearts. Using the fabric of our own beings, our knowings, movements, flowing of emotions, thoughts and intuitions, we become finely-tuned instruments resonant to the possibilities for connection and relatedness. Such connection allows insight and healing to flow through the channel of our relationship.

Prophetic Witness

In my own work as a pastoral counselor in a mental health clinic, most of my clients have experienced severe trauma and relational impoverishment. The attempt to engage relationally with my clients brings me face-to-face, heart-to-heart, with deep woundedness and the reality of the profound cruelty and violence which human beings can do to each other. I wrote the following journal entry as an attempt to put into words my own feelings and anguish about the pain and struggle of one particular client who battles strong suicidal impulses.

> You hold out to me our bleeding, broken world carved into your body and soul. A silent scream rips the cloth of reason, tenderness and solidarity we keep on weaving, again and again. In your soul the tension of a fragmented, violent and violated spirit battles the fierce tenderness of life striving to resurrect itself. The extremes of human experi-

ence and expression make up your being—radiant beauty, crippling torment, corrosive rage, fierce determination, simple loving trust, unbearable longing, deep joy in life. Despair and hope, violence and horror, faith and love. I see them move across the landscape of your face and I am changed.

In loving you, my humanity has been stretched wide. I have called out for a God who can hold the depth and breadth of all you are and all you have experienced. My own heart has grown as you have allowed me to be present with you. If you must go, know that I will continue the struggle. I will grieve for you. I will rage at your going and the violence that has taken you. I will hold even more furiously to a fierce love for life and for bearing tenderly with one another. I will not give up hope.[4]

We live in a violent world, and a suicidal world, one intent on destroying that which sustains it. In our work as pastoral caregivers we encounter the effects of such violence in the bodies, hearts, and souls of those with whom we work. As pastoral care givers, we witness to the pain and suffering in our world. Such witnessing can bring us to the edges of our own faith.

We also live in a world of great beauty, immense joy, and profound connection. As pastoral care givers, we are also witness to the radiance and resilience of the human spirit, to courage and hope, to the possibility of love and new life even in the midst of suffering and death.

To The Beautiful Ones Who Have Been Broken

> Your beauty haunts me
> As you shatter in anguish
> Pain slashing ragged edges
> Through the fabric of your being
> I cry out

Who has done such sacrilege to body and soul?
Who has the right to defile
Your radiant beauty
Now shot bright through fragments?[5]

Quaker spirituality affirms that the spirit of the living God is at work not only in our hearts, but in the world, transforming, redeeming, and restoring right order in our social relationships. It testifies that there is a power at work "in this dark night,"[6] liberating, healing, birthing new life in our midst. The "ocean of light and love" moves over the "ocean of darkness."[7] Ministry is part of this work of transformation. It is activity which makes real the presence of God in concrete acts of caring and justice. Ministry is the action of the Spirit in the world, tending wounds, feeding one another, liberating each other from confinement and oppression, resisting with one another evil and injustice, birthing new life and deepening the bonds of human community.

Quaker spirituality is a prophetic spirituality, calling us into concrete acts of caring and justice. It calls us, and those with whom we work, out of structures and practices which sustain violence and cruelty into a life of peace where we bear tenderly with one another in the power of the Spirit. Our inward discernment leads to outer actions, which move us toward mutuality, justice and harmony, and through which we take our part in the transforming work of God.

Pastoral caring from a Quaker perspective must, therefore, be prophetic as well as sacramental and relational. We are called into the world of others through the voices of pain we hear. We are challenged ethically and spiritually by what we witness. In line with our Quaker tradition, we are called to speak and act without violence as we witness to the truth that we see and hear. We are called to respond to the relational woundedness of our world and to engage the task of healing broken hearts, souls, bodies, and relationships.

In turn, we offer ethical challenge as well as centered presence and relational encounter to those with whom we work, calling them to more loving ways of relating to themselves and to others. We hope to move individuals toward creative and compassionate action. Beyond our concern for any one individual's healing and empowerment, we have a concern for their moral agency which is part of our common well-being. We hold up people's power to act creatively or destructively in relationship and work, and to learn to relate and act in creative rather than destructive ways. We have a concern for helping ourselves and others recognize, create and sustain loving and just relationships with one another. We are faced with the choice that we all have: to respond to one another either with tenderness and caring or with rejection, indifference, or cruelty. Our work as pastoral care givers is to help others choose life not death, to choose blessing not cursing, tenderness not cruelty.

In order to do this, we need to understand the ways in which all of us have been impacted by the violence of the social relations and systemic injustice in which we live. Personal change is ultimately linked with social change through our ability to use our collective power to create more loving and just communities. We seek to help all of us learn to love one another better, to create interpersonal relationships and social structures which embody respect and caring, which are committed to our common welfare and which provide opportunities for creative work, healthy intimacy, and mutual empowerment. We listen for the particular ways in which we, and the people with whom we work, may be led to particular manifestations of this common work. Our work of pastoral care takes its place as part of the healing work of God in our world.

Concluding Remarks

How might these themes of centered presence, relational engagement, and prophetic witness play out in particular pastoral care relationships? In my work at a community mental health center I am constantly challenged to use these themes as reminders and touchstones for my work.

When I remember the theme of centered presence, I am reminded that my encounter with others is a form of worship, that I am called to center into that place where I meet with another in the presence of God. I may hold myself and my client in the Light before our session and at times of worship during the week. During the session itself, I may enter into a time of silence and prayer, either known or unknown to my client. When I find myself distracted, confused, angry, or afraid in response to my client's words or actions, I center myself in our common connection through the Spirit.

The challenge of relational engagement reminds me that each person with whom I work has inherent value and is worthy of respect and attention. I work with clients from so many different backgrounds and experiences. They share worlds with me I would otherwise never know: worlds of poverty and violence, worlds of faith and creativity, worlds of despair and bleakness; survivalists, new age channelers, foresters, students, single parents; those involved in prostitution, or struggling with addiction; those lost in delusional nightmares they cannot release, or incapacitated by deep depression or paralyzing anxiety; all share their experience of human living. I find myself humbled by discovering our common humanness as well as each person's uniqueness. I am blessed to be able to journey with each person. My call is to treat each person, each encounter, with utter respect. My task is to find a way to meet with each person at a level where connection can be felt and caring can flow. To do this, I must meet them eye-to-eye, centered in my own humanness, open to theirs. I try to enter this process openly, willing to engage in a genuine relationship where I may be met and transformed.

As clients heal from the effects of trauma and violence; as they identify the differences between abusive relationships and healthy intimacy; as they give voice to the pain, shame, and anger within them; our dialogue often turns to other issues. We begin to examine questions of how to understand the presence of both good and

The King's Library

evil in the world; how to live in the world in ways which are healing and loving; and what it means to develop a centered sense of oneself and a living spirituality. In these dialogues, we work together to understand the particular challenges and sufferings each person is facing within a broader context of meaning and purpose. We identify the "promptings of love and truth" arising within and listen to what actions may be being called forth. In such conversations, I am reminded of the prophetic witness that roots my pastoral counseling in the broader work of the Spirit.

> You come to me in faith—anxious, hopeful, guarded—
> unsure of how you will be met, what might come. I see you,
> another of my faces, heartbeat of life reaching for itself.
>   I welcome you into this sacred space, with gentleness. I
> hope that life will flow between us, and restore us each to
> our own, with renewed faith in the humanity we share.
>   Blessed Be.[8]

Notes

1. Maureen Graham, Personal Journal.
2. John Woolman, *The Journal of John Woolman*, edited by John Greenleaf Whittier (Secaucus, NJ: Citadel Press, 1961), 142.
3. Margaret Fell, location unknown
4. Maureen Graham, Personal Journal.
5. Maureen Graham, Personal Journal.
6. "The Epistle from the World Gathering of Young Friends" (Boston, MA: Mosher Book and Tract,1986).
7. George Fox, *The Journal of George Fox*, Rufus M. Jones, ed., (Richmond, IN: Friends United Press, 1694/1976), 87.
8. Maureen Graham, Personal Journal.

II. "Opportunity" and Pastoral Care

Bill Taber

Editor's Note: This chapter is edited from a talk which was presented at the 1998 Conference for Quakers in Pastoral Care and Counseling, held in Richmond, Indiana. The talk was given out of a context of waiting worship, with a return to silence afterwards. Following the talk and a period of worship, a sample "opportunity" was demonstrated. Thanks to Naima Solomon for transcribing the talk from a tape and to Joelen Bergonzi for the initial editing.

I'VE BEEN STRUCK THROUGHOUT THIS WEEKEND with the sense that this gathering might be thought of as a continuation of the Quaker ministers and elders meetings of old. A minister speaks the received Word of God out of silent worship. An elder is a companion to the minister, helping to give quality to the silence out of which vocal ministry comes. The elder's function is illustrated in this story.

Not long after I had been recorded as a minister in Ohio yearly meeting, I needed to attend the regular meeting of ministers and elders in our local Meeting. I was a little late getting there. I can remember rushing up the brick walk to the Meeting house. As I walked in the door, my heart was beating hard from the exertion; I was still breathing heavily. As soon as I walked in the door of the inner room of the Meeting house, where the ministers and elders were meeting, I could feel as if I were entering a zone of peace. And by the time I took my seat, I had entered into that state of "waiting worship," of peace, even though my body hadn't settled down. That example demonstrates how a gathered meeting of ministers and elders provides a climate that one can walk into, a climate in which the Quaker technology of the shifting levels of

16

consciousness is being demonstrated. Sometimes we need to be able to find the place where we can enter that deep quiet with other people who know it. Elders hold, shape, and open that place.

The elders didn't speak in Meeting very often, but they had experienced this quality of being. And it was so important for the minister to be able to make contact with that special level of consciousness, to know the difference between enthusiasm and that inward motion which rises from the still depths. That motion also has power, but it's different from ordinary enthusiasm. We who are called to speak and lead need that gathering of ministers and elders, that touchstone place to recalibrate our "spiritual instrumentality." It's important to find those people who don't talk about it, but who live the silence in a way that you can feel.

The Quaker worship "opportunity" is another way of experiencing this deep silence. A tradition that goes back to George Fox and the earliest generation of Friends, it has continued until this very day in the Religious Society of Friends. In its simplest form, an "opportunity" is a meeting for worship between two people, or among just a very few people. It can be held at any time. Ordinarily it is at a different time and place from the regular Meeting for Worship. It can be very short, and it might take place in some unusual circumstances.

My great-grandfather, who was a Quaker minister in Ohio, was being taken to the train in Salem by a group of young people in a buggy. As they were going along the road, he asked them to pull the buggy over and have an opportunity right there beside the road. Opportunities could occur in the living room, when a visiting minister was present. In the midst of conversation, a hush would fall over the room—not just an ordinary pause in the conversation, but a hush which Quakers could recognize as a beginning of that shift in the levels of consciousness. All conversation would cease, and the people would remain in silence for fifteen minutes, twenty minutes, or half an hour, even in the middle of dinner.

Every Quaker child knew about this once upon a time. A Quaker child knew that visiting ministers, if they came to the home, would probably ask for an opportunity. Even if they didn't ask for it, it would just happen. Opportunities could also be requested. We can assume that John Woolman as a young man sought out opportunities with older friends, mentor-type Friends, seeking advice. He would go and call on an older Friend, perhaps by pre-arrangement. They would have a time of quiet, and then perhaps John Woolman would "open his mind" to this Friend. They would have a quiet conversation, growing out of a time of quiet together.

In traditional Quakerism, if one Friend had a concern that another Friend was doing something wrong that would hinder his spiritual development, she or he would arrange for an opportunity between them. This would be a form of eldering, but they would begin by sitting together in the quiet, in that altered state of consciousness in which love is clearly present. Surrounded by this level of consciousness, the concerned Friend would speak out of great love so that in many cases the other person would not be offended, for the intention of love would be evident. I've been involved in a couple of opportunities when people had concerns for me. Each time I've been grateful that I could feel their love in a way which felt uplifting, rather than being put down or offended.

We often assume, in our modern context, that traveling ministers in the past, like John Woolman, had a checklist of concerns to share at each new house or meeting. Often Friends travel that way today, and I think that's quite appropriate, sometimes. But, in traditional Quakerism, a minister traveling under concern would not know ahead of time what the content of the next opportunity might be. John Woolman describes that attentiveness in his journal. He was used as an instrument again and again in the slavery issue, and on many other issues as well, but he never assumed ahead of time just what the Spirit would require him to say.

After I was recorded as a Friends minister, I found that my gift increased considerably, and I often spoke in Meetings, sometimes for five, ten, or fifteen minutes. While not appropriate in most of the unprogrammed meetings that we attend now, but at that time in Ohio, ministry of that length was appropriate, especially if there was what the old Friends would call "suitable matter." Often my ministry would apparently touch people very deeply—it wasn't uncommon for people to come up and say that I had spoken to their condition.

Then there came a time when I began to discover that there was a wall going up between me and the other people in the Meeting if I tried to speak. I would still have leadings that seemed to be very accurate. I knew exactly what that Meeting needed to hear, but the minute I got up and started to speak, I could feel that it was worse than not speaking at all. Then I read something in Ann Branson's journal that said:

> A minister who does not wait for the special anointing each time does more harm than good, and will create confusion in his [sic] own mind, as well as in the mind of the whole Meeting.

I thought, "Well, perhaps I am meant to be silent."

Soon I discovered that I could pray silently for the manifestation of the insight that I had about the Meeting, that it would occur without my speaking, or that somebody else might speak. Gradually I realized that I was in for a time of deeply resting in the Spirit, and learning how to radiate God's love and peace in a kind of ministry without words. And that eventually felt right.

It dawned on me that my gift in the ministry had really depended on the faithful spiritual presence of women and men in a Meeting who had never spoken at all; people who were not even thought of as leaders in the Meeting; individuals who knew intuitively and instinctively by long practice, by faithful dedication, this Quaker technology of shifting levels of consciousness which is at the heart of Quakerism. They made it possible for fools like me to speak. The minute I realized that, I could begin to speak again.

For many years I had known intellectually and intuitively that a minister is but an extension (like an arm, a leg or a mouth) of the Meeting, of the body of Christ. I still had to learn that lesson deep down inside. Once I knew that, then I could speak.

I want to tell the full story of how I first discovered the minister's belly. I happened to be sitting beside a weighty, elderly Friend from North Carolina who was moved to preach to the woman's Meeting at Yearly Meeting time, when we still had separate men's and women's Meetings at Yearly Meeting. I had been named as his companion, even though I was a very young man wearing a sports jacket and all, very unusual at that time. I sat beside him as he began to get, as a pastoral friend in New England once said, "steamed up," getting ready for his message. He stood up and he preached powerfully to these women, and I could just sort of imagine his belly going up and down—he had an ample one.

Only years later did I connect that with what I came to understand as the "minister's belly." John Woolman talks about it when he says "the first motion was love." Again and again, as we read the Quaker journals, we come across that term, or the idea, that before the individual is moved to speak to the group, he or she feels a great love radiating out to the people. Finally I came to realize that was an important key to Quaker ministry, I hope to all ministry. It is that the person has a "minister's belly." It doesn't matter what size it is. I visualize this as a radiant energy coming out from the viscera to the people. And when I've talked with people who practice yoga, they would agree that the belly is where it comes from.

That's a very good touchstone if one is wondering about speaking, whether or not one has a sense of love. The inward motion is where it all begins; that's why it's so useful to have a touchstone meeting, or a friend, a mentor, an elder to whom one can go, and just sit and find this place. The leading to speak ultimately comes from the inward motion, which seems to come from deep down in the pool of consciousness. It arises as pure thought, pure concept, at first, without any emotion at all. As the leading to speak rises to the surface, it may express itself with various emotional connotations. If we resist, as we often do, being a mouthpiece of the Holy Spirit, we may get the shakes and the quakes as the last aspects of it.

Experienced ministers often come to discover how the inward motion begins to rise. And it's powerless; it's seen as so little, so ineffectual, but as it rises to the surface, we come to recognize its validity against other kinds of motions that rise too within us. The skill of the Quaker technology of shifting levels of consciousness is so important in Quaker ministry in helping us recognize the validity of the inward motion.

We use the term "waiting worship," or "deep silence"; we use the term "covered meeting," or "gathered meeting." You can have a gathered meeting in which nothing is said. You can have a covered meeting in which nothing is said, but there comes a quality to the silence that an experienced Friend feels. It's so important that our ministry come not just from the belly, and not just from the heart, although the heart is very important. The ministry comes from a deeper source. I sometimes call it an expanded state of consciousness, a metaphor of the experience, but more or less inadequate to describe it.

With the encouragement of a teacher, I probably began experiencing "opportunities" when I was in high school at Olney Friends. Some of us as juniors and seniors tried to meet in the morning before breakfast for times of worship. I don't think very much happened then, but at least we were going through the motions. Once after I had spoken in Meeting as a senior, the superintendent, the father figure in the old Quaker boarding schools, called me into his office, and we had a little opportunity. I don't remember much of what we said, but I do remember the silence that we had. He said at the end, "Well, William, now we have dedicated thee." He was a recorded minister himself from Middletown Meeting in Pennsylvania. And I can still remember as I walked back to the dormitory how beautiful the stars were that night. He helped me come into my own ministry. And this, of course, is part of the tradition in Quakerism. Every generation mentors the next. And we need plenty of ready mentors.

Later on, I remember a Friend who was a student at Earlham School of Religion when I was a student. She was what I would call a psychic sensitive, but a strong Christian, and we got on very well from the very beginning of our time at ESR. I remember a time in the spring semester when I began to think I perhaps needed to get some psychological counseling, to see whether I needed to get some things straightened out. I talked to her about it, as she had been a Christian counselor herself, and she said, "Well, why don't we have a few sessions ourselves first, before you do anything like that?"

So, we arranged for a time to meet, five or six times in the remainder of the spring term, and I can still remember the first session. We started in silence together, after we agreed that I would open the conversation when I felt ready, so it was a kind of opportunity. When I felt ready, I knew exactly what I was going to say, but some other words came to me that I could speak. So I had a choice: either say what I had planned to say about what I thought was my problem, or to accept and speak these words that were coming in from the side. I chose to accept the inspiration, and that's the way it worked for the rest of the five or six sessions that we had. It felt like it was ministry to myself.

Again and again as I would be feeling these things that I needed to say, she would be all ready to start doing her counseling, and I would say, "Wait a minute, something else is coming through!" And so, we both realized that we were learning—she was learning that she as a counselor didn't need to do as much work, and that she could trust the process; and I was learning something about the process that was very exciting to me.

The other person that was important to me was someone who was not technically an elder at Stillwater meeting. I sometimes embarrassed her by calling her a "True Elder." She was a very humble person, but she also was psychically sensitive, strongly Christian, and an unprogrammed Quaker. I often went to her for opportunities. I could feel so strengthened by that climate—the ministers' and elders' climate, that state of expanded consciousness. I would ask a question out of the silence, and before she said a word, I knew the answer. I began to realize then that one of the gifts that an opportunity can bring is that if a person has some experience in this expansion of consciousness, then she brings a climate of clarity. In the presence of such a person the normal cloudiness in the mind is brushed away; I'm given greater clarity in the mind.

From the very first of being with this group this weekend, I could sense, all around the room, individuals, some very powerfully, who have the possibility of projecting a climate around the people who are with them. It's a love that is more than just emotional love. It's a deep caring. It's a ministry, even though you don't say a word.

In an opportunity, if one is in this expanded state of consciousness—for which we could give various theological names, not the least of which would be "in the presence of the Holy Spirit"—thoughts will come, in the midst of a conversation. I've heard at least one counselor here describe the same phenomenon in the counseling session, when she would not know what to say next. She would pray, secretly, and then she would always be given what to say. In my experience with opportunities, I would be listening with two ears—one to the person, and one to Something beyond. Often I would get the idea that there was something I should say, or something I should ask, which seemed almost off the wall, or I was almost shy of asking, but invariably if I did, it seemed to be the right thing.

I first learned about the absorptive mode in dealing with students at Olney Friends School. Being a rather shy and sensitive person, it's often difficult to deal with strong personalities, especially if they're threatening to me. And so I discovered somehow that if I used what I call the absorptive mode, or the non-reactive mode, I could deal more usefully with the individual in front of me. It is a worshipful mode actually; a form of non-verbal prayer state. It's not quite as deep as we get sometimes in meeting for worship, but the same faculty or phenomenon can be used in an opportunity as well. In a counseling session, one can be in this state all the time if one feels it's right.

The absorptive mode is my metaphor of describing how, if someone is speaking to me in a certain way, I absorb their words with my body, rather than with just my mind. It's as if the words go right through me. And of course it's important to remember that I don't absorb those words, but it's as if I am. I don't let the negative emotions lodge in me. Then I turn on what I call the "divine vacuum cleaner." That is simply another metaphor that describes the work of Jesus Christ in this universe. There is something which is forever recycling negative stuff. Any negative emotion we put out can be absorbed by that incredible center of light and life in the universe.

Let us think also about the non-reactive mode. In that mode I'm consciously not in the mode which is so common in our culture—to react, to control—instead I am just observing. There is another state of consciousness, which one of my students at Pendle Hill calls "soft-eyes." In effect I take off my glasses, or blur my eyes, and look at the world in a slightly softer way, so that the boundaries are less sharp.

Though you are not absorbing that pain or negativity, you are paying very serious attention to it. It's a relaxed attention, not a self-conscious attention. When we come into the Quaker technology of the shifting levels of consciousness, the expansion of consciousness, we are by definition experiencing a relaxation of the egocentric, individualistic character that is such a burden sometimes in this culture. That relaxation makes it possible to pay attention without being anxious about it.

When we are in this state, the Holy Spirit gives us as much time as we need. That's the way it feels, so I don't have to react for a moment, and I may have only microseconds, but those microseconds expand enormously. It's as if the real time is laid aside, and I am given all the time I need. I examine my own possible reactions, which might be fear, anger, or reacting as I would to Aunt Minnie, or something of that sort. I'm able to discard that because I have time. I'm more able then to see what the person before me is really trying to say, where that person is hurting, rather than how it's going to affect me. I have all the time I need. Then, especially if I'm having trouble with Aunt Minnie or anger or fear, it's very important that I turn on the divine vacuum cleaner as well to absorb my own emotions, so that they don't get in the way. It's important that I recognize them.

We as individuals are different, and what we have the capacity to bear will vary. It's so important then to have a good mentor, a spiritual friend, or a spiritual director so that one can sort all of this out. "Friends should not engage in business beyond their ability to manage." Some people are born with such sensitivity that the pain they bear is incredible.

Here is another metaphor: Suppose my aperture of consciousness is this large, normally, but when I go through a time of expanding consciousness, now the aperture is much larger. Let us suppose that when the aperture of consciousness is small, I have a bee sting. That bee sting takes up most of that aperture. It's an incredible pain; I can hardly bear it. Now I expand the aperture of consciousness. The bee sting is still the same kind of pain; I still feel the pain, but it seems smaller, relative to the expanded aperture—and so it is more possible to live with the pain.

That takes me back again to Jesus. Only that incredible expansion of consciousness would have made comprehensible what Jesus did on the cross. Romans 8:28 tells us, "All things work together for good, for those who love the Lord, those who are willing to be called according to the divine purposes." Pastoral counselors, chaplains, who are present with pain, are following that calling.

In pastoral counseling, in what ways does opportunity occur in the counseling session? Sometimes it is asked for, or it just happens; it just arises. Would that occur more often if we were more open to the spirit? I have talked with psychotherapists now and then who have said, "Oh, that's what happens in my sessions. I have the same sense of an invisible spiritual connection." They have described the same sense of feeling a powerful sense of empathy. I think it's quite possible, if we have the spiritual discipline in practice, we can carry that state of consciousness with us into the session. The only thing that keeps it from being an "opportunity" is that the other person may not be familiar with Quaker practice, but that person will still be experiencing it.

III. Discernment:
The Soul's Eye View

Felicity Kelcourse

NOW, AT THE TURN OF THE MILLENNIUM, three strands of awareness divided since the Enlightenment—the physical, psychological and spiritual—are being rewoven. The materialistic focus that has driven industry and revolutionized our scientific understanding of the world has left us rich in things but poor in spirit. Consumer culture suggests that only what can be measured, bought and sold is of value. Experience teaches us otherwise. Without loving relationships, without a sense of purpose, life loses its meaning. We have a deep hunger, a soul hunger, for a different way of being in the world. In our times, as in times past, there is a need for discernment. Discernment is understood here as a way of knowing that allows the soul to be our guide.

What is the soul? In *The Care of the Soul: A Guide for Cultivating Depth and Sacredness in Everyday Life*, Thomas Moore avers that soul defies definition.[1] Following Ann Ulanov and Paul Tillich, I imagine the soul as a door to the Eternal Now through which God can come at any time.[2] Thomas Kelly, in keeping with the Quaker understanding of "that of God" in everyone, describes the soul's perspective in *Testament of Devotion* when he writes:

> Deep within us all there is an amazing inner sanctuary of the soul, a holy place, a Divine Center, a speaking Voice, to which we may continuously return. Eternity is at our hearts, pressing upon our time-worn lives, warming us with intimations of an astounding destiny, calling us home to

27

itself. . . . It is a seed stirring to life if we do not choke it. It is the Shekinah of the soul, the Presence in the midst. Here is the Slumbering Christ, stirring to be awakened, to become the soul we clothe in earthly form and action. And He is within us all.[3]

Kelly speaks as one who knows the soul's point of view experientially. To understand what soul might signify, one can begin by giving it attention and hope that one's efforts of study and reflection will eventually be met by the more intuitive knowing Kelly's words imply.

In some languages, the word for soul is indistinguishable from the word for psyche or mind.[4] Although the distinction is in some respects arbitrary, I find it helpful to distinguish psyche from soul, with psyche being that aspect of self that is influenced by heredity and environment; soul the eye, or door, through which I see God. Psyche and soul exist on a continuum with psyche leaning towards the pole of body, the physical self, and soul, "that of God" in us, leaning toward spirit. The Ulanovs have made a useful distinction between soul as the spiritual aspect of individual identity and spirit as found in community, "when two or three are gathered together."[5]

My own theory of persons is informed by Friends' understanding of human nature and depth psychology. Psyche mediates between our outer and inner worlds but also between a personal unconscious constellated by individual history and a collective unconscious that constitutes the deeper symbolic underpinnings of the mind. The soul is that part of us that sees past phenomena to noumena, what Rudolf Otto calls the "non-rational emotional perception" of religious experience.[6] Reason structures and contains the study of soul but reason alone cannot fully apprehend what the soul knows.

I first became interested in discernment in relation to my own suffering. At the age of 34, after several experiences of pregnancy loss, I began to face the idea that I might never give birth. I come from a large extended family with 21 first cousins where family and fertility are the norm. The idea of being a childless woman was anathema. We had begun to consider adoption but at first all doors seemed closed. (Two years later, after our first attempt fell through, we succeeded in adopting our daughter who has been with us from birth.)

Energized by a wave of anger, I impulsively applied to doctoral programs and was stunned to find myself accepted to the program in Psychiatry and Religion at Union Theological Seminary with a full fellowship for the fall of 1989. I felt uncertain and confused. How could something that sounded so wonderful be the fruit of anger that felt unacceptable? Assent to this invitation, one that could not be deferred, meant uprooting my husband in a way that was disruptive to his career. To undermine my husband's professional development would further confirm my status as a "bad" woman. How could I decide between a choice that might be good but felt "wrong" or a choice that felt "right" but might in fact be bad? Though I prayed for guidance, I could not honestly say that I felt clearly led to either choice, to go or to stay. Perhaps the static from the psyche was too loud for the discerning silence of God to be heard. My study of discernment began with this dilemma.[7] How could I distinguish the voices of culture, family of origin, and the predilections of personality that hold such sway over the psyche from the stirrings of the slumbering Christ, the speaking Voice that inhabits the sanctuary of the soul?

Eventually I arrived at a resolution. Before sharing that resolution as an experiential example of the discernment process, I first consider the dialogical process of discernment itself, in general and through the earliest course of human development. I will then illustrate discernment through the biblical account of Jesus' encounter with the Samaritan woman at Jacob's well (John 4:1-42) and examples from psychotherapy.

Understanding Discernment

Our English word "discernment" comes from the Latin, *dis-cernere*, to sift apart. In the Bible, the Hebrew words we translate as discernment (*byn, binah, tebhunah*) are synonymous with insight, understanding, and wisdom. The word conveys the idea of *giving attention to God's deeds*. This is the spiritual connotation often given to the idea of discernment.

In the Greek New Testament, words translated as discernment (*kritikos, anakrino, diakrino*) are associated with making decisions, judgments—right or wrong, good or bad. But inherent in the process of discernment is a dialogue, an art of attention. The idea of sifting suggests a boundary that allows some things to be held back and others to fall through, like a prospector panning for gold. When a confused mass is separated, attention is given to differences and the process of dialogue can begin.

Discernment is a dialogical process, a method, a way of knowing. My understanding of the *process* of discernment that precedes judgment is that it involves first of all a separation or tension between things, people, or qualities of awareness, giving attention to what each side has to say. To the extent that the process of discernment is dialogical, it can be compared to Jung's "transcendent function" in which the tension between opposites in the psyche builds until it finds resolution in a third entity that transcends the opposition.[8] The results of discernment, the decision or judgment, may or may not bring unity, but the process of discernment requires separations that struggle, through dialogue, to find resolution.

In relation to clinical concerns this is the very work of communication we encourage couples to do. Couples (and faith communities!) tend to avoid direct disagreement because disagreement is painful. But the avoidance of disagreement leads to resentment, repressed hostilities and, ultimately, painful divisions. In marriage and family therapy, couples are encouraged to express openly their wants, feelings, needs, and desires but to do so in a manner that recognizes the other's right to respect when disagreements arise, without resorting to accusations or blame. While divisions that defy resolution are sometimes inevitable, important opportunities for dialogue and movement toward a new level of unity are clearly missed when the sifting process of discernment is avoided.

Quaker history offers many examples of interpersonal dialogues leading to new understanding. I think of John Woolman's conversation with a dying slave owner who wanted Woolman to include the disposition of slaves in his will. Woolman's response was a model of clear disagreement in a context of respect for difference. Woolman didn't say to the slave owner, "You're a bad person for keeping human beings as property." He simply said, ". . . I could not write any instrument by which my fellow creatures were made slaves, without bringing trouble on my own mind."[9] Woolman's respectful attention to this distinction between himself and the slave owner allowed his potential adversary to enter into dialogue with him and at length to appreciate the wisdom of Woolman's concern.

Individual psychotherapy, "the talking cure," is in essence a multi-layered process of dialogue. On one level there is the conscious intersubjective dialogue between therapist and client, on another the unspoken semi-conscious or subconscious dialogue that flows between them beneath their words like the underground portion of a river. There is also an intrapsychic dialogue at the interface between conscious and subconscious knowing that occurs continuously within the heart, mind and soul of each participant. It is little wonder that communication in the therapeutic hour can be both intense and obscure. Before sessions I ask God to be present in the *temenos* or sacred space of therapy, helping us each to hear the voice of the true Self, the call of vocation. This conscious invocation of God's presence invites the soul's perspective to join the intrapsychic and intersubjective dialogues of each participant.

Psyche, Soul and the Process of Discernment

Discernment includes both process and decision. If the process of discernment is a dialogical art of attention, what do we give attention to and why? If the purpose of our attention is to find healing, wholeness, integrity, then we must look towards the center, towards "that of God" in us. Jacob Boehme had a religious experience in which he looked into a pewter plate and saw his own eye looking back. The soul is our window from time into the Eternal Now, the eye with which we see ourselves as *imago dei*, God's reflection.

As Friends, we give attention to the Light of Christ in each of us, to God as the Presence in our midst. In the context of faith, discernment is inextricably linked to our relationship with God; the purpose of discernment is to know and to do God's will. *If the soul is the window, the eye through which God's light enters psyche, mind and body, then the sight of the soul is essential to discernment.*

But the center, the dwelling place of the soul, is not easily reached. To find the soul's sight clearly is a gift of grace. Often we must wend our way through dark forests or a barren wilderness in the psyche to find the fountain of wisdom we thirst for, the well of living water. How will we know when we have reached our goal?

I find the distinction between psyche and soul clinically useful in distinguishing between the many "voices" one hears in sessions and within oneself. In the example I gave from my own experience, one voice urged me to take the difficult leap of faith required to begin doctoral work, another counseled caution. A traditional aid to discernment found in Quaker journals is to choose the path that requires a "cross to the will." If "I" don't want to follow a particular leading, whether it be to speak from the silence or travel in the ministry, then the more challenging direction is probably the one God intends.[10] But in this case each choice, to go or stay, offered a cross of a different kind. There was apparently no "easy way out" to avoid. In such cases one can draw on the community's discernment by calling a clearness committee or muddle through, continuing one's internal dialogue in hopes of an eventual resolution. (For those who are not familiar with the practice of clearness committees, Patricia Loring's Pendle Hill pamphlet on the subject offers a useful introduction.)[11]

With clients one frequently uncovers semi-conscious dialogues between parental dictates, cultural constraints, and the voice that urges one on towards the difficult choices healing requires, breaking step with the old to make space for the new. In clinical practice, I think of the voice that holds *hope* as being the voice of the soul. Naturally this voice is more easily identified in another than in oneself.

No doubt we have each faced similar dilemmas in our own lives or, vicariously, as therapists and pastoral care givers, through the struggles of those we serve. As persons of faith our conscious desire is to know and to do God's will. Our clients may be less clear about whether faith is possible or whether there is a God who could hear them and speak to them in any meaningful way. What if God takes the form of an abusive stepfather, forever smacking you to keep you in line? What if God is an emotionally distant mother, critical, full of judgment, unavailable for nurture so that the child grows up riddled with loneliness and self-doubt, never able to go home? Who can find any help from such a God? Hope, as the soul's perspective, is easily missed when one lacks receptivity. In such cases we must hold for our clients the hope they are too fearful to acknowledge, lest it be snatched away. And we must also have a place to bring our own doubts and hopelessness, a community of faith to shelter us when inner storms rage and it feels as if the light beyond the clouds will never return. Just as a child cannot grow a self in the absence of love, so we cannot find the light our souls long for without a community to sustain us in being. Care givers too require the holding environment provided by supervision, friends, family, and faith communities if we are to remain receptive to hope in the face of despair.

How is the soul's sight to be identified and recovered if it has been obscured? To answer this question I offer a developmental understanding of the soul's eye view. In my experience, *hope, receptivity, and intuition* are each essential ingredients for a fruitful process of discernment, as opposed to dialogues that are prematurely foreclosed. In general, I consider discernment to be fruitful when it results in greater clarity in relation to self, others, and God, with improved inner balance between one's own conscious and unconscious knowing and improved outer balance between the individual and his or her community.[12]

Developmental stages of emerging psyche and soul: nurturing the soul's eye view

Soul is that part of us that sees and knows God. The soul lives at the divine Center. There can be no integrity without the voice of the soul, no sense of vocation without the soul's direction, no fruitful discernment without the soul's eye view.

If the soul sees and knows God, what does the soul see?

As Christians we make affirmations of faith. We say that God is good, that God is love. If these affirmations are fundamentally true, then the soul continually sees God's goodness and love for us. Just as the sun continues to shine on a cloudy day when the earth is dark, so the soul receives the Light of Christ, even when the ego or conscious self is shrouded in desolation. This helps to account for persons suffering from life-long depressions, from preoccupations with suicide or self-destructive behavior who, against all odds, find themselves at a therapist's door. The soul holds *hope, receptivity* to the Light beyond the clouds and mediates *intuitions* of an unseen but dimly remembered time when we were as one with God.

If we could only keep to the soul's eye view we could float in trust, free from fear all our days. But for most of us the genetic and environmental inheritance of the psyche is a maze through which we must find our way to arrive at the soul's true appreciation of God. Too often the god representations derived from introjected parental imagos block the way to God for both therapist and client.[13] So God the Father, Mother, Creator becomes god the drunk, god the unholy terror, god the absent, unavailable father, god the poisonous mother.

As Friends we make a curious affirmation of faith. Against all evidence to the contrary—innocent children who suffer and die, nations rent for centuries by ethnic hatreds, the degradation of God's glory in creation, the ubiquity of divorce, senseless natural disasters—we affirm that God is good, that the universe can be trusted. This is the essence of an early prophetic opening of George Fox, echoing the prologue to the gospel of John (1:5):

> I saw also that there was an infinite ocean of darkness and death, but an infinite ocean of light and love, which flowed over the ocean of darkness.

This is the soul's eye view. The soul knows and rests in the goodness of God. Such a view is quite different from Jung's understanding of the collective unconscious in which all symbols are bivalent, both good and bad.

Here we have the basic tension between the sight of the psyche and the sight of the soul. The psyche knows torture as well as delight, fear as well as joy. The soul knows, as its core reality, only bliss. Yet in this life the two are inseparable and completely essential. A neurologist, Antonio Damasio, gives detailed physiological evidence for the mind's complete dependence on the body in his book *Descarte's Error: Emotion, Reason and the Human Brain*.[14] Whether a similar analogy can be made between soul and its dependence on the psyche is unclear to me. In any event, the fact that we make distinctions, for the purposes of awareness, need not result in a hierarchical dualism which places mind over body, male over female, soul over psyche. None of these pairs can exist without the other. In this life there can be no mind without body, no soul without psyche or embodiment.

What most of us experience, within the first two to four years of life, is a fall from grace in the psyche that is comparable to the expulsion of Eve and Adam from paradise. Paradise is the country of the soul at one with God. Sin is the state of separation from God in which the Light of Christ is hidden from view and the self feels alone, cast out, bereft. One of Fox's more arresting images of sanctification is that we move back through the sentinel angel's flaming sword into paradise,[15] what Ricoeur calls a second innocence.[16]

Out of my own experience of early pregnancy loss I offer the following imaginative description of the soul's eye view from conception through the beginnings of language:

1) Prior to conception the soul exists like a drop of water in the sea of being. Though it has its own being and integrity, the soul is not separate from the enfolding love of God. Like Friends whose souls unite to form one spirit in a gathered Meeting for Worship, it is surrounded by a community of others, joined to them as one. We need not think of the soul as "disembodied" at this point. Traditional Christian doctrine holds that there is a bodily resurrection after death, despite the empty corpse that the departing soul visibly leaves behind. What the soul's body might be before birth or after death is a mystery. Like God and love itself, the soul is both real and unseen.

2) At conception intrauterine life begins. The soul has moved from the sea of being to the dark waters of a mother's womb. As an embryo with a developing body it swims, overhears the voices of its parents, and dreams. Perhaps the beginnings of distinction and dialogue are there ("this is mother's voice, that is father's voice"), but for the most part the unitive consciousness that bathes in love continues. If the mother is addicted to drugs or alcohol or finds herself in frightening, dangerous circumstances the soul may struggle even before birth to retain its vision of the love of God.

Both the body and soul of the developing child can be damaged by such experiences. The mother's holding environment, and the community's holding of the mother, is essential to the well-being of the child.

3) At birth the child is separated from the body of its mother and begins to have even more definite, potentially traumatic experiences of physical, emotional, and spiritual separation from its origins in the sea of being where it suffered no separation from the love of God. If the mother has had a positive experience of pregnancy in an emotionally supportive environment, the dreaming child in utero will have few anticipatory fears about "outside" and "other" voices. I put these words in quotes because some developmental psychologists believe the newborn is "symbiotic," having no ability to clearly distinguish between self and other.[17] Others believe the child has a rudimentary sense of self from birth, if not before.[18] In any event, the child at birth experiences a rupture from the protected precincts of the mother's body and discovers the terrors of physical helplessness for the first time.

Freud recognized this implicitly when he observed in *The Future of an Illusion* that our emotional need for God stems from a deep-seated fear of our own fundamental helplessness, beginning at birth and continuing throughout life, especially evident in times of suffering and loss.[19] Freud believed that our need for God and religion, "the universal neurosis," stemmed from nothing more than our childhood longings for a loving mother and father to hold and protect us. I believe that Freud was accurate in his observations but wrong in his conclusions. Any "neurosis" that is "universal" must be normal. Our fears of helplessness are well founded, our need for God's loving protection very real.

We do long, at the deepest levels of our being, for the "everlasting arms" that can keep us from falling. Some of us were blessed with loving parents whose tender physical and emotional attention to us as infants came as close as any love in this world can to the enfolding, inexhaustible love of God. Others of us, clients and therapists both, were not so lucky. But even those of us who suffered various degrees of physical and emotional deprivation from birth knew that we were missing something.

If the sight of the psyche, our embodied experience and heredity, were all we had to go on, how would we know on some deep level that loving care was our birthright, that we were wronged when that birthright was damaged or withheld? We know because our souls tell us, at the core of our being, that there is more to life than neglect and abuse. If we can hold on to this knowing we can hold on to life and the hope for healing transformation. If we lose hope we slide towards the lure of a quick death by suicide or slow death through addiction and other self-destructive behaviors. How we are "held" by our parents, extended family and community, physically, emotionally, and spiritually, can either help us or hinder us in retaining our memories of the soul's eye view.

4) In the oral phase of development the infant still has limited mobility and physical coordination but is developing a lively curiosity in the world and a hunger for emotional connection. At this stage parents bond with their infants through eye contact and cuddling, instinctively engaging the infant with high-pitched sounds and repetitive games that give the infant pleasure and form the rudiments of interpersonal relatedness in later life.[20] In effect, if all goes well, the familial environment formed by those around us loves us into being.

It is humbling to realize how utterly dependent each of us has been on the loving care of others. Mere food and shelter are not enough. In studies of children orphaned during war, developmental psychologist Rene Spitz observed that children who received adequate physical care but were deprived of physical and emotional affection lost their will to live and died from emotional neglect.[21] Just as the child is physically nurtured by a happy feeding experience at the breast, so he or she is emotionally fed in essential ways by the warm physical presence and loving gaze of parents and family. One could say that the infants Spitz studied

died of a broken heart when the nourishing love they expected and longed for was denied.

Erikson Erikson described the basic developmental challenge of the oral stage in terms of trust and mistrust.[22] Clearly, if we are "disappointed in love" at this early stage in our development it will be difficult to open our hearts in love to others, difficult to trust that the light of God's love is always available to help us grow.

5) The task of the toddler, or anal stage, as Erikson sees it, is autonomy versus shame and doubt. Now the child is mobile, beginning to take charge of his or her own basic bodily functions like eating and elimination. If all goes well the child is able to experience a developing separate and independent sense of self while retaining a positive connection to a family that both accepts the child and sets limits in a consistent, loving manner. During this time the child also begins to speak. Language, as Stern notes, is a two-edged sword. It serves to connect the child to family and culture but it also disconnects the child from the amodal quality of pre-verbal perception. Amodal perception engages the whole person more vividly than mere reason or ordinary rational thought. Art, poetry, music, being in love, and religious experience afford opportunities for adults to re-experience what the pre-verbal child may feel all the time, a vivid interconnectedness of sense and feeling. In amodal perception red tulips "shout" with color, a symphony sends chills down the spine, poetry allows us to feel the textures of another's being through words. In religious experience mystics of all ages have known the paradox of being one in loving union with God and still an individual self who can descend from the mountain top of revelation to speak of that noetic encounter in ordinary life.

I believe that as children, especially before language, we experience the vivid intensity of loving union with others and all creation. The eye of the soul is still one with all it sees. Gradually, as we are disappointed in our experiences of love, we shut down most of our aliveness into the quasi-torpor and depression that often passes for a normal middle-aged existence. But unless the soul's sight has been thoroughly blinded, there is always something within us that hungers for more.

Discernment and Soul: the Woman at the Well

In *Waiting for God* Simone Weil writes that ". . . prayer consists of attention. It is the orientation of all the attention of which the soul is capable towards God. . . . There is a real desire when there is an effort of attention. . . . (D)esire alone draws God down." [23] She speaks of the soul's longing for God that focuses the soul on God with the rapt attention of lovers in the Song of Songs. As lovers desire the loving presence of the other, the soul longs to revel in the presence of God.

The clear-eyed soul hungers for a glimpse of God, the Beloved, and the psyche hungers for its own wholeness. We intuit on some level that our conscious understanding is only the tip of the iceberg. If we dive into the watery world of dreams we learn to understand ourselves in a deeper way, developing more compassion for ourselves and others. Jung presents the need for the conscious mind to be in dialogue with the unconscious:

> If attention is directed to the unconscious, the unconscious will yield up its contents, and these in turn will fructify the conscious like a fountain of living water. [24]

Weil writes from the soul's perspective of attention to God in prayer. Jung speaks of the psyche that gives attention to the unconscious but does so with an implicit awareness of the soul's eye view. Being a pastor's son, Jung was no doubt aware of the biblical allusion he suggests with the phrase "living water." [Life-giving water for Zion was a prophetic theme (Zechariah 14:8, Ezekial 47:1f); water is also an essential symbol in John's gospel.] Jesus said to the Samaritan woman at the well:

> If you only knew what God is offering and who it is that
> is saying to you: Give me a drink, you would have been
> the one to ask, and he would have given you living water
> (John 4:10, JB).

The Samaritan woman may have been a person so damaged in
her relationships with others that she came to draw water in the
heat of the noon day sun rather than risk encountering members
of her community at dawn or dusk. She may have kept her hope
unconscious the way a neglected child hides her favorite toys for
fear of losing them. Yet she answered the Jewish stranger boldly
when he said "Give me a drink." He then proceeded to offer her
"a spring of water welling up to eternal life." Without clear awareness of what Jesus was offering, she reached for this water with the
full desire of her wounded being. A moment of intuition, based
on her hope that the stranger had something of real value to offer,
came to her just before she said to Jesus "Sir, give me this water,
that I may not thirst, nor come here to draw." Despite the defen-
siveness and anger common in those who have been abused, forever failing to find love because they feel unworthy, some unconscious knowing stirred this woman's hope and intuition enabling
her to trust a stranger. She was receptive to Jesus' mysterious offer.
She returned to her townsfolk saying: "Come, see a man who told
me all that I ever did. Can this be the Christ?" and because of her,
many believed (John 4:7-42).

As a psychological metaphor, the Samaritan woman who comes
alone to the well in the heat of the day can be understood as
that part of ourselves that is scorned, despised, cast out. Isolated,
bereft, she thirsts for meaning and comes to draw wisdom from
the unconscious depths where hope abides. Her thirst, her desire
for life brings her face to face with the Christ. Their encounter, at
a spot where water wells up from underground in a high and arid
land, transforms her. Jesus confronts her honestly and directly with
the truth of her life but does so without condemnation or rejection. Through their encounter she finds transformation. She re-

turns to her community bearing good news and is scorned no more. Having been transformed in her own eyes, she is transformed in the eyes of her community as well.

Three aspects of the process of discernment are illustrated by this story. Despite her history of abuse and neglect, the Samaritan woman had hope that her longing for love might one day be answered. Though her relationships repeatedly failed she kept trying. The love we feel for each other is the earthly counterpart of God's love for us. As we are able to draw near to ourselves and others in clear-sighted, loving acceptance, we draw near to God. The Samaritan woman's relationships were a repetition of earlier failures, yet she still hoped to love and be loved, to "get it right."

The woman at the well also had an intuition that the stranger had something of value to offer her. When Jesus piqued her curiosity by saying "If you only knew what God is offering. . . . " she was quick to respond, like a small child reaching for her mother "Sir, give me this water. . . . " Perhaps most important, she was receptive to the good she sensed in Jesus. Somewhere at the core of her being she carried the memory of being bathed in love and she reached for the living water Jesus offered as for life itself. And in so doing she found herself transformed.

Discernment and Soul: Contemporary Examples

Any therapist who has worked with couples in distress recognizes the anger and despair of love lost. Harville Hendrix believes that in marriage we hope for a second chance to win the love of the parent from whom we felt most estranged. We are therefore unconsciously receptive to persons with the characteristics that remind us of that parent. Our intuition tells us that if we can find our way through the flaming sword of past parental disappointments, the paradise of God's accepting love can be regained.[25] When our new love, our hope for salvation fails to meet our deep longings, we feel bereft. The only choices appear to be depression, furious confrontation, or distance and divorce. The connection between pre-Oedipal, pre-verbal love and the acceptance we crave is so strong that most couples find it difficult to believe that dialogue can do any good. They want the other to change, now!— nothing else will do.

The journey of life-long partnership is rather like the life of faith. Those who first undertake a conscious partnership with God, sincerely desiring to be led and sustained by God's daily guidance, are likely to be fed with milk at first. Prayer is an unfailing source of comfort and answers to prayer seem clear. Later, things become more difficult. It is as if God says to us, "Now that you're ready to be weaned, I expect you to decide on your own. I'll be nearby if you need me, but the decision is up to you." Just as the toddler begins to explore the world by moving away from the mother, so growing in faith may require us to move away from easy certainties and assurances, hoping that God is present even when unfelt and unseen.

So too in partnership and marriage, couples begin with an intoxicating sense of unity that is like heaven on earth as it replicates their souls' longing and answering bliss in the arms of the Beloved. Later it becomes necessary for the couple to stand farther part, to find their own way in the world, still in partnership, hopefully, but not as closely identified as before.

Looking back from the vantage point of several years on my own dilemma, I see my confusion as overdetermined. The simplest version might be to say that my values were in conflict with the direction that growth into greater wholeness required. But the values that seemed so difficult to reconcile, as for example the value that a "good woman" places her family's needs above her own, were not simply discarded in the course of the inevitable disruptions that followed my decision for doctoral studies, but transformed.

During one snowy week in January when my family was away, I prayed through the spiritual exercises of St. Ignatius. In these exercises one is given a series of images, largely drawn from the life of Christ. The instruction is to hold these pictures in the mind's eye and give them attention. In two instances, to my amazement, the images came alive. They were no longer like a flat picture in a book but a living scene of which I was a part. In the first I saw the Holy Family, the infant Jesus with his parents, and beheld their love for him. I understood this as a metaphor for human love to which all families and all persons are called—to worship that of God in one another just as loving parents adore and delight in the life of their newborn child.

The second scene, so vivid that I could only bear to look on it for an instant, was that of Jesus' agony on the cross. His physical, emotional, and spiritual suffering was so great that I vowed in that moment never to add to that suffering by harming another if I could possibly avoid it. Being far from perfect, I fall short of this resolve daily. Both visions, the Holy Family and the crucified Christ, point to a perfection of love and sacrifice that one might well labor one's entire life to approach. The point of our life's journey is not to arrive at perfection, but to keep the goal clearly before us, ever desiring to recover the sight of the soul. In this example of discernment I approached the exercises with *hope* that they might give me the guidance for which I longed. Because I was *receptive* to the images as a vehicle for discernment, I did receive, in two instances, a deeper *intuition* of their spiritual significance as a guide for living.

Like God's answer to Job, I did not receive the specific answer I was looking for: "Do this, don't do that." What I did receive were visions to live by and the same assurance of God's presence that answered Job's long lament. Met by God's response, after all his suffering, Job could still respond "I repent of dust and ashes" (Job 42:6).[26] After receiving God's response to his cries he was finally able to come to terms with suffering as a mystery and re-enter life, knowing that God would be with him always.

Conclusion: the Essential Unity of Psyche and Soul

A client once raised some difficult issues toward the end of his session. To break the tension between his words and the painful feelings that they elicited, he told this joke:

> Q: "What did the guru say to the hot-dog vendor?
> A: "Make me one...with EVERYTHING!

The joke is bittersweet because it names a deep longing. My client longed to cut through the shame that had mired him in self-hatred all his life, separating him from others, from himself, and from God. I share his longing and I also share his frustration; the divine Center that calls us, that draws us, that embraces us in moments of unexpected grace can be so difficult to reach, so hard to see and hear.

How can we be "one with everything" when we can't even be one with ourselves? We long for the freedom of wholeness but cling to the comforting confines of a familiar lack of health. We long to be open and trusting of others including God as Other, the Presence in our midst, but we fear loss of self, loss of control. Our integrity is too often a house built on shifting sand; we comfort ourselves with an illusory sense of our own goodness by ignoring, projecting, or repressing whatever aspects of self we deem to be unacceptable and dark.

We long to be one with everything, with ourselves, with others, with God, but we don't want to do the messy work required to get there. As twenty-first-century Friends we have a tendency to look back nostalgically at our glorious past. We celebrate the resurrection and ignore the crucifixion. We forget the years of lonely struggle George Fox endured before his early prophetic openings. Most of us go through such struggles not just once but many times. We may find that as our sphere of light enlarges, our awareness of the darkness beyond it grows as well. Through the dialogue of discernment we often find more questions, not easy answers.

Despite the potential usefulness of separating the hopeful soul from the more pessimistic voices in the psyche, it is also true that distinctions have their limitations. The very idea of "soul" has been criticized as a theoretical abstraction that detracts from the essential unity of those aspects of being we label mind and body, psyche and soul.[27] Perhaps if we could see Creation and ourselves as God sees, we would see that oneness, the interconnectedness of all things, is more real than the distinctions and divisions that seem so insurmountable. We live with the tension between a mystical view which finds the divine Center, a loving Creator, at the heart of life and the more temporal, divided perspective that generally serves to get us through the day.

Jung notes that distinctions are necessary for consciousness; without them thought itself is impossible. But consciousness is not synonymous with God. In considering the dialogue of psyche and soul we do well to remember that thought and language are always one step removed from the ineffable being of Creation. If our ultimate goal is to minister from the divine Center, discernment is essential in moving us towards our goal, but only as the means, not the end. Our end as persons of faith is the state of awareness Julian of Norwich knew when she said "And all will be well, all manner of things will be well."[28] Julian's beatific vision is the sight of the soul. Her felt unity with God may be like a distant mountain peak, glimpsed from afar, but we know it is there. The dialogue of psyche and soul can show us the way.

Though we are not the Christ and may seldom find ourselves or those we serve as vividly affected by a pastoral encounter as the Samaritan woman was by her dialogue with Jesus; yet, as the Light of Christ lives in us, we can expect such transformations to occur. As we journey through the seemingly barren wilderness of the damaged psyche with our clients and within ourselves, hope, intuition, and receptivity can guide us in the process of discernment, leading us ever onward through life's valleys toward the mountain vistas of the soul.

May we ask for hope even in the dark night of the soul when hope seems lost. May we seek those sparks of intuition by which the still, small voice of the Holy Spirit guides us. May we knock insistently and then be receptive to whatever greets us from the other side of the doors we have closed within ourselves and against others. The knowledge of God's love for us lives within us all, at the core of our being. We can answer the psyche's deepest fears only as we hold fast to the sight of the soul, reweaving our humanity at the turn of the millennium, Now.

Notes

1. See for example Thomas Moore, *The Care of the Soul: A Guide for Cultivating Depth and Sacredness in Everyday Life* (New York: HarperCollins,1992), xi ff.

2. Ann Ulanov, unpublished address, Union Theological Seminary (New York, New York, 1991) and Paul Tillich, *The Eternal Now* (New York: Scribner, 1956/1963).

3. Thomas Kelly, *Testament of Devotion* (New York: Harper and Row, 1941), 29.

4. Cf. German - *seele*, and French - *l'esprit*.

5. Ann and Barry Ulanov, "Senses of the Soul: the Meeting of Spirituality and Psychotherapy." Conference held at Christian Theological Seminary, Indianapolis, IN, 4/30-5/1, 1999.

6. Rudolf Otto, *The Idea of the Holy* (New York: Oxford University Press, 1923/1958).

7. Felicity Kelcourse, *Discernment: the Art of Attention in Spirituality and Psychotherapy* (Ann Arbor: University Microfilms International, 1998).

8. C.G. Jung, *Collected Works*, vol. 8, "The Transcendent Function" (Princeton, New Jersey: Princeton University Press, 1934/1954).

9. John Woolman, Phillip Moulton, ed., *The Journal and Major Essays of John Woolman* (New York: Oxford University Press, 1971), p.51.

10. William Penn, *No Cross, No Crown*, Ronald Selleck, ed. (Richmond, Indiana: Friends United Press, 1682/1969).

11. Patricia Loring *Spiritual Discernment: the Context and Goal of Clearness Committees*, Pendle Hill Pamphlet 305. (Wallingford, PA: Pendle Hill Publications,1992).

12. Felicity Kelcourse, *Discernment*, 58-74.

13. Ana-Maria Rizzuto, *The Birth of the Living God: A Psychoanalytic Study* (Chicago: University of Chicago Press, 1979).

14. Antonio Damasio, *Descarte's Error: Emotion, Reason and the Human Brain* (New York: Putnam's Sons, 1994).

15. George Fox, *The Journal of George Fox*, Rufus Jones, ed., (Richmond, IN: Friends United Press, 1694/1976), 97.

16. Paul Ricoeur, *The Symbolism of Evil* (Boston: Beacon Press, 1967).

17. Margaret Mahler, *On Human Symbiosis and the Vicissitudes of Individuation*. (New York: International University Press, 1968).

18. Daniel Stern, *The Interpersonal World of the Infant: A View from Psychoanalysis and Developmental Psychology* (New York: Basic Books, 1985).

19. Sigmund Freud, *Standard Edition of the Complete Psychological Works of Sigmund Freud*, 21, 3, The Future of an Illusion (London: Hogarth Press and the Institute for Psychoanalysis, 1927).

20. Daniel Stern, *The Interpersonal World of the Infant.*

21. Rene Spitz, "Hospitalism: an Inquiry into the Genesis of Psychiatric Conditions in Early Childhood," *Psychoanalytic Study of the Child*, 1 (1945): 53-72.

22. Erikson Erikson, *Childhood and Society* (New York: Norton, 1963).

23. Simone Weil, *Waiting for God* (New York: Harper and Row, 1973), 110-111.

24. C.G. Jung, *Collected Works,* vol. 14, Mysterium Coniunctionis (Princeton, NJ: Princeton University Press, 1955-56), 163.

25. Harville Hendrix, *Getting the Love you Want: A Guide for Couples* (New York: Harper and Row, 1988).

26. J. Gerald Janzen, *Job,* Interpretation: A Bible Commentary for Teaching and Preaching (Atlanta, Georgia: John Knox, 1985), 254-259.

27. Naomi Goldenberg, *Returning Words to Flesh: Feminism, Psychoanalysis and the Resurrection of the Body* (Boston: Beacon Press, 1990).

28. Brendan Doyle, Introduction and versions, *Meditations with Julian of Norwich* (Santa Fe, NM: Bear & Company, 1983).

IV. Pastoral Care Across Cultures:
A Quaker Model

Bill Ratliff

OUR LIFE TODAY consists of living with persons from many parts of the globe. Work, school, and the market now include persons with a variety of accents, skin tones, and modes of cultural dress. Pervasive in urban areas, small towns and rural areas increasingly experience this multicultural variety. In worship on Sunday morning we may sit beside a person recently emigrated from Mexico. In a committee meeting, we may discover that there is a member born in Russia who came here with parents as an infant, another member who lived in Kenya with missionary parents, and another recently returned from working for three years in Saudi Arabia. In cities, faith groups from other countries have negotiated meeting in the buildings of established churches. How do we relate to these persons in a way that honors them for who they are? More specifically for this chapter, how do we effectively care for such persons within the context of our faith community?

Pastoral care has generally been defined from the perspective of white, educated, upper-middle class Euro-American men who have written and published the primary texts in this area. As we become more aware of the diversity of cultures and people around the globe and often in our own Meetings and churches, we are seeing that these old paradigms of relating and caring for others do not work for everyone. My personal transformation began in the early 1980s on a study tour of China. I suddenly realized much of what I studied and currently practiced as a pastoral counselor would be irrelevant in that country; the Western value of personal introspection and focus on the self is not a Chinese value.

This necessary transformation occurs only when we can get outside our own culture. As David Augsburger puts it, "One who knows but one culture knows no culture."[1] Minority persons become bicultural to survive; they have to learn the rules and language of the majority culture if they are to traffic there. We in the majority culture can stay insulated in our circumscribed world of home, work, and faith community; we can adjust to working with them without being impacted by their worldview.

In order to care effectively for persons different from us, we have to be able to bridge the differences, to some extent, in order to understand them. Bridging those differences means that we have to be able to leave the "comfort zone" of our world, and risk seeing the world from the other's point of view. We enter into the lives of other people through empathic imagination. Many ways exist to do this, in addition to living in another culture. We can read novels and historical accounts of other places and times, look at art, listen to music, watch a series on television, or study the context and times of the First or Second Testament of the Bible. Any such activities can provide a cross-cultural experience, if we enter deeply into it. With any of these experiences, we can remain a tourist, that is to make a quick, cursory excursion of the highlights. Just as with actual travel, in our imagination also, our intellect may take the journey, while our mind and heart stay at home. Reading, music, art, television—all can provide entertainment rather than a view from the inside.

We can really enter another culture and allow the worldview of that culture to soak into our skin when we see, at least for a moment, the world from another perspective. When that happens, we are changed. "To 'pass over' is to enter a new world; to 'come back' is to return a different person."[2] Indeed, this transformation can be spiritual, as one writer notes: "Passing over and coming back, it seems, is the spiritual adventure of our time. . . . One has to pass over, to shift standpoints, in order to enter into the life of Jesus, even if one is a Christian, and then one has to come back, to shift standpoints again, to return to one's own life."[3]

At one and the same time we are like everyone else, we are like some others, and we are like no other.[4] First, there are many universals that are true about every human being: we all live and breathe and need food, shelter, relationships, and meaning to life. Until recently theology has tended to focus more on the universal truths such as love, peace, sin, and salvation than pastoral care has. Second, we are like *some* other people, in terms of specific characteristics having to do with language, culture, and personality traits. Both pastoral care and theology have traditionally ignored this area. Yet these cultural variations are important in the way we view troubles and joys and what kind of care is needed. Third, also true is that we are unique as a human being; we are like no other, in terms of physical, mental, and emotional characteristics and in terms of the particular combination of genetics, experiences, and background that come together in making us who we are. Pastoral care has focused and excelled in this area. Pastoral care and theology can benefit from tending to the second truth, mining its riches to make our care-giving more effective.

In this chapter I propose how Quaker faith and practice can provide a helpful way of approaching another culture, to learn what gives meaning, and then to care more appropriately. Worship is central to Quakerism and to this model. George Fox, the founder of Quakerism, provides two pillars for a cross-cultural approach. The early American Quaker, John Woolman, and his initial travel to a Delaware tribe of Native American Indians at Wyalusing exemplifies the model. Finally, I explore the implications of worship, Fox, and Woolman's visit for our efforts at pastoral care across cultures.

Quaker Way of Worship

Genuine worship, of any form, takes us beyond the boundaries of our limited self. At these moments we view ourselves outside ourselves, perhaps as God might view us. In worship we can transcend the self, or can be given a new self, as the writer of Ephesians points out:"You were taught to put away your former way of life, your old self. . . ."[5] This kind of worship provides a crucial foundation for going beyond the boundaries of the self, that is required in entering into another culture. It also guards against our temptation to be a savior to persons in need by keeping our pastoral care realistic, limited, and appropriate to the particular person in her or his context.

For Quakers who take their faith seriously, weekly Meetings for Worship lie at the heart of who they are and what they do. Whether an unprogrammed Meeting, with the gathered community waiting in silence to hear a divine word, or a pastoral Meeting, with the gathered community proceeding through a service of worship, true Quaker worship is an encounter with the holy. The silence present in Quaker worship is a distinctive mark. Unprogrammed worship is silent, with persons standing to speak, recite, sing, or pray as they are led. Pastoral Meetings will have periods of silence before and/or after the prepared message. When people speak out of the silence, it is called vocal ministry. Indiana Yearly Meeting describes worship in the following way:

> Worship stands neither in forms nor in the disuse of forms; it may be without words as well as with them. Both silence and vocal exercises are recognized and valued not as ends, but as means toward the attainment of an end, which is the divine blessing upon the individual and the congregation.[6]

John Punshon, Quaker author, teacher, and speaker, calls this weekly experience of worship ". . . a grueling and exciting exposure to the searching wind of the Spirit."[7] The Credo of the Earlham School of Religion, a Quaker seminary, is "We hold that

Christ is present guiding and directing our lives, and that we can know and obey Christ's will." Regular and sustained soaking in the gathered community for worship makes Christ's presence more real in our lives and experience. Out of that sense of Presence, we can more readily discern, with the aid of the community, Christ's direction for our lives.

The community coming together in expectant waiting has always been central to Quaker worship. The community supports us in the difficult, exhilarating experience of opening ourselves to the holy Other; the community assists us in discerning God's call and leadings. The Quaker community, like all faith communities is not perfect, but as John Punshon notes, "The church is imperfect because we all belong to it."[8]

Over time, worship forms and transforms. Many Quakers have disobeyed civil laws that they believed were unjust, have ministered to those in prison and to Native Americans, and have resisted all forms of violence and war and slavery. Their actions grew out of deep, sustained worship and careful, prayerful discernment in the community.

Worship is key to understanding God's call and to being effective pastoral care givers, especially in cross-cultural situations. The ways George Fox and John Woolman approached worship inform the connections between cross-cultural pastoral care and worship.

George Fox

George Fox (1624-1691) is the acknowledged founder of Quakerism. The son of a Leicestershire weaver, he had little formal schooling, and left home at age 19 in search of meaning to his life. He did not find it in the clergy and churches of the established Church of England. Neither did he find it among the ministers of the other, dissenting churches. Then a powerful experience changed his life. His own words best describe his experience:

> And when all my hopes in them (the preachers from the dissenting movement) and in all men were gone, so that I had nothing outwardly to help me, nor could tell what to do, then, Oh then, I heard a voice which said, "There is one, even Christ Jesus, that can speak to thy condition," and when I heard it my heart did leap for joy.[9]

He began to travel the countryside, preaching to whomever gathered to listen. Out of his experience with God, he fearlessly confronted the religious and civil authorities. This led to numerous persecutions and imprisonments. But his message of having access to God without the intervention of priests or church institutions sounded a fresh and exciting call for his day, to which crowds of persons eagerly listened and responded.

In the same year as his conversion, 1647, Fox had to deal with inner temptations and wickedness. He cries to the Lord, asking why he should be this way:

> And the Lord answered that it was needful I should have a sense of all conditions, how else should I speak to all conditions; and in this I saw the infinite love of God.[10]

Fox, in dealing with his own humanity, receives the empathy necessary to understand other persons. His problems and wounds have become ways to understand other people. Through it all is God's love. His ministry then proceeded from the position of being *with* the people rather than being *over* the people, as he had earlier experienced other priests and ministers. Fox models another way of learning empathic imagination. In facing his own inadequacies and awakening to the witness in himself of God's love, he is empowered to see more of the truth of other persons, not judgmentally, but with love for them as well.

Later in his spiritual formation inwardly and ministry to others outwardly, he most fully articulates the paradigm for care his experiences of the Inward Teacher have taught him:

Friends, in the power of life and wisdom, and in the dread of the Lord God of life, and heaven, and earth, dwell, that in the wisdom of God over all ye may be preserved, and be a terror to all the adversaries of God, and a dread, answering that of God in them all, spreading the Truth abroad, awakening the witness, confounding deceit, gathering up out of transgression into the life, the covenant of life and peace with God. . . . Bring all into the worship of God. . . . So the ministers of the Spirit must minister to the spirit that is transgressed and in prison, which hath been in captivity up to every one; whereby with the same spirit people must be led out of captivity up to God, the Father of spirits, and do service to him and have unity with him, with the Scriptures and one with another. And this is the word of the Lord God to you all, and a charge to you all in the presence of the living God, be patterns, be examples in all countries, places, islands, nations, wherever you come; that your carriage and life may preach among all sorts of people, and to them. Then you will come to walk cheerfully over the world, answering that of God in every one; whereby in them ye may be a blessing, and make the witness of God in them bless you. (*Journal*, 263)

It's as if his own wrestling with his temptations and wickedness gives him the knowledge that deceit and transgressions hold people in captivity and through a mutual awakening out of love among people, God's presence can be manifest in particular lives. Negative experiences in others' responses to his attempts to awaken the Spirit did not shake his trust in God. In fact, it is in being faithful to these negative experiences, patiently waiting out deceit and distrust, through worship, that the deep joy and cheer is born. In Fox's experience as described in these two pillar statements of his faith, we have a powerful model for pastoral care givers and counselors, particularly in a cross-cultural setting.

Quaker history has referred to "that of God" as the Inward Light or the Seed or the Seed Christ. Seeing that of God in others produces a profound respect for all humans, because they have that of God just as we do; they have access to the truth just as we do. We are truly equal, no more, no less. This attitude has profound implications for meeting others who are different from us. John Miller, retired professor at Earlham School of Religion, describes the Quaker foundation for multi-cultural education, which can also serve as a foundation for cross-cultural pastoral care:

> Because of the Quaker experience and belief that there is that of God in every person, that the Seed Christ is present in the heart of every human, Quakers have always had a point of contact with people of differing cultural inheritance, language, or religious practices. The Quaker experience and testimony to the Inward Light points to an inherently non-provincial place of meeting other persons. This is why meeting in silence is crucial to all genuine forms of Quaker meeting, whether unprogrammed or programmed. In this setting the cultural inheritances can be abandoned and the Inward Light of Christ allowed to illumine the community God is trying to create among people of divergent cultural practices and beliefs.[11]

The Quaker foundation for cross-cultural pastoral care is built first on a particular, central understanding of worship that harkens back to Fox. Worship provides the spiritual foundation for our daily lives, as well as for any new adventure. Worship guides us into this new area of cross-cultural pastoral care, if we are called to this kind of care, and helps us discern the call. Worship provides the support and perspective necessary in approaching people from another culture, and worship leads us home, where we can rest, reflect on the experience, and learn from it.

In walking cheerfully over the land and seeing that of God in others, as Fox suggests, we are enabled to trust strangers and strange cultures. Indeed, we are encouraged to take the risk to cross boundaries of familiarity and security in order to venture into another culture. At the same time, we have a basic respect for others, which leads us to treat them as we ourselves wish to be treated.

John Woolman's Visit with the Native Americans

John Woolman embodies the basic Quaker attitude of respect for the "other" and desire to answer to the witness in that person or culture different from what he knew. Born in 1720, John Woolman grew up the fourth of 13 children in Burlington County, New Jersey, less than 20 miles from Philadelphia. His father was a farmer and fruit grower. Throughout his life John felt a keen sense of God's presence, and occasionally of God's absence. An active prayer life and a firm belief in divine providence, in which God directs the destinies of persons and nations, firmly convinced him of the need to act from the revealed truth of God. His inner life of the spirit was combined with an outer life of action. He developed a primary concern for the condition of slaves and worked for the abolition of slavery among Quakers and others. He did this through personal confrontation with individual slave owners as well as worshipping and speaking in various meetings and larger Quaker gatherings. He also wrote an essay, *Some Considerations on the Keeping of Negroes,* as well as an antislavery epistle sent by Philadelphia Yearly Meeting of 1754 to all Quaker groups in Pennsylvania and New Jersey.[12] Philadelphia Yearly Meeting in 1758 adopted a formal statement, at the insistence of Woolman:

> . . . urging Friends to free their slaves, arranging for the visitation of slave holders, and decreeing that anyone who bought or sold slaves was to be excluded from participating in the business affairs of the church.[13]

He made many trips throughout the land in early America and to England at the end of his life, on behalf of his many concerns.

When he was tempted by wealth, Woolman became a tailor so that he could live simply and without luxury. The growing luxury and the growing poverty in this country concerned him through his life. He expressed his economic views in an essay, *A Plea for the Poor*. He was also concerned about issues of war and peace. During the French and Indian war, he encouraged Quakers to remain pacifist. He refused to pay taxes levied by England to help underwrite the war.[14]

As part of his concern for peace, Woolman undertook a hazardous trip of reconciliation to the "Indians." At age 36 he began keeping a journal, which he continued until his death. This record of his life and spiritual concerns and activities has been influential to many people, Quaker and others alike, through the centuries. His journal records his trip to visit the Delaware Indians in 1762. We turn now to the events surrounding that trip.

Journey to Wyalusing

John Woolman writes in his Journal that he had felt love for the "natives of the land" for many years.[15] In fact, he had referred to "Indians" or "natives" four times prior to this record of his trip.[16] (Throughout his writings, John Woolman uses the word "Indian," as was common for his time. While not acceptable today, "Indian" will be used throughout the rest of this chapter.) In August 1761, he met some natives from an Indian town called Wyalusing, about 200 miles from Philadelphia. He conversed with them through an interpreter and found that they were acquainted with the divine power. This experience apparently increased his "inward drawings" until they came to some ripeness, as he called it. "Drawings" is a sense of guidance or mission usually to a particular act rather than to a lifelong occupation.[17] He had shared his inward drawings with no one except his wife until this point. Then in the winter of 1762 he laid it before Friends in his local Meeting, as well as two regional Meetings. Friends united in supporting him in his drawings and apparently also in his choice of an Indian guide or pilot.[18]

The night before he was to leave, he was awakened by a man reporting that the Indians had taken a fort west of Philadelphia and had killed and scalped a number of English. His response was to turn to the Lord for guidance. Afterwards, his mind ". . . settled in a belief that it was my duty to proceed on my journey. . . ."[19] He did acknowledge that there was great searching of heart and strong cries to the Lord that only the pure spirit of Truth be sought. He committed himself to the Lord and set off on June 9, 1763, along with traveling companions including his friend Benjamin Parvin who decided to go with him. This was almost two years after his first meeting and conversation with the native people.[20]

Meditations While Traveling

Woolman records two instances of empathic imagination toward the Indians as he journeyed to visit them. One night they camped near some large trees which were peeled and on which were recorded stories by the Indians of battles. As he thought about the miseries of these proud people and the way hatred grows in the mind of children of nations engaged in war, ". . . the desire to cherish the spirit of love and peace amongst these people arose very fresh in me."

Woolman's desire to cherish the spirit of love and peace among these people describes well the heart of pastoral care and the motivation for taking arduous journeys in understanding others. They must all be done in the spirit of love and peace. If that is not present, nothing else matters.

Three days later he was riding over barren hills and began meditating on the change in the circumstances of the Indians when the English came and took the best land. He thought about the difficulties of the natives and the Negroes, and a love and heavenly care for them came over him. He was concerned not to give any just cause of offense to blacks from Africa and the native inhabitants. The phrase "not to give any just cause of offense" is taken from Paul's writings in the New Testament, as Michel Birkel helpfully pointed out to me.[22] Woolman uses this phrase in several places as a kind of technical term, in reference to dealing with slaves and also with Native Americans. According to Woolman, these people, as people in all other cultures, will judge us by what we do rather than by what we say. They will judge our professed Christian faith by the way we behave. He asks us to reflect on what danger we are putting people in, by the way we act and live. He was clear that God has equal regard for all humankind and that the English were spreading a wrong spirit. ". . . the seeds of great calamity and desolation are sown and growing fast on this continent."[23]

Several times during the trip, Woolman would think about what he was doing, and would end up feeling quiet and content. During one day, for example, when rain kept them in their tent all day, he found space to think about the nature of what he was doing. He records that "love was the first motion. . . ."[24] From that love arose a concern to spend time with the Indians, so that he could feel and understand their life and spirit. He also wanted to learn from them, and thought perhaps he could help them by ". . . following the leadings of Truth amongst them."[25] The troubles of war and bad weather he saw as a good opportunity to season his mind and bring him more into sympathy with the Indians. He ended up quiet and content.[26] On another day trees fallen across their path and swamps in other areas hindered their progress. He thought about this and felt himself a sojourner in the world and believed that God would support him. So he came to a perfect resignation, or what we might call a sense of deep peace.[27] At least two other times Woolman reconsidered whether he had done the right thing in coming at this time. Each time he concluded that he had followed God up to this point, and he was given quietness in his spirit.[29]

A few days later he became weak, and with the news of warriors on the march near them, he had a fresh trial of his faith. As he described it, ". . . my cries for help were put up to the Lord, who in great mercy gave me a resigned heart, in which I found quietness."[30] A "resigned heart" is not negative for Woolman; rather it means a letting go that results in peace.

Stay at Wyalusing Indian Settlement

Eight days after beginning, they reached Wyalusing. Their Indian pilot told them to sit down at the edge of the settlement while he went to tell the others that they had arrived. A deep inward stillness developed over them as they sat on a log. An Indian woman of "modest countenance" with a baby came and sat near them. They felt the nearness of God.

He and his friend were invited to a house where about 60 people were sitting in silence. After they sat together in silence a short time, he stood and explained the concern for their good which prompted his visit. He used only a few brief sentences. Then he presented his certificate from his Quaker Meeting, which probably indicated that he was traveling on behalf of the Meeting which supported him.

Woolman convinced a Moravian missionary, who was already there, that he was not in competition, thereby dealing with another cross-cultural issue. By mutual agreement, John Woolman joined the missionary's worship time with the Indians. He was moved to speak, with interpreters helping. In one instance he felt his mind covered with the spirit of prayer, so he told the interpreters to stop, since he knew that if he prayed rightly, God would hear him. At the end of the meeting, Papunehang, a chief of the tribe and a Christian converted by the Moravian, said "I love to feel where words come from."[31]

The following day he was meditating on the state of the Indians and:

. . . a near sympathy with them was raised in me; and my heart being enlarged in the love of Christ, I thought that the affectionate care of a good man for his only brother in affliction does not exceed what I then felt for that people."[32]

This statement shows how deeply Woolman cared. For Woolman, a "near sympathy" means a close feeling with another person, according to Birkel. At other places, he speaks of a "feeling condition of others," which means much the same thing. This basic feeling of identity with the oppressed, whether slave or Indian, comes for Woolman from worship.

Although the situation remained dangerous, nonetheless he felt joyful that the Lord had strengthened him to come. He was quiet in several of the meetings, and when he spoke, he did so in short, plain sentences. Having stayed four days, he felt at liberty to leave. Those who had gotten to know him through attending the worship services came to him to shake hands. He then went to those who did not come to the services and also shook their hands. Upon leaving, he believed that a door remained open for faithful disciples to labor among them.[33] His belief has proved true, since history has shown an ongoing interest on the part of Quakers for the Native Americans.

He returned home, having been away 18 days. Woolman sums up what he gained from the journey in the following way:

> [But] I was not only taught patience but also made thankful to God, who thus led me about and instructed me that I might have a quick and lively feeling of the afflictions of my fellow creatures whose situation in life is difficult.[34]

From his writings, it is clear that he wants to enter the suffering of people, in order to educate himself and others and to promote the ongoing redemption of the world. We can only hope to have such gifts of patience and empathy in our cross-cultural forays. What powerful, galvanizing motivation for entering the terrain of cross-cultural pastoral care!

Implications for Pastoral Care Across Cultures

In looking at the nature of Quaker worship, two statements from George Fox, and John Woolman's journey to the Indians, we find several guidelines for our own journeying across cultures, whether for our own enlightenment or to offer pastoral care. We need to immerse in worship; listen to the call; discern whether it is from God; be open to each other; remember that there will be difficulties and trying times; have the support and accountability of the community; and finally be grateful to God. Each one will be elaborated below.

Worship

As we have seen for Quakers throughout history and for John Woolman specifically, everything proceeds from worship. Regular, deep worship with a faith community is the bedrock upon which life and work are built. Much of Woolman's journal recounts his experiences in worship, his inward leadings and struggles, and his meetings with individual and families, which often included worship in the home. As Bill Taber notes in his chapter, "seeking an opportunity" was the early Quaker way of worshipping with an individual or family. Profound speaking to the condition of the individual or family often came out of worship, embodying pastoral care of them.

Pastoral care, when done with sensitivity and in depth, is not easy. In listening to someone, the issue often is not what to say but how much we can bear. Challenges rise exponentially when attemptiong to offer this kind of pastoral care to a person of another culture. From worship we get the courage and the resources to dare to provide care. As a result, all of pastoral care emerges from, is bathed in, and returns to worship.

Expecting God to be present and give us what we need in caring for another, when we do not have an ongoing relationship with God, is presumptuous. Worship must be a regular part of our lives, so that when the occasion for pastoral care arises, the God who provides the resources and love is readily present in and between us.

The unprogrammed style of waiting worship seems to speak to persons from many cultures, especially to native peoples. With the aboriginal people in Darwin, Australia, as well as the students from the South Pacific island countries who come to Pacific Theological College in Suva, Fiji, I experienced a deep, centered silence quickly settling over the gathered worshipping community. Deep vocal ministry often emerges.

While visiting Nungalinya Theological College in Darwin, Australia, which trains aboriginal people for church leadership, I was invited to lead the morning worship service. Since the students were not familiar with Quakerism, I spent most of the time explaining the history and testimonies of Friends. Near the end, I invited the gathered group into a brief time of open worship. A deep silence fell over us and a few students spoke or prayed with real power. They responded so positively that the principal asked me to lead the following two worship services and use the entire time for open worship! Beyond Friends, the World Conference on the Environment in Brazil a few years ago began with silence, the one way in which all participating countries could agree to participate.

Listen to the Call

Out of genuine worship, we will feel many kinds of nudges, calls, or inward drawings. Anxiety about what God may demand of us can result in ambivalence about worship. We know and have heard that God supplies the resources necessary to follow the call, but we step out in faith each time we follow a call.

When the call comes, we need to *listen*, to take it seriously. Woolman certainly did that throughout his life and particularly in relation to his call to visit the Delaware Indians. He felt a love

for them for many years; after his conversation with them, he began to feel the call more strongly. Then the call or inward drawing came to a kind of ripeness. This experience of Woolman's suggests that there are stages in a call, beginning with interest or
love, proceeding to grow stronger with certain life experiences.
The call then matures to the point where it demands more
focused attention on our mental horizon and then action.

At any time along the way, the call could have been squelched.
Especially in the early stages, we can easily dismiss such nudges as
unrealistic or only silly daydreams. Life may be good and we may
be doing good things, so why pay attention to a niggling thought
in the back of our minds? The fantasies and fleeting thoughts in
our minds have a lot to teach us, if we pay attention. The call to
provide pastoral care across cultures must be listened to, if it comes.
And like Woolman, we will need to continue to listen and perhaps re-evaluate it throughout the time of pursuing it.

Discern the Call

Once we hear the call, we then have to discern from where the
call comes. It may be solely from our need to feel special or loved
or powerful. We know now that personal motives are always involved, but more needs to be present, for it to be a genuine call
from God. A real call from God builds on our past experiences,
though perhaps not directly, uses our gifts and desires, and challenges us in a new way.

This discernment first begins inwardly, as we listen and pay
attention as it ripens in us, as it did in Woolman. Woolman, at
an earlier point in his journal, speaks about the ". . . necessity of
keeping down to that root from whence our concern proceeded."[35]
We need prayerfully to attempt to see who is doing the calling, to
get to the root. A faith community can help us with that. At some
point we can bring our inward drawing to the community for clearness. A faith community has resources and perspectives that will

raise new questions which we may not have considered. A Quaker Meeting would then enter into a time of corporate discernment, in an atmosphere of worship. The belief is that God's Spirit, who may have given the initial call, will also lead the Meeting gathered in worship to that same truth. If the Meeting does not confirm our own call, then we may put our call on hold, re-assess what we thought was a divine call, or proceed only with great caution and after other consultation. If the community feels clear that the call is from God, then we can proceed much more freely and easily.

Quakers often use a clearness committee to aid in such discernment. It has traditionally been used when a person is considering joining the Quaker Meeting or considering marriage. Clearness committees are now used for assisting in making other important life decisions. In consultation with the person asking for clearness, the leader selects the committee members. A "weighty" or mature Friend may be asked to clerk the committee, which is made up of several persons carefully and prayerfully selected for what they have to offer to such a process. Once the persons are selected and a time set to meet, the person asking for clearness will often write a description of the issue she or he is dealing with, including some history and context. The person may simply share verbally the information at the beginning of the meeting. Then the committee enters into a time of silent worship. Members may speak out of the silence, if they feel led to do so. The group focuses not on solving the person's problem but in listening to God in the context of this issue. The clerk discerns when to end the worship, after which there is some time for more general discussion and for the person asking for clearness to talk. The committee may decide to meet again, if their work does not appear finished. This process is especially good in discernment for major life decisions, but can be useful in many ways in pastoral care.

Training programs, consultants, and supervisors, as well as therapy may all be useful in discerning the call. Talking with family and friends is always helpful and important to do. John Woolman spoke only with his wife before he brought it to his Meeting, then to two larger regional meetings of Quakers. And it was almost two years between the time that he began to take seriously his inward drawing and the time he left on his journey.

I found when I felt called at age 43 to do something different with my life, that it took two years of discernment before moving into teaching. Prayer, personal counseling, conversations with friends, family and my pastor, and trying on different possibilities occurred during that time. Discernment is not a quick process, especially when major change is contemplated.

Open to the Other

As was stated earlier, every person except ourselves is "other." In relating to any person outside ourselves, we are to some extent crossing cultures. The more differences that exist between us—in terms of gender, sexual orientation, race, age, life experience, socio-economic class, able-bodiedness, education, culture, basic value system—the more difficult understanding can become. On the other hand, the more subtle the differences, the easier they are to overlook. For example, a person from England may look and sound fairly similar to an Anglo-American, but to assume therefore that the English person is like the Anglo-American is to make a profound mistake. John Woolman, at one point in his journal, states "It's good for thee to dwell deep, that thou mayest feel and understand the spirits of people."[36] In dwelling deeply in the Spirit of God, we are more able to be open so that we can feel and understand others.

Openness to the other, the care receiver in this case, is a crucial factor in the success of pastoral care. Openness does not mean necessarily agreeing with the other persons, or merging with them so that our own boundaries blur or disappear. It does mean being able, at certain times, to see the world through their eyes. Open-

ness means coming to the place where we, through empathic imagination, can enter the person's world and sense why they feel and
respond as they do. Different from sympathy or empathy, David
Augsburger coins a new word for this ability, *interpathy*, which he
describes as:

> . . . an intentional cognitive envisioning and affective ex-
> periencing of another's thoughts and feelings, even though
> the thoughts rise from another process of knowing, the
> values grow from another frame of moral reasoning, and
> the feelings from another basis of assumptions.[37]

He later describes it as ". . . the intellectual invasion and the emotional embracing of what is truly other."[38]

One day after eating at a local restaurant in Suva, Fiji, it occurred to me that I had gotten the attention of the server through
a subtle nod of the head, as Fijians do. Without realizing it, I had
not used the more obvious American way of verbally summoning
a server, often accompanied by a hand gesture. Then I knew that
I had taken another step in cultural immersion.

This kind of openness and interpathy does not come easily, in
my experience, and occurs as a gift, when one is grounded in personal identity and in God and is really open to another culture. It
takes the ability both to know oneself and to set one's own agenda
and needs aside for the moment. We are unable to be this open and
interpathic all the time; we need to come back to ourselves for rest
and refreshment. We require good self-care, especially when in a
foreign culture or caring for persons who are culturally different.

To come to this point of being able to be open may require
personal counseling and/or spiritual direction, as well as ongoing
consultation and support. If we are attempting to care for a person
from a culture different from ours, we may need help to understand
the person, in terms of a cultural interpreter, someone from that
culture who can teach us or answer our questions. Listening carefully to the person we are trying to care for must be the starting

place. Admitting our blind spots to that person and asking for their patience and help is important to do at the outset. We may find that we simply do not understand the person and will have to admit that and help them find another care giver more suitable.

Inevitable Difficulties

As Woolman so clearly shows, even when we have a clear call from God, setbacks, difficulties, and trials will still occur. The life of Jesus shows us that what others may define as success is not guaranteed when we follow God's call. Our task, as we know, is to be faithful to what we perceive to be God's call.

Sometimes, like Woolman in his reflections while spending a day in his tent, we can use adversity as an opportunity to review our motivations and test our leadings. We may ask, given the hardships that we can never fully anticipate but which now are upon us, is this really the thing to which God is calling us? The answer may not be clear. We often wish that God would write God's will clearly in the sky, or speak to us with a loud, discernible voice! In the midst of ambiguity, and in remembering the earlier discernment process and original motivation, we check in with others, share our honest doubts, and pray.

Near the end of Woolman's life, he really struggled with whether to travel to England. He talked to many people, prayed about it, went to the ship and talked to the owner, was on and off the ship several times. He had misgivings about staying in the luxurious guest quarters while the crew lived in steerage. He also had scruples about the ornateness of the ship. He explained his misgivings to the owner and eventually decided to live in steerage with the young crew. When he settled down on board, he wrote, "I felt a satisfactory evidence that my proceedings were not in my own will but under the power of the cross of Christ."[39]

In his trip to the Delaware Indians, Woolman confronted news of warring Indians who had taken a fort and killed and scalped the English, difficulty with the weather and the path, his own weak health, and his fear of the Indians when he arrived at Wyalusing. He took these difficulties seriously and reflected on them, listening to what they might be saying to him. We can do the same thing. The difficulties do need to be heeded; responding to a call from God does not mean being foolhardy in the face of reality. Perhaps because we feel divinely led, we can feel more free to examine nondefensively the meaning of events that occur to us, to see if God is speaking to us through them. But then, like Woolman, we are also free and enabled to stay on course. At other times we may need to change course. Expecting difficulties to occur will make them less disappointing and perhaps less traumatizing when they in fact happen.

Community Support and Accountability

For most indigenous cultures around the world, community is central, more so than in the developed countries of the West. Unless we have lived in such a culture for a while and glimpsed the centrality of community, we cannot conceive of this way of life.

In Fijian villages, for example, women gather at the birth of a baby, and the infant is held in a woman's arms twenty-four hours a day for the first week of life outside the womb. The mother, while pregnant, has woven a special mat that the baby lies on, in the arms of various women, during that time.

The traveling minute, or the certificate as Woolman called it, is one way that Quaker Meetings have of blessing a trip, as has been mentioned earlier. Upon return, the person often presents the minute to the Meeting, with messages appended to it from the different Quaker groups where she or he has been. Often the Meeting will then hear a report from the person. This process can be an effective way to assist the returned traveler to re-acclimate to his or her own culture and community.

From the beginning and all the way through, we need community, for any pastoral care but especially for pastoral care across cultures. At first, we need community to help us with discernment, as noted earlier. Then, when we begin to follow our call, we need structure and regular ways to stay in touch with our primary community. Woolman took friends with him, so there was a kind of community available. Many today stay in touch around the world by e-mail. When college students are away, for example, the church or Meeting can stay in touch through sharing of newsletters and other information and in welcoming them back at holidays, and perhaps in working with them to offer activities in the summer.

When living in another culture, we need to stay in touch with our home community, find a community in the new culture, and get back in touch with our home community when we return. When adverse experiences occur, we then have a place to go to process them and have persons pray with us. A support group or community on site is also important, if we can find or assemble one. Staying in touch with our home community while we are away will also help remind us who we are as we live in the new culture. In returning, the home community can be very helpful as we debrief and attempt to integrate the experience. Most people want to hear only a few sentences about our trip when we return, so members of our faith community will have to learn how to listen and care for us during this time of cross-cultural transition. The re-entry process into our home culture can be more difficult than the adjustments required in entering another culture.[40]

It took me almost a year before I re-acclimated to being back home, after nine months in Fiji. I did much journaling, talking with friends, seeing a spiritual director and praying. Nothing seemed to speed up the painful process of not feeling at home. Then one day in worship at Earlham School of Religion where I teach, I felt that the sun came out in my spirit. I knew then that I was back, and I was thankful and relieved.

The point is that we are not traveling alone or following a call from God completely on our own. God and others are there with us. Like the disciples walking back to Emmaus, discussing the crucifixion in Jerusalem, we too may find that a fellow-traveler is Jesus.

Gratitude to God

Meister Eckhart states that "If the only prayer you say in your entire life is 'Thank You,' that would suffice."[41] An attitude of gratefulness is not only recommended for life in general, but is particularly important in pastoral care across cultures. Our attitude makes a big difference in the way we approach a new experience and the way we negotiate through it. After wrestling and struggling, Woolman usually ended up grateful for adversity, which produced a quiet, centered peacefulness in him.

We can be grateful that we are called to a life of worship, in which we are called to particular tasks in the ongoing work of creation. We can be grateful that a community of faith is available to help us in discernment and in support and accountability. We can be grateful for the diversity of the world and of human beings, where we can be open, through God's grace, to learning and living together and helping one another. We can be grateful when we are allowed to provide care for another. We can be grateful when we are allowed or invited by persons of a different culture to enter their world. We can be grateful when we return home and rest. Perhaps, like Woolman, we can even be grateful for the adverse times when our mettle is tried and we grow stronger in responding to challenge. We might even be given patience and a deep feeling for others, as was given to Woolman after his visit with the Native Americans.

The result will be transformation—a changed perspective, certainly, and perhaps a changed life. We may feel more robust, more in touch with people, more global in our awareness, more a disciple of the God who calls us and keeps us. Then we have the possibility of offering effective pastoral care to people of other cultures.

Notes

1. David Augsburger, *Pastoral Counseling Across Cultures* (Philadelphia: Westminster Press, 1986), 18.

2. Augsburger, *Pastoral Counseling Across Cultures*, 37.

3. John Dunne, *The Way of All the Earth: Experiments in Trust and Religion* (NY: Macmillan Publishing Co., 1972), ix-x. In Augsburger, *Pastoral Counseling Across Cultures*, 36.

4. Augsburger, *Pastoral Counseling Across Cultures*, 9.

5. Ephesians 4:22-24, New Revised Standard Version.

6. *Faith and Practice of Indiana Yearly Meeting of the Religious Society of Friends* (Dublin, IN: Prinit Press), 35f.

7. John Punshon, *Encounter with Silence: Reflections from the Quaker Tradition* (Richmond, IN: Friends United Press, 1987), 36.

8. Punshon, *Encounter with Silence*, 127.

9. John L. Nickalls, ed., *Journal of George Fox* (Philadelphia, PA: Philadelphia Yearly Meeting, 1997), 11.

10. *Journal of George Fox*, 19.

11. John Miller, "Multi-cultural Education: A Vision for ESR," unpublished paper, 1990, 3.

12. *The Journal and Major Essays of John Woolman*, Phillips P. Moulton, ed., (New York: Oxford University Press, 1971), 6-12.

13. *Journal of John Woolman*, 13.

14. *Journal of John Woolman*, 4-16.

15. *Journal of John Woolman*, 122.

16. *Journal of John Woolman*, 84, 85, 99, 100.

17. *Journal of John Woolman*, 314.

18. *Journal of John Woolman*, 123.

19. *Journal of John Woolman*, 124.

20. *Journal of John Woolman*, 125.

21. *Journal of John Woolman*, 126.

22. I Cor. 10:32, II Cor. 6:3.

23. *Journal of John Woolman*, 129.

24. *Journal of John Woolman*, 127.

25. *Journal of John Woolman*, 127.

26. *Journal of John Woolman*, 127f.

27. *Journal of John Woolman*, 131.

28. *Journal of John Woolman*, 129f.

29. *Journal of John Woolman*, 132.

30. *Journal of John Woolman*, 132.

31. *Journal of John Woolman*, 133.

32. *Journal of John Woolman*, 134.

33. *Journal of John Woolman*, 134.

34. *Journal of John Woolman*, 137.

35. *Journal of John Woolman*, 96.

36. *Journal of John Woolman*, 112.

37. Augsburger, *Pastoral Counseling Across Cultures*, 29.

38. Augsburger, *Pastoral Counseling Across Cultures*, 30.

39. *Journal of John Woolman*, 165.

40. Craig Storti, *The Art of Coming Home* (Yarmouth, ME: Intercultural Press, 1997).

41. *Meditations with Meister Eckhart*, Intro. and Versions by Matthew Fox(Santa Fe, NM: Bear & Co., 1983), 34.

V. Out of the Not-So-Silent Gathering:
Meeting for Worship As Pastoral Care

Deborah Suess

Introduction

PASTORS WEAR A MULTITUDE OF HATS: preacher, administrator, teacher, pray-or, counselor, interpreter, organizer, worship leader, evangelist, mediator, pastoral care giver. Although in programmed Quaker Meetings the pastor is considered to be one minister among a congregation of ministers, the one "released" into full-time church work carries a large portion of the ministerial responsibilities.

Pastors who remain in ministry learn to discern and delegate. They help identify others' gifts and nurture their leadership skills. They work with ministry and counsel committees or spiritual elders to choose priorities. Also, they give God thanks that their roles often intermingle. For instance, when a pastor works with her outreach committee on a systematic way to do follow-up with visitors, she is an evangelist, teacher, and administrator. Or when a pastor discusses with first-time parents how we might "officially" welcome a newborn into Meeting, he is doing the work of worship planning, interpretation, and religious education. And as he carefully listens to the parents' hopes and dreams for their little one, he is extending pastoral care.

The ministry of pastoral care is one ministry that I believe undergirds and extends into all of our other tasks. If pastoral care is indeed "the broad ministry of mutual healing and growth,"[1] then pastoral care becomes the work of every believer and certainly the call of the local pastor. When programmed Friends hear the term "pastoral care," however, what picture generally comes to mind? Most likely it is an image of a minister sitting in her study counseling and praying with an individual or couple. Although such direct one-on-one care is very important, we need to expand our understanding of how and where pastoral care occurs.[2] *In particular, I believe programmed Friends benefit from a clear acknowledgement that powerful and effective pastoral care ministry can consistently take place during Meeting for Worship itself.*

Worship as a resource for pastoral care is indeed good news. It is good news for the pastor who in terms of time simply can not offer regular individual care to every attender. It is also good news for those in the pew who, for a variety of reasons, are not comfortable asking for and/or receiving one-on-one pastoral attention. In the words of William Willimon, Professor of the Practice of Christian Ministry at Duke University:

> Worship offers the pastors a unique opportunity to "discern the spirits" and to answer the perennial, "What's going on here?" . . . In most churches, that Sunday morning gathering will offer pastors the opportunity to see, be seen, and be with more of their parishioners for a longer period of time than any other activity of the church. While there, in worship, those people will probably act, think, speak, perhaps sing, respond, and feel in more complex, revealing, and significant ways than in any other activity of the church. Most of them go there voluntarily to receive and to give, to be with others, to be with themselves, to confront the faith and to avoid the faith, to be with God and to hide from God. And always their pastor is there . . . leading them in worship.[3]

Worship as Central; Pastoral Care as By-Product

Worship provides the foundation for spiritual community. While the Sunday morning Meeting for Worship offers us a weekly opportunity for corporate pastoral care, we must always keep in mind that the primary purpose for Meeting is to worship God. We gather as Friends to listen corporately to the One who can "speak to our condition." We gather to commune with our Beloved. Friend Thomas Green writes, "Worship is essentially an act of adoration, adoration of the one true God in whom we live and move and have our being."[4] Or in the words of the Westminster Cathecism written in the language of its time, "What is the chief end of man?" The response: "To glorify God and to enjoy him forever."

Meeting for Worship functions primarily to attend to God. William Willimon, although a strong proponent of "worship as pastoral care," warns us that if our liturgy (Meeting for Worship) simply becomes a means for achieving pastoral care goals, then our worship:

> . . . is being used and thereby abused. God is not to be used for our own purposes, not even for our own good purposes. My thesis . . . is not that we should use the liturgy as a new method of pastoral care but that the liturgy itself and a congregation's experience of divine worship already functions, even if in a secondary way, as pastoral care. The pastoral care that occurs as we are meeting and being met by God in worship is a significant by-product that we have too often overlooked.[5]

While it is important to maintain theological clarity regarding our "primary" goal in worship, in practice any attempt to separate worship from pastoral care seems artificial. *Pastoral care and worship interact; one builds upon and strengthens the other.* As discussed below, a worship experience will often minister to one's emotional, psychological, or "pastoral care" needs, as well as to one's spiritual needs. When this happens, the gathered community's silence or vocal ministry will often deepen, for "though their parts are many, they form one body" (1 Corinthians 12: 12). As a way for programmed Friends to make fuller use of the natural link between pastoral care and worship, let us first consider our current order and style of worship.

Why Do We Do What We Do?

When it comes to planning their order of service, clergy in "high church traditions" such as Lutherans and Episcopalians are generally clear about why they do what they do in corporate worship. They have studied the specific historical and theological underpinnings for the "call to worship," a "prayer of confession," and "the response." They know why, for instance, a collection is taken at a certain place in the liturgy and why the service ends with a benediction and not a prayer.

In general, programmed Friends in North America are not as clear. Our particular style of worship reflects our relatively recent beginnings. In the second half of the nineteenth century, the "great revival" significantly influenced several yearly meetings. Revivalists and evangelists came from both within and outside of the Religious Society of Friends and introduced new elements into the worship services, such as the enthusiastic offering of public testimonies, hymn singing, and planned Bible reading. As a result of their powerful work, Friends Meetings (primarily in the Midwest) were flooded with converts. What was to be done to nurture this overwhelming influx of new believers? How could local Meetings ground the newly "convinced" in Quaker faith and practice while also trying to meet the increased demand for dynamic preaching and pastoral care? For the majority of Midwest Meetings the response was two-fold. The 1860s and 1870s saw a gradual move to include some preplanned Scripture reading or preaching during worship. Then during the 1880s, Meetings began to hire ministers.[6] "No longer confined to their narrow sectarian traditions, Gurneyite Friends in America increasingly acquired most characteristics of such popular evangelical denominations as the Baptists and Methodists after 1860."[7]

In the last 140 years, programmed Friends have become a hybrid of sorts. We are deeply rooted in the Religious Society of Friends, yet we have borrowed generously from other Christian traditions. My farmer friends inform me that cross-pollination can potentially lead to a more vigorous and sturdy product, and I believe that can be the case for programmed worship. Such vigor and strength can come from educating ourselves about the worship elements we have adapted from other denominations in conjunction with evaluating how these worship elements can best serve pastoral Friends.

Evaluating Programmed Worship

How do we evaluate our "order of worship" in terms of its effectiveness to guide us Godward while allowing for its natural by-product—pastoral care?

Jack Kirk, Quaker pastor, offers this advice:

> . . . the music, Scripture readings and sermon in a programmed meeting should not be performances drawing attention to themselves, but they should point people to God who is beyond and moving in the midst. In fact, all items included in the Sunday bulletin of a programmed meeting should be evaluated on the basis of whether or not they enhance the experience of communion.[8]

From her experience at Reedwood Friends Church in Oregon, Celia Mueller suggests the various elements of programmed worship—hymns, special music, offering, prayers, Scripture readings, and prepared message—should facilitate both ministry to one another and direct communion with God:

> It has been my experience that thoughtful placement of a prayer or hymn in a worship service can enhance true wor-

ship. Again, speaking from my Reedwood experience, we have identified three significant needs that must be met in the corporate worship experience. First we have the need to interact with each other; second we have the need to interact with God and lastly, of utmost significance, is the need to be open to God's interaction with us.[9]

With that in mind, let us consider the question: *How does our current order of worship draw Friends "spiritually outward, upward and inward" while at the same time create an atmosphere where pastoral care "naturally" happens?*

One Programmed Meeting for Worship

At West Branch Friends Church (Iowa Yearly Meeting, Friends United Meeting) our order of worship has evolved, and it will continue to do so as the Meeting inevitably changes. The following is meant to serve neither as a template nor as a recommendation, but simply as an example of one Midwest programmed Meeting for Worship. Currently a typical Sunday bulletin at West Branch Friends Church (WBFC) will read:

CALL TO WORSHIP
WELCOME & ANNOUNCEMENTS
JOYS & CONCERNS
PRELUDE
SILENT REFLECTION
PRAYER
HYMN
SCRIPTURE READING
CHOIR
CHILDREN'S MESSAGE
SERMON
SILENCE FOR CENTERING PRAYER
OPEN WORSHIP IN THE MANNER OF FRIENDS
OFFERTORY

HYMN
BENEDICTION
Postlude

In most Quaker Meetings, no matter what the bulletin says, worship leaders attempt to be sensitive to the Spirit's guidance during the worship hour and make changes when appropriate. Many programmed meetings emphasize this point by using the language "*Suggested* Order of Worship" at the top of their bulletin.

Assembling Together

> Worship is the symbolic expression of the Christian faith. As the church gathers for worship it provides a picture of the body of Christ. The ministry of hospitality offered as the church gathers for worship communicates the reality of fellowship in Christ and welcomes the stranger into the body.[10]

Before the first hymn is sung or a word of welcome offered, "the ministry of care" has already begun. Care starts in the parking lot when a trustee waits out in the cold to assist one of our elder members get past the icy spot on the sidewalk. Care continues in the entrance hall with a welcoming handshake or a genuine "It's good to see you." In fact, for some these caring acts in coming together will be the most significant and healing part of the entire worship experience.

If ministry begins as we gather, what should this gathering look and sound like? In the words of the Quaker query: how do we best prepare our hearts and minds for communion with God and fellowship with one another? Is it advisable to assemble in silence? Or maybe gather to the soothing melody of an organ prelude? Then again, in the words of Psalm 100: should we enter God's gates with thanksgiving and God's courts with praise?

Seth Hinshaw, pastoral minister of North Carolina Yearly Meeting, addresses this well-worn dilemma. He argues on one hand that "unseemly visiting and chatter" can be a distraction to our time of preparation. But on the other hand: "Would it be going too far to say that individuals who assemble with gloomy countenances are not true witnesses?"[11] West Branch Friends Church (WBFC) has experimented with various ways to address this particular issue. I personally lean in the direction of asking for "silence upon entering the Meetingroom in preparation for worship." When I am tempted to get legalistic or demanding about pre-service silence, however, I am reminded of the following story:

> . . . a young pastor labored heroically to get his loquacious congregation to keep silence during the moments before the service began. Time and again he told them, "The noise before the service is irreverent." One Sunday. . . he really lowered the boom on them. . . After the service was ended . . . an old farmer approached him. "Young man," he said, "I heard what you said about our talking before the service. Let me tell you what I was talking about. As I entered church, Sam told me about Joe and Mary's milk cow, how she had jumped the fence and tore her udder. Well, I knew that Joe and Mary needed that cow for milk for their kids. So I told Sam that, after church, we'd get one of my cows and take it over there to Joe and Mary's house and take their cow to the vet. Now, after I told Joe and Mary about that, I was ready to worship."[12]

May God help us not to be rigid about how we and others need to worship on any particular Sunday!

The issue remains: how do we try to meet the "gathering needs" for both connection and silence? There is no easy answer to this dilemma. To encourage silent centering, our Meeting no longer has organ music as a prelude to the worship hour; instead, instrumental music follows our time of announcements, joys, and concerns. We also encourage those on the facing bench to be seated and silently centering by 10:25 a.m. As a result, sometimes it is completely still when I offer our Call to Worship at 10:30 a.m. Other times, there is a friendly, chatty buzz going on when the "worship hour" arrives. This is particularly true if we are welcoming a first-time visitor or a returning Friend after a time away.

The dilemma always remains, for what meets the needs of one can be disturbing for the other. Tolerance, flexibility, and a willingness to try to understand another's heart-felt position are requirements of community. Our Meeting will probably continue to discuss this issue from time to time and experiment with differing ways to "gather." Whatever we do, the need for connection with one another must be honored in some manner, since it is in those gathering moments that some among us will be significantly touched and feel cared for. We turn now to look at each element of a typical worship format at West Branch Friends Church and consider its role in facilitating pastoral care.

Call To Worship & Welcome

At 10:30 a.m. the worship leader invites the meeting to stand and join in a brief "Call to Worship." This is generally a chorus, hymn, or a short Scripture reading that articulates why we gather: to worship and praise God. The call also serves to draw us together and remind us that everything that follows, including the announcements and offering, are part of our service of praise to God.

Recently for our call to worship, a verse of a familiar hymn was sung:

> For the beauty of the earth,
> For the glory of the skies,
> For the love which from our birth
> Over and around us lies;
> Lord of all, to Thee we raise
> This our hymn of grateful praise.[13]

A middle-aged member of the Meeting who is struggling with an incrementally debilitating disease expressed how important it was to begin the service with such praise: "I may not be feeling 'happy' right now. But I can still genuinely offer thanksgiving for the beauty of the earth." The call to worship does not ask us to be thankful for all of our circumstances, but asks us to look to the One who is both within and beyond us.

After the call to worship, all are welcomed to Meeting, especially the visitors. In the past, guests were either introduced by regular attenders or were asked to introduce themselves. We discovered, however, that while some enjoy this kind of welcome, other visitors are uncomfortable with that level of attention. As a result, our welcome now varies from week to week as we try to be sensitive to this concern. In addition, the following is printed weekly at the top of our bulletin in bold print:

> A Note to Visitors: Welcome! We are glad you are here and we hope your hour with us this morning is a blessing. For information about this Meeting (Quaker word for church), please take a pamphlet or two from the literature rack in the lobby or feel free to contact the pastor at 643-5598. We also invite you to sign our guest book in the lobby.

Joys and Concerns / Prelude / Silent Reflection

> The ministry of pastoral care is rooted in common worship, for genuine sensitivity to mutual needs naturally develops as Christians hear God's Word. . . and join in common prayer. . . . The acts of naming an affliction, of turning a sorrow into a prayer, and of proclaiming the hope that Christians have in Christ all minister to those who suffer. In worship, Christians rejoice with those who rejoice and mourn with those who mourn, ministering to each other in Jesus' name.[14]

After the welcome and introductions come the announcements, joys, and concerns. This sharing time provides an important opportunity to "rejoice with those who rejoice and mourn with those who mourn." What a blessed gift to be able to say to the congregation: "I give thanks for my grandson who came into the world seven weeks early but is now doing fine." "Today for the third year in a row, I will be participating in the Cancer-Survivors Walk." "Thanks to everyone who has encouraged and supported me as I have sought guidance on what to do next. I have just got the official word that I have been accepted into seminary and it feels right." Sometimes such announcements will inspire applause from even us reserved Quakers. Often phone calls, handshakes, hugs, or notes will follow.

Some request prayer for themselves or others. "I'll be undergoing a particularly intense round of chemotherapy this Thursday. I would appreciate your thoughts and prayers." " My niece's husband died suddenly leaving two young children without a father. Please pray for Ruth and her family." Or the twelve-year-old who stands to say: "We are very sad that Chloe, our dog, was injured and will now be blind in one eye." Such "concerns" not only solicit intercessory prayer, but like the "joys" they also provide a connecting point with others and an opportunity for follow-up pastoral care. The pastor, elders, or whoever wishes may offer a prayer, send a note, bake a pie, or make a call as follow-up.

In sharing both joys and concerns, we tell our story, or a brief portion, in a worship setting. This gives us an opportunity to connect publicly our story with the Divine story, and in doing so we may discover new meaning in our experience.[15]

A note of caution: Meetings may need guidance on what is and is not appropriate to share in this setting. Some people are very private and do not want their concern mentioned in public. Others appreciate having their need mentioned as long as it is announced carefully. As the pastor, there are two ways in which I try to model appropriate ways to communicate joys and concerns. First, if a parishioner tells me of a need that seems appropriate to share with the congregation, I will specifically ask them: "Would you like me to list this as a prayer concern in the bulletin or would you rather keep this private for now?" Second, when I announce concerns from the pulpit, I will occasionally include language such as: "Jane has given me permission to share this concern with you today." Third, I regularly make references in my prayers to the "unspoken needs" of the meeting. Such modeling is important since appropriate boundaries, regarding sharing information, help create healthy communities.

This 5-8 minutes of community sharing at the beginning of the service indeed "builds up the body of Christ." Such sharing helps draw us together as a worshiping community, where people feel acknowledged and cared for. Reedwood Friends Church (North West Yearly Meeting in Oregon) tried at various times to "remove active fellowship" from their worship hour since there were numerous other opportunities where it could take place. They discovered, however, that:

> when this need is not addressed intentionally, that is when we do not assign it a place in the worship experience, it transpires at inappropriate times. For example, if people have not found ways to express their connectedness before we enter our period of open worship, prayer requests, sharing, announcements and testimonies will find their way into open worship and we will be distracted from doing the listening and/or speaking that we are called to do there. Having a time to greet one another, share announcements and prayer requests and the like, help us reestablish community.[16]

After the announcements, welcome, joys and concerns, the worship leader invites the Meeting to "take these joys and concerns to God in prayer during the prelude and in the silence that follows."

Pastoral Prayer

> In programmed meetings there is almost always a pastoral
> prayer. This may not be offered by the pastoral minister; it
> may sometimes come from an elder or other leader in the
> meeting who is aware of the spiritual condition of the con-
> gregation and who can gather up and express the deep
> needs and longings of the members in such a way that ev-
> eryone feels involved as a participant.[17]

Sometimes the pastoral prayer I offer indeed gathers us, and
sometimes it simply does not. Sometimes I agree with those
who argue that the pastoral prayer should be replaced by shorter
prayers throughout the worship hour. William Willimon writes
the following:

> I have two main objections to the pastoral prayers I hear;
> they are not prayers and they are usually not very pastoral.
> Protestant pastors have long been berated for turning their
> public prayers into sermonettes with the eyes closed, cliché-
> ridden, vague ramblings prayed at people or about people
> rather than for people. This is far different than a priestly
> effort to bring the congregation before God.[18]

Although Willimon's critique has merit, my experience is that
prayer, whenever offered, which honors the thanksgivings and
concerns of the people, has the potential to offer healing and hope.

The following are some guidelines to consider when preparing
a pastoral prayer.

1. There is no rule against planning ahead of time what words or
   images the worship leader will use. Some people are comfortable praying extemporaneously, others prefer to write it out.
   The question is not: "Which is best or right?" But rather: "What
   preparations do you need to make in order to articulate a prayer
   to God on behalf of the Meeting?"

2. We pray as spiritual leaders (clergy or lay) who know our congregation. Over coffee we have listened to them worry about their children. We have held their hand at the hospital. We have reminded them of their worth and beauty after a divorce hearing. Although our prayers NEVER betray a confidence, our Sunday intercessions reflect the fact that we know and love one another.

3. We need to be careful, when speaking to God on behalf of the congregation, not to assume everyone is feeling the same way we are. For instance, on one gorgeous April Sunday, I prayed: "God of new beginnings, we feel grateful for this glorious day and we are full of the hope that spring brings." Later that day I found out that one attender had just been diagnosed with cancer and in that moment was not "full of the hope that spring brings." Elaine Ramshaw writes that "liturgical scholars call this the mistake of subjectivization. They object to it not only because it risks inaccuracy and alienation, but also for the more theological reason that it focuses prayer on the praying person's state of mind, rather than on prayer's proper object, the work of God."[19]

4. We pray using a variety of images for God. "Language is always influential and formative, but it may be especially influential in times of prayer, because at these times ideally, the whole person is involved. . . ."[20] We need not exclude traditional and often beloved language for God such as Dear Heavenly Father or Loving Lord. Rather we can expand our vocabulary for God to include names such as Eternal Friend, Breath of Life, God-With-Us, Living Word, Beloved One, and Brother Jesus. For many in our meetings "expansive language" is genuinely not an issue. But there are others who are desperate for new images and language that "invites them in."

So—let us pray. Let us pray with sensitivity, preparation, awareness, and an expectation that God indeed hears our prayer.

Psalms, Hymns and Spiritual Songs

> . . . be filled with the Spirit, as you sing psalms and hymns
> and spiritual songs among yourselves, singing and making
> melody to the Lord in your hearts, giving thanks to God at
> all times and for everything in the name of our Lord Jesus
> Christ. Ephesians 5: 18b, 19.

Never underestimate the power of song to move a meeting
Godward. In the last four years I have taken several informal
surveys among (primarily) programmed Quakers to learn about
"worship preferences." I asked various groups: "If you *had* to choose
just one element of worship that draws you most consistently
Godward, what would it be? You have three choices: the sermon,
the open worship, or the music." Each time, music scored in either first or second place. Music plays an important role in the
spiritual lives of programmed Friends.

Music can encourage, lift up, heal, and challenge us. Theologian Karl Barth (clearly not a Quaker) says praise is the mark of
the true church:

> The Christian community sings from inner material ne-
> cessity. What we can and must say quite confidently is that
> the community that does not sing is not the community.[21]

Singing is an experience like no other act of worship. As one Friend
put it, "No greater joy in my life has there been than to stand on
Sunday mornings and sing praises to the Lord."[22] Many times a
member tells me, "That hymn we sang on Sunday kept going
through my mind all week, and gave me hope (or strength or calm
or joy.)" The hymn "did the work" of pastoral care.

For years I was unaware of the deep impact music and singing
can have on Meeting for Worship. As with many Quaker pastors,
I have had no formal training in leading worship through music.
That may help explain why I have been so impatient with the
"hymns vs. choruses" and the "traditional vs. contemporary

music" debate that is going on in many churches and denominations today. I now understand why discussions regarding music preferences are so passionate: for many Christians music and song are synonymous with worship.

As pastoral care givers, can we listen carefully as members speak about their musical preferences? Can we affirm that for many their spiritual longings are expressed most readily through music? How might we encourage members to listen tenderly to one another as they speak about the role of music (or silence, or Scriptures, or other elements) in their spiritual journeys? Although there will never be enough music for some and never enough silence for others, we can assist in a dialogue process that promotes understanding and respect for diverse worship needs.

The chance to help select hymns provides the pastor with an important care-giving opportunity. We can schedule hymns that affirm the wide range of our human experience. We can sing the traditional songs of praise and thanksgiving, adoration and love, assurance and trust, faith and hope; then we can go one step further. On occasion we can also sing the following:

* Psalms of laments that express our grief and questions:

> How long O Lord will you forget an answer to my prayer?
> No tokens of your love I see, your face is turned away from me;
> I wrestle with despair . . .

> How long, O Lord, will you forsake and leave me in this way?
> When will you come to my relief?
> My heart is overwhelmed with grief,
> by evil night and day.

> How long, O Lord but you forgive, with mercy from above.
> I find that all your ways are just,
> I learn to praise you and to trust in your unfailing love.[23]

*Prayers of confession:

> If I have wounded any soul today,
> If I have caused one foot to go astray
> If I have walked in my own willful way, Oh God, forgive! ...
>
> Forgive the sins I have confessed to thee;
> Forgive the secret sins I do not see;
> O guide me, love me, and my keeper be, Oh God, forgive![24]

*Hymns of assurance:

> Our God has said, "Behold, I make all things new,
> I shall forgive your sins, and shall rejoice,
> and shall rejoice in all I do.
> . . . Just like a mother shall I give comfort;
> I'll nurture and carry you,
> Celebrate your joys and share with you the hurting tears,
> So I will comfort you . . .[25]

Music should reflect a thoughtful use of language. For some, changing the words of old and dearly loved hymns is offensive and disturbing. For others, singing hymns which exclusively use male imagery for God or humanity is offensive and disturbing. Our Meeting has addressed this issue by including the following suggestion (adapted from a statement developed at First Friends Church in Richmond, Indiana) in the bulletin:

> Most of our hymns were written before inclusive language was a consideration. As is helpful to you, please feel free to change nouns and pronouns and sing the hymns in a manner that enhances your worship.

It makes for interesting singing at times, but it at least achieves a level of hospitality to all.

The Sermon

> A good time to address . . . core issues is when people are not in the midst of death, divorce, or illness. The pulpit is one of our greatest aids in pastoral care. It is an occasion to teach, to give pastoral direction, to interpret scripture and world events, and to give people a sense of the preacher as a pastoral care giver. Even if we do not intend this, our sermons tell people a great deal about who we are and whether they can come to us with their concerns or not.[26]

Preaching points listeners to the Living Word. In the words of Quaker minister, Howard Macy, ". . . in God's power, preaching can help us worship."[27] As a pastoral care giver, I am always grateful when my sermon not only helps us worship but also lends comfort and support, offers new ideas, direction or hope. While I generally do not write my sermon with a specific situation in mind, neither are my sermons written in a vacuum. The words are often composed (literally) between phone calls, meetings, worship gatherings, counseling sessions, hospital visits, and bulletin preparation. My messages reflect my experience.

Howard Macy in his article, "Vocal Ministry in the Programmed Meeting" affirms the interplay between preaching and pastoral care:

> . . . part of the work of preaching becomes a gathering up of our lives—of our corporateness, of our experience in the world, and holding them in the context of God's life among us. This is where preaching and pastoral care intertwine. One can hardly preach effectively without also having the kind of presence with people that lovingly gathers and understands their triumphs and struggles, their dreams and disappointments, their times of hope and despair. Out of the gathering and sharing of our lives, preaching can convey the response of the Eternal Word who is among

us. Through preaching we can hear fresh and specifically appropriate words of guidance and encouragement, of rebuke, forgiveness, and comfort, of new dreams and new tasks. We can hear God's call to life in this world.[28]

This "intertwining" of preaching and pastoral care happens not only when the pastor preaches, but also when a member of the Meeting speaks. This is especially true when the message-bearer shares from his or her own spiritual journey. For that reason, I believe we need a variety of voices speaking from a multitude of experiences. Congregations which hear only one preacher and one perspective for forty-eight out of fifty-two Sundays are simply missing out.

Programmed meetings can encourage a variety of voices. At WBFC we plan for wide vocal ministry in four ways: First, we have a minimum of 15 minutes of open worship each Sunday, allowing enough time for messages to arise out of the silence. Second, once a quarter we have an extended period of open worship (30-40 minutes) in lieu of a prepared sermon, thus increasing the opportunity for others to speak. Third, once a month someone other than myself is asked to bring a sermon. Generally the invited person is an attender or a member from meeting. Fourth, our ministry and counsel committee remains open to adjusting our worship plans if a traveling minister is in our area with a message to share.

At the conclusion of the sermon, the worship leader at WBFC steps to the side of the pulpit and invites the Meeting into a time of silent reflection.

Silence for Centering Prayer/ Open Worship

Perhaps the greatest worship need in pastoral Friends meetings today is the rediscovery of creative silence . . . Creative silence is a holy and expectant hush before God until, in one way or another, the message of

God comes through. The meeting which has lost the creative use of silence in worship, whatever else it may have retained, has lost an essential element in Friends worship.[29]

Elsewhere in this book is a thorough discussion of pastoral care as it relates to unprogrammed worship, which is based on open worship. Therefore little needs to be said here, except to encourage pastoral friends to continue to cherish and preserve this vital element of Friends worship.

Over the last several years, WBFC has increased the time given to unprogrammed worship. We have also experimented with various ways to deepen this portion of our service. In order to allow time for Friends to center down before vocal messages are offered, we now have a period of uninterrupted silence right before open worship that is called "Silence for Centering Prayer." During this 4-5 minutes, the worship leader remains standing. When the worship leader sits down, we move into open worship during which people may speak as they are moved by the Spirit to do so. Although it is hard to document, it appears that this time of uninterrupted silence has served to deepen our open worship experience.

Benediction

As your pastor raises her hand in blessing, you can feel the power, the power of one human being upholding another, the power of one person saying to another, "The Lord is with you." This isn't a prayer to God or a pious human wish. This is a statement of fact. This fact makes re-entry into the world possible. You don't know what you will encounter tomorrow at work. . . . What new challenges, higher hurdles, tougher tasks will come your way? You don't know. All you know is, "If God is for us, who is against us?" (Romans. 8:31). All human life, all community, is built upon this foundation.[30]

Kathleen, a convinced Friend, agreed to bring the morning message. Since she was preaching, I asked if she would also like to do the benediction. She readily agreed. When it came time to close Meeting, Kathleen stood up tall, looked directly into the eyes of the congregation, lifted her hands in blessing, and proclaimed:

> May the Lord bless you and keep you,
> May the Lord's face shine upon you and be gracious to you,
> The Lord lift his countenance upon you and give you peace.

I was stunned. I had never seen the raised hands of blessing before at a Quaker meeting. I also felt blessed. My response was not surprising, as the word benediction means blessing. Kathleen, thankfully, had never been informed that Quakers didn't do that kind of thing.

I realize I am now treading on dangerous territory. After all, who knows where such a "ritual" could lead? Might we fear that one day the pastor is raising her hands in blessing and the next day she'll be handing out bread and wine? I can appreciate Friends' hesitancies, but I believe that such a blessing could be appropriately and powerfully adapted for use by programmed Friends.

But why? Why not stick to the traditional closing prayer, with eyes shut and heads bowed? Why? Because many of us need a blessing. Many of us need a reminder that God goes with us and that God's face does indeed shine upon us. We need to look into the eyes of our pastor, friend, sister or brother and be urged to "Go in peace. Serve God, for the grace of Jesus Christ is with you."

William Willimon writes passionately about the need to reclaim the benediction. He describes a conversation he had with a woman whose congregation had just been sent a new pastor. When asked if she liked the pastor, she replied, "Oh, he is wonderful. He gives the best benedictions." Willimon was intrigued by her unusual reply and asked her to explain.

. . . the first Sunday he was with us, at the conclusion of the worship service . . . he stayed up front and said something like; "Now I am going to bless you. I want you all to look at me and receive my blessing because you may really need it next week." We all watched as he raised both hands high above his head, stretching out as if to embrace us, looking at each one of us, and almost like a father, blessing us . . . His benedictions have become the highlight of each Sunday as far as I am concerned.

Willimon continues:

Her testimony on the helpfulness of her pastor's blessing reminded me of a fine essay Paul Pruyser wrote a few years ago on "The Master Hand: Psychological Notes on Pastoral Blessing." Pruyser noted the potential usefulness of this ancient gesture as a means through which to "dedicate the individual to the divine providence."[31]

Friends may believe in divine providence, but is it appropriate for Quakers to extend the literal hand of blessing? Actually, in most programmed meetings we are already doing so at other times. At WBFC we regularly "lay hands of blessing" on those in need of special prayer. Generally this happens during the midweek Meeting for Prayer, but occasionally takes place during the Sunday worship hour. Also on those Sundays when we receive a new member into the Meeting, the clerks or elders are asked to join the new member up front and touch a shoulder or a hand as the words of blessing are offered. This is also true when someone is leaving our midst. I would propose that a Friends benediction is distinctively Quaker in this way: Any member of the Meeting has the authority to lift his or her hands in blessing and offer words of benediction.

Imagine with me the following scene: it's Monday morning and yesterday's Meeting for Worship feels like a lifetime away. We don't remember much from the sermon or even the Bible readings, but we remember the benediction. Before being sent out into our work-a-day world the clerk of Meeting extended her hands and blessed us saying: "Remember, God is with you always, even to the end of the age. Amen." These words attach to our inner being and become the abiding presence of God during the week.

Closing Queries

Many issues related to programmed worship and pastoral care I have not addressed in this chapter, including three specific areas that I am particularly concerned about. In closing, I offer these concerns as queries and I look forward to seeing how the Spirit continues to bring light and guidance.

1. The need for repentance, forgiveness, and reconciliation are major pastoral care issues. Most mainline churches have worship rituals and liturgies that give structure and regular opportunity for confession and assurance of pardon. Although Quaker pastors frequently deal with this issue by meeting with individuals or couples, how might Friends provide such opportunities in corporate worship settings?

2. Programmed Friends have joined with mainline denominations in celebrating Christmas, Palm Sunday, and Easter. We have less enthusiasm for providing worship opportunities related to Advent, Lent, and Passion week. What are we missing in terms of pastoral care when, for instance, we move directly from Palm Sunday to Easter? What might it look like for Quakers to create a Lenten and Holy Week worship experience in which we "walk the way of the cross?"

3. Many denominations have designed worship liturgies or "occasional services" which address specific pastoral care concerns. How do/might Friends conduct Meetings for Worship with a focus on a house blessing, healing service, the occasion of dying or moment of death, retirement or other life passages

in which God's presence and the care of the faith community can be made explicit?

4. How does the design of the meetinghouse impact the "act of gathering" for meeting? First Friends Church in Grinnell, Iowa, designed their meetinghouse in 1972 so that the entry room leading into the meetingroom is nearly equivalent in size to the sanctuary. It is heated and furnished in a way that encourages lingering and conversation. They have recently renamed this area the "Friendship Center." In addition to being handicapped accessible, how can our buildings honor our gathering/ connectional needs?

My prayer is that we address the above concerns in a manner that reflects with integrity the faith and testimonies of Friends.

Conclusion

Worship is the heart and soul of a Friends' Meeting. A carefully planned and sensitively led worship service draws us Godward and in the process provides genuine pastoral care. This ministry of care strengthens the meeting, helps create a healthy community and in doing so deepens a Meeting's worship experience. Worship and pastoral care are integrally linked. As caring communities of faith, may we grow in this awareness while we seek to worship God in spirit and in truth.

Notes

1. Keith Maddock, "Worship With Children: Openings for Pastoral Care," *Out of the Silence* (Wallingford, PA: Pendle Hill Publications, 2001), 134.

2. Elaine Ramshaw, *Ritual and Pastoral Care* (Philadelphia: Fortress Press, 1987), 13-14.

3. William H. Willimon, *Worship as Pastoral Care* (Nashville: Abingdon, 1979), 57.

4. Thomas Green quoted in Quaker Faith & Practice (Britain: The Yearly Meeting of the Religious Society of Friends, 1995), #2.07.

5. Willimon, *Worship as Pastoral Care*, 48.

6. Thomas D. Hamm, *The Transformation of American Quakerism* (Bloomington and Indianapolis: Indiana University Press, 1988). Elbert Russell, *The History of Quakerism*, (Richmond, IN: Friends United Press, 1979) 421-434. Richard E. Wood, "The Rise of Semi-Structured Worship and Paid Pastoral Leadership Among 'Gurneyite' Friends, 1850-1900," in *Quaker Worship in North America*, edited by Francis B. Hall (Richmond, IN: Friends United Press, 1978).

7. Wood, *Quaker Worship in North America*, 72.

8. Jack Kirk, "Worship that Comes from Programming in the United Meeting Tradition," in *Quaker Worship in North America*, edited by Francis B. Hall (Richmond, IN: Friends United Press, 1978), 90-91.

9. Celia M. Mueller, "The Nature of Friends Worship" in *Friends Consultation on Worship* (Richmond, IN: Printed Report, 1989), 33.

10. Nick Wagner and Peggy Lovrien, "A Theology of Worship and Hospitality" in *The Ministries of Christian Worship*, edited by Robert Webber (Peabody, MA: Hendrickson Publishers, 1993), 415.

11. Seth B. Hinshaw, *Friends Worship Today* (Greensboro: North Carolina Friends Yearly Meeting, 1991), 61, 38.

12. William Willimon and John Westerhoff, *With Glad and Generous Hearts; A Personal Look at Sunday Worship* (Nashville, TN: The Upper Room, 1986), 31-32.

13. "For the Beauty of the Earth," words by Folliott S. Pierpoint.

14. Robert Webber, *The Ministries of Christian Worship* (Peabody, MA: Hendrickson Publishers, 1993), 237.

15. Herbert Anderson and Edward Foley, *Mighty Stories, Dangerous Rituals: Weaving Together the Human and the Divine* (San Francisco: Jossey-Bass Publishers, 1998).

16. Mueller, *Friends Consultation on Worship*, 33.

17. Hinshaw, *Friends Worship Today*, 67.

18. Willimon, *Worship as Pastoral Care*, 216.

19. Ramshaw, *Ritual and Pastoral Care*, 88.

20. Janet Schaffran and Pat Kozak, *More Than Words* (Oak Park, IL: Meyer Stone Books, 1988), 5.

21. Karl Barth in *Church Dogmatics* (IV) as quoted in Willimon and Westerhoff, 61.

22. Hinshaw, *Friends Worship Today*, 88.

23. "How Long, O Lord", *Songs & Hymns for Blended Worship* (Carol Stream, IL: Hope Publishing Company, 1995), 87.

24. "If I Have Wounded Any Soul Today," *Worship in Song* (Philadelphia: Friends General Conference, 1996), 191.

25. "God Makes All Things New," *Everflowing Streams* (New York: Pilgrim Press, 1981), 75.

26. John G. Martin, "Pastoral Implications," *Lectionary Homiletics* (May, 2000): 4.

27. Howard Macy, "Vocal Ministry in the Programmed Meeting" in *Friends Consultation on Worship* (Richmond, IN: Printed Report, 1989), 50.

28. Macy, *Friends Consultation on Worship*, 48.

29. Keith Sarver in *The Quaker Image* as quoted by Hinshaw, 63.

30. Willimon and Westerhoff, *With Glad and Generous Hearts*, 150.

31. Willimon, *Worship as Pastoral Care*, 210-211.

VI. Friends Ministry and Addiction:
A Ministry of the Head and of the Heart

Ingrid Fabianson

ADDICTION IS SO PREVALENT IN THE WORLD TODAY that Friends in ministry will be called to address it in the families they serve. In the United States, almost one in five children grows up with a parent who is dependent on alcohol or another substance. Other addictions, such as gambling, sex, and food increase the numbers. Children of addicted parents are themselves at risk for falling victim to addictive behavior, not only because of environmental influences, but also because of apparent genetic predisposition. Children raised in addictive environments have a thirteen per cent to twenty-five per cent chance of becoming substance abusers themselves.[1] This epidemic of epic proportions has touched almost every family in our country.

Addiction challenges pastoral and psychological counselors because the behaviors of the addict are often amoral or immoral as in promiscuous behavior, lying, cheating, stealing, addicting others, assaultive outbursts, driving under the influence, and exploiting others. These actions challenge our own spiritual beliefs and ethical standards. How, then, does our Quaker faith which is rooted in integrity, simplicity, honesty, and peace, sustain and inform our ministry with such persons?

In my years of working with Native Americans and rural Kentuckians in the substance abuse field, I've found my Quaker faith not only sustains me in the presence of so much human suffering but, conversely, the suffering has deepened my faith. In this chapter, I want to talk about my spiritual approach to my clients and how my Quaker faith has sustained and guided me. I ask God to guide me as I reflect on my experience.

In the mid 1990s, I worked in Alaska with Yupik, Athabaskan, Haida, and Tlingit people. Part of my work was leading Critical Incident Stress Debriefings (CISD) with emergency personnel after particularly difficult emergency calls. Many emergencies resulted from poor judgment related to substance abuse or addictive behavior. Confidentiality is difficult to maintain because of the small population of Alaska and the active communication network between Native villages, so I will demonstrate the nature of the emergencies without going into specific detail. All names and identifying information used in this chapter are disguised.

In many Native villages, a primary form of entertainment is bingo. Innocuous as this sounds, bingo playing has become so addictive that families may neglect their children in order to play. Villages are full of dangers, from dog pens full of wild dogs to swiftly flowing streams, dangerous equipment, and freezing temperatures. During my stay there, an unsupervised child was devoured in a dog pen, while another child drowned in a swift river.

Other tragedies were more insidious. Young children inhale gasoline fumes and damage their brains. As a result of alcoholic mothers, children are born with fetal alcohol syndrome and suffer permanent brain damage. These wounded children and young adults have little tolerance for noise. One such person shot and killed a crying baby.

In my work in Indiana with people from Kentucky, I have met clients who were given grandfather's moonshine at age three. One had suffered seven years of incest by drunken relatives. Another person married an abusive and addicted spouse at age fourteen in order to escape the violence at home. I have also met the socialite who discreetly became addicted to painkillers and committed fraud in order to obtain them. I met Allen, with a Ph.D., who is such a chronic alcoholic he can no longer speak or walk in a normal way. Scott has been banished from his church for his gambling and sexual addiction. These are some of the faces of addiction. These are some of the tragedies.

In addition to my training in social work, my Quaker faith has sustained me. I believe everyone has access to the truth and everyone must be heard. As Maureen Graham notes in an earlier chapter, I, too, attempt to bring a centered presence to my work and serve as a prophetic witness to my clients' stories. I also use silence as a tool, letting the weight of the moment provide the space for openness and sharing. Like early Quakers in the prison reform movement, I attempt to view my clients through a peace and justice lens, searching for issues of inequality, injustice, and unresolved grief. Often "the way opens" with compassion and love. I am personally sustained by my faith community and certain practices: the practice of reflection, the peace of silent worship, listening for the guidance of the Spirit, respecting "that of God in everyone," and honoring the mystery of faith.

Practice of Reflection

Out of my Quaker faith, I have developed a personal spiritual practice that allows me to begin and end my day refreshed and centered. Each morning I spend one hour reading spiritual literature and sitting in silence. During the silence, I reflect on the day ahead, the work I am to do, the challenges I will face. I pray for myself and for others. In the evening, I close my day in prayer and reflection. I reflect on my clients and pray for them. At times I receive fresh ideas for treatment plans or new approaches. My practice flows out of this morning meditation and returns to reflection in the evening. The concerns of the day are thus less apt to distract me from my focus on helping others. This practice of reflection frames and informs my practice.

Peace of Silent Worship

As a Friend in the unprogrammed tradition, I worship in corporate silence. In the silence, I welcome God and give thanks for
the many gifts I have received. I ask for forgiveness and strength.
As the silence deepens, I make room for the Holy Spirit to fill me
and speak to me. I listen. This prayerful emptying before God
nourishes a deep part of me. I think of Thomas Kelly's use of the
phrase "refreshment of the spirit" to describe my experience in
silent worship. A deep place within me reaches down to living
water where I am nourished and sustained. This sustenance helps
me maintain a compassionate faith in people and a belief that
even the most tortured soul can heal and change. In the silence I
can reflect on God as a forgiving God who continually guides us
toward the good, who heals the broken, and who gives us opportunity to grow through service to others.

In the silence of corporate worship, I often find peace, a peace
that is beyond understanding. To rest in this peace for one hour,
in the presence of other worshippers, is to nurture the centered
presence that I need in order to respond compassionately to the
stories that I hear. The peace of silent worship is like being blan-
keted by the gentle wings of love. I do not always attain deep peace
but even on those Sundays when my mind is restless and my silence
disturbed by my thoughts, I come away with a degree of refreshment that sustains me through the week. As my days are framed by
private meditation, my weeks are framed by corporate worship.

Listening for Guidance

In silent worship and during reflection, a period occurs of deep
and active listening for the still, small voice of God. This voice
may be actually auditory, an image, a memory, a dream fragment,
an inkling, a hunch, an intuition, or a song fragment. God speaks
in many forms. I find it important to be attentive in the stillness
and to be open to obedient response. God also speaks through

others. My clients offer gifts of wisdom that uphold and guide me, if I am receptive. Their stories remind me of paths I could have taken and of God's activity in my life.

Respecting that of God in Every One

As noted in other chapters, George Fox, the founder of the Quakers, professed that the Light of God resided in every human being. This Light can be nurtured and fanned; it can be (almost) extinguished. The choice belongs to the individual. As a Quaker, I deeply believe that my clients contain God too. They have an inner sanctuary, a spiritual well-spring of divine presence and power although many have done their best to extinguish it. I try to connect them with their feelings by asking them about their values and beliefs. While some say they hate God or don't believe in a higher power, almost all of them will profess love for their children, their pet, their truck, or their heritage. In the confession of their love, I hope to remind them of that deep inner "shining place" from which hope springs. In the reminding, they can make choices: to fan the spark and choose a path of wellness or to return to cynicism and substance abuse. I tell them outright and bluntly that their core values still exist and if they want to live, they will need to choose to nurture their goodness back into existence.

The Twelve Step Program is a spiritual program based on the wisdom that if one surrenders their addiction to a Higher Power, one can heal. The statements in quotation marks are from the Alcoholic Anonymous literature, while the statements following the quotations are my interpretation and the way in which I use the Twelve Steps:

Step 1. "We admitted we were powerless over our addiction; that our lives had become unmanageable."

Awakening: the first awareness of how much we are being controlled by substances and how helpless we actually are.

Step 2. "Came to believe that a Power greater than ourselves could restore us to sanity."

Humility: a tender appreciation of our own vulnerability and our need for God influences our sense of self in a positive way. We move past shame.

Step 3. "Made a decision to turn our will and our lies over to the care of God as we understood God."

Courage and faith: these two attributes give us the strength to move forward on our healing path.

Step 4. "Made a searching and fearless moral inventory of ourselves."

Purgation: facing reality and feeling pain, perhaps for the first time. We begin to take responsibility for our actions.

Step 5. "Admitted to God, to ourselves, and to another human being, the exact nature of our wrongs."

Confession and prophetic witnessing: now we confess to another who witnesses our wrongs. Catharsis.

Step 6. "Were entirely ready to have God remove all these defects of character."

Surrender: we give our defects to God and surrender to God's will for us.

Step 7. "Humbly asked God to remove our shortcomings."

Faith: deepening personal maturity occurs as we trust in God to change and forgive us.

Step 8. "Made a list of all persons we had harmed and became willing to make amends to them all."

Responsibility: we honestly assess our past actions and recognize our integrity depends on making amends.

Step 9. "Made direct amends to such people whenever possible, except when to do so would injure them or others."

Retribution: we do our best to right our wrongs. We begin
to feel compassion for those we have harmed and for ourselves. Self-forgiveness begins.

Step 10. "Continued to take personal inventory and when we
were wrong, promptly admitted it."
Growth: we continue to grow in wisdom and integrity.
We have connected with an authentic self.

Step 11. "Sought through prayer and meditation to improve our
conscious contact with God as we understood God, praying
only for knowledge of God's will for us and the power to
carry that out."
Illumination: we have discovered the Presence of God

Step 12. "Having had a spiritual awakening as the result of these
steps, we tried to carry this message to other addicts, and to
practice these principles in all our affairs."
Spiritual maturity: living in the Presence of God and
giving service to others.

The Twelve Step program can provide all the mystical strains
of the monastic life; purgation, self-knowing, illumination, and
the unitive way as well as the simple steps of moving from an
ego-centered life to a life in harmony with universal love. This
spiritual program recognizes that of God in every person and the
healing powers of the Spirit. In my practice, the Twelve Steps are
strengthened by my Quaker belief in the "light of God within
every one" and in the power of God to guide humans toward the
best they can be.

I have seen men, who have been addicted to a variety of chemicals for over twenty years, cry like small children when they begin
the fourth step of inventory work. Often drawn to treatment by
failing health or loneliness, these committed men (and some
women) begin to access a spiritual well-spring within and, with
the help of counselors and chaplains, begin the long road back.

The Steps are the path. The steps give form and meaning to each small success. The steps are a road map to the Light Within.

Centered Presence

A counseling session is sacred ground. A bubble of rapport develops around the two of us and in this atmosphere of intimacy, I try to provide a centered presence. I lay aside my thoughts of the day and engage in active listening. If my mind wanders, I bring it back. I remember a vocal ministry in A Meeting for Worship that helps me:

> When the mind wanders, bring it back to the quiet. When the mind wanders, bring it back to the quiet. When the mind wanders, bring it back to the quiet. It is in the quiet where we find God.

When I remember to do that, I am gentle with myself and provide a more centered presence in my ministry. I also try to be aware of what my body language is saying; for example, am I leaning forward, attentively or are my arms crossed, defensively? I listen with my mind and with my heart.

I believe that a centered presence is felt by my client and builds trust. Sometimes I have to interrupt but it does not give offense if it comes from a place of clarity and charity. I am no saint: Sometimes I get bored and my mind drifts. I try to honor my own vulnerabilities as well.

Prophetic Witness

As I counsel clients, I center down into a deep place of active listening. From this place, I speak my truth. If a client is in denial, minimizing, being grandiose, or rationalizing his or her behavior, I call them on it. For instance, Greg told me his income was $48,000 a year. His records showed that he had just been fired from his third job due to alcoholism. I challenged his grandiosity by asking how he made so much money when he was, by his own admission, unemployed. He confessed his income was actually zero. Denial, minimization, and rationalization are so much a part of this disease; I am speaking "truth to power" when I confront addicts in the sense they are under the power of a cunning enemy. I speak truth in the face of their addiction.

I sometimes envision addiction as a pod creature from the movie *Aliens*. Addiction attaches to the soul of the addict in the same way those creatures attached to the body in order to reproduce; addiction, too, multiplies and grows, bursting out in acts of violence and exploitation. Addiction attaches to the core wound, to the empty, lonely places that want to be covered over and masked. Like a poisonous amoeba, it entangles itself in the whole being, stealing the ability to use good judgment, to connect with a transcendent Creator, to develop a sense of meaning in one's life. It obliterates conscience and values and love. Addiction makes true intimacy impossible because the authentic self is undeveloped and dried up. I envision this self as a hard, wizened stone that sits on the heart with a very small living center, slowly being extinguished by the cunning enemy addiction.

The disease of alcoholism is a dreadful disease. It steals insight. It silences conscience. Those who suffer from it are blind to their own destructive behaviors. This disease is chronic, progressive, and fatal if not put into remission. Addicts are often not able to hear the truth. They need prayer and they need someone who will speak truth to them. I personally do not believe in a confrontative form of treatment that tears down already fragile egos. Such treatment is particularly destructive to women addicts. I do, however, confront behaviors that are leading to their continued abuse of substances. I walk a fine line here—not to offend yet to open eyes. I do this lovingly. I use story. I tell about other people, how they suffered and recovered. I self-disclose when it seems appropriate, as discussed in the next section. I have no firm guidelines. Much of the work is intuitive. I try to determine the strengths of the person. What is there to build on? Where is love? How can I touch their feelings? I try to let them know looking at their losses will involve grieving and that it is alright to cry. I tell men how difficult I know it is in this society to show feelings yet how unexpressed feelings make us sick and lead to addiction. I try to reach the empty, lonely place inside of them so that together we can begin to empty it of its pain and refill it with hope. I use spiritual language when appropriate but mostly I use words like "search for meaning," "philosophy of life," "hope," "dreams for the future." I may ask questions like "Where do you feel most safe?" "What is most important to you?" I use simple tools, tools that help people recognize their goodness and their dreams.

The Gift of my own Woundedness

Carl Jung has been quoted as saying "the numinous enters through our emotional wounds." I do not know where that quote can be found but I believe it. My own spiritual growth has come through my wounds. I was raised in an alcoholic, non-Quaker family, and married dysfunctional, alcoholic men, and raised children, mostly alone. Periods in my life I used drugs, especially when I lived in San Francisco during the Haight Ashbury days of the late 1960s. I, too, tried to cover up the pain of faulty nurturing with chemicals. I also searched for happiness in others, true co-dependent behavior often seen in addicts. My last marriage was to a man with an antisocial personality disorder (sociopath/psychopath) who could have seriously hurt us if circumstances or God had not intervened. My own poor choices led me to The Religious Society of Friends in what I can only call a Spirit-guided way. In the midst of my suffering I prayed for guidance and God spoke the name of a Quaker woman who I had met briefly at a women's education meeting. I called her and she nurtured me back to sanity. Through her, I met my mentor, John Yungblut, and eventually became a Friend. I continue on my own path of healing and growth.

This personal experience informs my work in substance abuse treatment. I can remember what it is like to be caught in an addictive pattern, yet I am healed enough to be present for others.

Peace and Justice

This lens presents the hardest challenge when working with addicted persons in de-tox treatment. The behaviors of addicted people often offend my Quaker beliefs in honesty, fairness, truthfulness, kindness, unity, peace, stewardship, civic responsibility, mutual care, and justice. Addicted people may lie, cheat, and steal in order to get their needs met. They may be grandiose and use violence.

How, then, do I cope? Education in addictions has helped. I have learned that some of the characteristics of the disease of addiction include low self esteem, an inability to cope with stress, immaturity, and an inability to relate as well as to respond to others. Addicted people tend to have a low tolerance for tension, an inability to make responsible decisions, and a deep, underlying sense of inadequacy.[2] These characteristics, combined with unhealthful dependencies on others to define who they are, leave addicts vulnerable to bad decision-making. Knowing this, can separate the person from the disease and see "that of God within" each one. Rarely do I encounter someone whose light has been completely extinguished.

Inequality is often another justice issue as well. Many of the people I work with are suffering the prejudice of racism, classism, and systemic hatred directed toward the marginalized. The clients from rural Appalachia have rarely completed the eighth grade, many cannot read, and some have suffered various forms of abuse within the family system. They are relegated to the lowest rungs of society and are thus working dead-end jobs in factories, often third shift. The Native clients I worked with were also poorly educated, living in small isolated villages, and unable to find work other than subsistence hunting. Substance abuse provides both sets of clients with some sense of freedom in an otherwise limited world. Knowing this, I can respond with compassion rather than judgment. They are suffering from systemic injustice as well as inner pain.

I can certainly become impatient with their patterns of denial and egotistical behavior. Yet, I try to speak to the "place within that shines." This shining place is where one's ". . . deepest wisdom and best instincts come from. . . . It's connected to the whole universe. It's ancient, loving, noble. . . . It's what other people mean when they use words like conscience, or soul, or God."[3] I try to see the face of Jesus in each of my clients. I try to kindle the "shine," the deep spark of wisdom and self-respect that is within.

I do this by using prayerful language, listening with deep respect, mirroring and repeating the good I hear and see, and by using silence to allow the full weight of disclosure to be heard. Marginalized people are often deeply spiritual, so that I may pray with the client if he or she is receptive.

Compassion and Spiritual Nurture

The grief I see in my clients' lives has deepened my capacity for compassion and care. In this way, my clients are a gift to me. Most addicts are sensitive people who are in denial about their feelings. They have suffered losses that may include health, property, employment, relationships, self-respect, and hope. They have also lost productive years of their lives by existing in a chemical haze. Spiritual crisis and alienation result, with symptoms that include feelings of emptiness, profound aloneness, depression and anxiety, anger, and guilt. Connections with others have been severed. They use drugs to drive away an empty core self.

In order to live sober lives, they must now feel the pain of these losses and reconnect with the spiritual dimensions of life. This can be an enormous task. They not only need to rebuild their lives but they also need to create a new life from the ashes of the old. Years of abusing chemicals have stunted maturation. They may no longer know what they believe or value. In my work, I lead a group session titled "Search for Meaning." Here we discuss various spiritual dimensions including our philosophy of life, concept of deity, sense of transcendence, and self-actualization and identity. My Quaker faith has helped me create an experience whereby the group members begin to think in terms of life values, integrity, meaning and purpose of life, and faith. Some clients have never thought about these subjects. Others are so angry at God that they swear and curse at God. My Quaker belief that we create our own personal relationship with God allows me to be tolerant in the face of such rage and also to maintain a non-judgmental, centered presence.

"Be Where the Client is"

This social work mantra lies at the heart of my counseling style. The phrase instructs us to begin where the client is NOW. It also means assessing the environmental circumstances of the client. Is the person homeless? Is he or she struggling with responsibilities for an aged parent or sick child? What is the client's employment situation? Do they have health issues? These questions must be answered if we are to treat the whole person. Spiritual work also requires that we treat the whole person—the mental, physical, spiritual, and emotional aspects. Thus my social work practice informs my spiritual practice and vice versa.

Unity with Nature

My own love of the natural world led me to the Friend's Committee on Unity with Nature. Many addicts understand the place nature plays in their search for peace of mind. When I ask them where they find peace in their lives, they often mention taking long drives in the country or solitary walks in the woods. Some hunt wild mushrooms and ginseng for pocket money. Some addicts, who cannot tolerate people, feel very close to pets. Nature has sustained me through many trying times and I often recommend time in natural settings for people in recovery.

Mystery

My Quaker beliefs sustain me as I work with clients in the mystery of faith and healing. Quakers believe "the way opens" if one listens for the still, small voice of God. I, too, find that the way of healing opens in an equally mysterious way. Sally Bryant speaks to my condition when she says "Quakers hold that the mystery out of which we come is the mystery in which we live, the mystery into which we go." This speaks to my condition. I am strengthened by the mystery of life. The unknowingness of it keeps me open to the unexpected in my clients and in my life. The result is an ability to tolerate ambiguity and to be free of expectation. Miracles happen. Divine revelation occurs. They are part of the mystery. That of God in each of us can be a guide to find and follow the truth, at any time and in any place. Thus my faith keeps me open to the potential for change in my clients and open to "miracles" in the healing process.

Case Illustrations

The following cases are composites from several experiences, as a way to protect the privacy of the persons. The names and other identifying information have been changed.

Heather

Heather, a twenty-eight-year-old white female, came into the hospital addicted to pain pills and strung out on cocaine. She had been gang-raped in a near-by city by members of a gang. The perpetrators injected her with hard drugs during the rape and she became addicted. She also suffered physical pain and soon found herself dependent on Oxycontin, a prescription drug widely available on the street, as a way to gain relief. She was also developing agoraphobia, a fear of open spaces, and anorexia, as well as experiencing panic attacks and depression. She was diagnosed with post-traumatic stress syndrome as well as addiction to substances. She admitted herself to the hospital when a friend confronted her with her growing addiction.

When I spoke with her, she could not stop crying. Her life was in turmoil and she was about to lose custody of her child as well as lose her job. She was also experiencing withdrawal symptoms. As I listened to her history I heard that she was from a rural Alaskan village, had a tenth-grade education, and had been in an abusive relationship for ten years. She had been sexually abused by an uncle from ages six to ten.

In the course of our work together, we often sat in silence. My centered presence seemed to strengthen her resolve to change her life. The silence gave her time really to hear herself and her manner of thinking. She was surprised how negative and frightened she had become. I became a witness to her rage and validated her right to feel it. At times in her story I simply couldn't speak. Then I would wait for the guidance of the Spirit. During one session I could only say "I am so sorry this happened to you." In this phrase she saw the terribleness of the rape and began to understand her innocence. She was a gentle, wounded person who wanted more for her life. She wanted to be a nurse. I saw the "shine" within her, the resilience and determination to contribute to society. I hold her in deep respect.

Her child is mentally disabled. She had no extended family in the area and was leaving her partner of ten years. We talked about loss and spiritual alienation. She was full of longing for a healthy relationship, with God, and with a partner. She was losing hope in her ability to live a rich and rewarding life. When long-term treatment was suggested, however, she wasn't interested. "I can do it on my own," she said. Her refusal was partially due to the cost of long-term treatment. Affordable mental health and substance abuse services for low-income people are in scarce supply; a definite peace and justice issue in our wealthy society. So I recommended free services to her such as Narcotics Anonymous (NA), The National Alliance for the Mentally Ill (NAMI), and the local Mental Health Association's support groups. I hope she followed up.

I reflected and prayed about her and I still do. I set aside time to remember her and in my reflection I honor her suffering, giving it dignity as I hold it in the Light of God's presence. With Heather, I ask the Holy Spirit that she make choices that are best for her and perhaps she will eventually pursue a self-help group, counseling, and long-term treatment. I pray she has the strength and incentive for self-care.

Herb

Every addicted person comes with a story. Some, like Heather's, are heartbreaking. Others, like Herb, are simply exasperating. Now sixty-seven years old, he started drinking at age three, when his grandfather served him moonshine. Growing up in Kentucky hill country, he quit school in the third grade, when his family needed him to run liquor in the mountains. He developed skills in ginseng and mushroom hunting; he also developed a life-long addiction. Herb never went back to school and now lives with an alcoholic son in an old trailer. He is on disability pension because the alcohol addiction has affected his gait, and he cannot walk or stand for any period of time. As a veteran he periodically goes to the Veteran's.Administration (VA) hospital for treatment. He has never remained sober for more than one month. Herb uses humor to hide the pain of his addiction. Jolly and laughing, he comes to various de-tox units every six months or so, dries out, and then, when he is feeling better, goes back to drinking. He has no intention of quitting.

How do I maintain hope in the face of such repetitive, self-destructive behavior? I simply accept the right of each adult human being to make his or her own choices. I can challenge, confront, witness, pray, and be a calming presence but I cannot make someone stop drinking. Herb and I maintain a relationship of affection. He knows I care for him because I treat him with kindness and respect. He also knows I know he will not quit drinking and that it will probably kill him. We accept that knowledge about each other. Herb makes me think of Will Campbell's statement in *Brother to a Dragon Fly* "We're all bastards but God loves us anyway."[4] Herb has made bad choices for his health yet remains a lovable rascal in his own right. Some day I will read his obituary and be sad he died too young.

Herb and Heather's lives, as well as the other people I see, make me question my personal way of life. I am grateful for the queries of Baltimore Yearly Meeting that serve as a guide for my own behavior and choices. "Query Five: Personal Way of Life" asks these questions:

> Do you live in accordance with your spiritual convictions? Do you seek employment consistent with your beliefs and in service to society? Do you practice simplicity in speech, dress, and manner of living, avoiding wasteful consumption? Are you watchful that your possessions do not rule you? Do you strive to be truthful at all times, avoiding judicial oaths?
>
> Do you strive to develop your physical, emotional, and mental capacities toward reaching your Divinely given potential? Do you cultivate healthful and moderate habits, avoiding the hazards of drugs, intoxicants, and over-indulgence generally? Do you try to direct such emotions as anger and fear in creative ways?[5]

Such questions provide me with material I can ponder and they keep me on the right track. I have used the queries in my Spirituality Group to serve as a guide for people who need a model for ethical living. The development of integrity needs to be instilled from an early age; if a person misses this teaching because of living in a dysfunctional family, they need to be taught. The Quaker Queries provide good role modeling for clients who are disabled by childhood deprivation. The Queries are wise and thought-provoking.

Summary

I believe my Quaker faith informs my pastoral care on many levels, providing me with personal strength and opportunity for continuing spiritual development. Quakerism also gives me resources with which I can help others. I am a more effective counselor because of the use of silence, the practice of reflection, prophetic witnessing, and belief in the deep mystery of faith. I am able to attend to my counselees with a centered presence because I listen for the guidance of the Spirit and because I respect that of God in everyone. Quaker faith encourages me to look at people through the lens of peace and justice that I may understand the eroding consequences of racism, classism, and poverty. It supports my social work training and allows me to see the addicted person in a spiritual light, respecting where the person is and observing the environment which informs and influences the person. The practice of silent worship has deepened my personal connection with the Divine so I can help others as they work the Twelve Steps and try to surrender to an unknown God. My personal experience with addictions and spiritual intervention feeds my hope that all humans can change. I am closer to knowing my own truth and thus can come from a more authentic place within my self. My clients recognize this settledness in me which assists in building trust and rapport. I know the "way opens" if we are quiet enough to read the clues. God sends lures; we decide whether or not to be caught.

Being a Quaker influences and informs my ministry. The Light continues to hold me and to call me to my deepest longing: to serve God and to have a peaceful heart. To serve God and to have a peaceful heart are gifts I also want to give my people. This ministry is a ministry of the head and of the heart.

Notes

1. Adult Children of Alcoholics Support Group Hand-out. No credit given.

2. Notes from an Aurora Treatment Center Lecture, Reid Hospital, Richmond, IN, March, 2000.

3. Donella Meadows, "What Does It Mean to Be Human"? as excerpted in *Earth Light. The Magazine of Spiritual Ecology*, Spring 2001, Issue 41, 14.

4. Will D. Campbell, *Brother to a Dragonfly* (New York: Seabury Press, 1977) 220.

5. Baltimore Yearly Meeting, *Faith and Practice*, Query Five, as cited in Newsletter. Goose Creek Meeting, Lincoln, VA, May 2001.

Reflections on Practice

The Leaven

The Parable of the Leaven.

THE kingdom of heaven is like unto leaven, which a woman took, and hid in three meaſures of meal, till the whole was leavened.

Matthew, Chap. xiii.
v. xxxiii.

VII. Family Therapy,
Quaker Style

Judy Owens

MY GOAL IN THIS CHAPTER is to explore how my Quaker beliefs and my clinical work have influenced and informed each other. I am trained as a family therapist rather than as a pastoral counselor or chaplain. Although I am speaking from a very personal perspective, my hope is that other clinicians will find my efforts helpful as they seek to clarify the intersection of their spiritual and their professional lives. As a Quaker, my understanding of my faith is rooted in my own internal experience, and may therefore be somewhat idiosyncratic.

I will first say something about my own background, the way I do therapy as a Quaker, then discuss some current relevant writing in the family therapy field, and finally present a case study.

My Background

I feel blessed to be both a Quaker and a family therapist. I am often able to experience congruence between my work life and spiritual life.

My training in family therapy coincided with my early attendance at a local Quaker Meeting and with the beginning of my remarried family. From the distance of nearly twenty years, these three unfolding developments seem to be a happy circumstance, or a propitious leading. All three paths influenced each other in important ways that I am just now understanding.

My husband and I began attending Quaker Meeting in 1982. I was pregnant with our first child, and my son from a previous marriage was 9 years old. During our courtship we discovered, among other common interests, that we both had been looking for an alternative to our Protestant upbringings, and had always intended to visit a Quaker Meeting. The warm welcome our family received, the living out of social concerns, and the rich quiet we found in our first Meeting for Worship all added to our growing sense that we wanted to be a part of this Society. Since we live in the greater Philadelphia area, the Meeting we found is unprogrammed, which means our Meetings for Worship are silent, with messages coming from those attending as they are "led," or moved by the Spirit. Each of us is a minister, and we share responsibility for functions of the Meeting, such as over-sight (administration and pastoral care), religious education, and worship and ministry, through committees of members and attenders.

The same year that we began attending a Quaker Meeting, I had begun a post-master's clinical program in family therapy at the Family Institute of Philadelphia. My master's degree in coun-seling had led to work with teenagers in an innovative alternative program. I loved the work, but felt hampered by my inability to reach the families of our clients. A co-worker's excitement about family therapy training, along with my husband's encouragement, helped me to pursue the three-year program.

For a few years, the demands of adjustment to a remarriage and new baby, as well as the reading, papers, and clinical hours of the training program, kept me too exhausted and busy to attend Meeting regularly. We kept returning, though, and in 1983 helped form a parent support group. Through this group we became more acquainted with other families in the Meeting, and learned more about Quakerism. In the years since then, we have felt more and more part of the life of the Meeting. We became members, taught First Day School (Quaker "Sunday School"), served on committees, and with the help of our Meeting, sent our two children to the elementary school under our Meeting's care.

In the meantime I became more immersed in the systems thinking that is central to family therapy. I was particularly drawn to the theories of Bowen and Nagy, and worked with other remarried and single-parent families, as well as families referred for school-related problems and general couples work. I worked in a neighborhood counseling service that offered subsidized clinical services to people who might not otherwise receive therapy, and later became that agency's director. A few years later, I joined Philadelphia Yearly Meeting's Friends Counseling Service, which makes counseling available to members and attenders of Quaker Meetings on a sliding scale basis. Eventually I became an approved supervisor and clinical member of the American Association of Marriage and Family Therapy, and lectured and supervised other therapists. I am currently licensed as a Marriage and Family Therapist. For many years I maintained a private practice and administered the neighborhood agency. Recently I joined The Penn Council for Relationships as the director of the New Jersey office.

Quaker Family Therapy

There are, no doubt, as many ways to do "Quaker Family Therapy" as there are Quaker family therapists. Having now served nearly ten years on the Philadelphia Yearly Meeting Friends Counseling Service, I have had a chance to hear many Quaker therapists discuss their work, and I believe some basic similarities exist.

Belief in the "Inner Light" allows Quaker family therapists to trust in the client family's own internal healing capacity. We can create a healing environment, trusting the family to know what it needs to do in order to get better. When reminded of their underlying strengths, parents often know what their children need, and partners know how to love each other. We can take a respectful stance toward our families quite naturally since we know there is "that of God" in each member.

Knowing that each family member has "that of God" influences a Quaker family therapist in another way. We tend to be non-hierarchical and to see the value of each person's views, needs, and contributions. Validating the perspective of the youngest member does not mean devaluing the parents' role, however. We can model empathic, active listening, and help parents take the children's views into consideration as they make decisions for the family.

Quaker theology can also give therapists a useful perspective in this multicultural age. We start from a respectful stance when Meeting with minority families or with families whose backgrounds differ from our own. Since Quakers believe that truth may come from many sources, we enter into a session curious and interested, rather than feeling we have solutions to dispense.

The Quaker tradition of social activism can also be helpful in family therapy. A systemic view that gives credence to the role of poverty, racism, gender inequality, and other aspects of our culture can help us understand our clients more deeply. We can help our clients understand themselves better by giving them a context for some of the issues facing them. I have sometimes found that being aware of what our Religious Society and other activists are doing to counter deep, cultural problems keeps me from feeling so hopeless about my clients' lives.

When working with a Quaker family, we know a faith community exists with the capacity to offer various kinds of support. A family in crisis may be reminded that their Meeting can "hold them in the Light," prayerfully calling for spiritual guidance and Presence for them. We may ask permission to contact their Meeting's overseers and explore available resources. One possibility may be to establish a clearness committee, which is well described in Bill Ratliff's chapter. Such a group of concerned people can provide the spiritual and community connection that an individual therapist cannot provide. Other resources may include setting up a called Meeting for Worship with the family, or providing practical assistance with meals or transportation. We can encourage the family members, adults and children, to use the quiet of Meeting for Worship to sustain them through difficult times, whether that means calling on God's help or taking some time for a thoughtful review of the issues. We can ask if there are Friends in their Meeting with whom they would feel comfortable talking about the current problems, either for emotional and spiritual support or perhaps some possible solutions. With their parents' support and encouragement, children may seek out a Meeting elder, First Day teacher, or a sensitive peer to hear them out or offer another perspective.

I also encourage my non-Quaker clients to tell me about their faith communities, and explore with them how their churches and clergy can be part of their healing. My favorite example involves a long-term client recovering from depression and addiction. Despite her ambivalence about God after her daughter's death, she continued to feel a pull to explore her religious beliefs and to sing in the Lutheran church choir. I encouraged her to engage in a dialogue with her pastor about her doubts and needs, and they developed a close, supportive relationship. Eventually we expanded her therapy to a group support meeting with the two of us, her pastor, and her boss, who also struggled with addiction. We recently acknowledged that the group serves to nurture all of us, and I have learned and benefited from the pastor's warm and thoughtful ending prayers.

In addition to accessing the religious community's potential help, sharing the problem offers other benefits. Therapeutic value often exists in breaking the secretive, shameful silence surrounding many family problems such as alcohol/drug addiction, school failure or family violence. The family may discover that they are not alone with their struggles and may develop a deepened commitment to the community that has helped to sustain them.

Family members of all ages gain self-esteem and a sense of their own value when asked to return some service to the Meeting. When working in conjunction with a family's Meeting community, I can remind the Meeting that the family still has strengths. They can be invited to work on a committee, teach a class, cook a meal, plant a garden, talk to another Friend in trouble, or help on a service project. Growth and recovery can also occur from active involvement in a Meeting.

With Quaker or non-Quaker families, my own need to stay centered and to listen for spiritual guidance is constant. I am increasingly aware of my clinical work as a form of ministry and of the sacredness of the clinical hour. I often take time between sessions to breathe, center, and envision light surrounding myself and the families, as they arrive and depart. When a family's struggle touches me deeply, perhaps because of some similarity with my own life, I may spend some time in Meeting for Worship to ask for guidance for them and in our work together. Having several Quaker colleagues with whom to confer is also helpful.

Family Therapy Literature

During my formal training 15 years ago, little was said about the spiritual health of families. It was as if "serious" family therapists did not use language of the Spirit, or they would be discredited.

Dan Gottlieb, the president of the Family Institute of Philadelphia when I was a student there, was an important exception to this rule. Dan served as my supervisor in my third year of clinical training and for some years afterwards. He has since become the host of a public radio program, and has written *Family Matters; Healing in the Heart of the Family*.[1] A clinical psychologist specializing in family therapy, Dr. Gottlieb believes and teaches that healing occurs in the context of authentic, caring, and safe relationships. As he states in his book:

What I tell my students is that their first and primary responsibility is to create an environment of safety for the families they work with. . . . The world feels unsafe to most of us, and I think relationships feel unsafe. Even our families feel unsafe. But an *experience of safety* is healing. . . . I think part of the way we create safety is through *respect*— respecting the integrity, respecting the dignity, respecting the inner psychic strength of people. I respect the ability of people to manage their own lives and I respect the human spirit . . . I think all people in the helping professions are somewhere on the continuum of healer. No one becomes the ultimate healer—that would be some divine spirit. But we can move on that continuum.[2]

I absorbed these basic ideas about therapy from Gottlieb without being aware, at the time, of their radical nature. Now I see more clearly that I was blessed with a mentor whose philosophy fits very well with Quaker beliefs.

In recent years, family therapy journals, books and conferences increasingly sound a theme of the spiritual nature of our work. Following are ideas from this growing literature that aid my effort to integrate Quakerism into my work with families.

In *The Shelter of Each Other, Rebuilding Our Families*, Mary Pipher outlines how families can strengthen connections to each other and overcome "this family-unfriendly culture." Her goals of family therapy include becoming "purveyors of hope and . . . respect," promoting moderation and balance, and fostering humor. She feels family therapy can help families build good character, control consumption, violence and addictions, diffuse anxiety, and cope with stress. Pipher stresses that a therapist's job is to promote authenticity and creativity, teach empathy, discourage secrets, promote openness, and encourage facing pain directly. We can also help families develop a strategy to make good decisions, clarify thinking, connect families to others, and "teach . . . [families] how to protect themselves with their values, use of time and places, celebrations, stories and metaphors."[3] These confirmations and others provide encouragement and clear ideas to clinicians, including myself, wishing to include spiritual aspects in their work.

Another theoretician whose message is congruent with Quaker thought is William Doherty. In an address entitled "Psychotherapy and Moral Responsibility" given at the International Contextual Conference at Allegheny University in November 1997, Doherty encouraged family therapists to keep in focus the ethical dimensions of therapy. He framed a therapy session as a "moral consultation," an opportunity to explore with a client the "moral terrain of issues."[4] Doherty calls for a shift from the value-less, self-oriented approach that he feels has been prevalent, and likewise to avoid the prescriptive stance sometimes linked to religious counseling. The "quintessential question," Doherty states, is, "How will what you're doing affect others?" A family therapist, as a caring, prudent and moral person, can discuss with divorcing parents how their conflict will affect their children, or discuss with an adult child the complex questions surrounding the decisions of care for an aging parent. Doherty develops these ideas further in his recent book, *Soul Searching, Why Psychotherapy Must Promote Moral Responsibility.*[5]

Today's mail brought a brochure describing an upcoming workshop on "Spirituality and Psychotherapy" being offered by Harry Aponte. In *Bread and Spirit, Therapy with the New Poor,* Aponte includes an understanding of spiritual issues in his discussions and case studies. In a chapter on forgiveness, Aponte movingly describes a family's and their therapist's struggle with incest in terms of a search for redemption and healing of souls.[6]

Case Study

I'd like to describe briefly therapy with one family as an example of some ideas I have outlined. Names and some details have been altered to preserve the family's confidentiality. Several years ago, Beth called to ask if I could see her two young daughters who were having trouble dealing with the aftermath of their parents' divorce. The final decree had been issued six months prior to the phone call. May, 11, and Anna, 8, were struggling in school, fighting with each other, and getting angry with their mother. They spent regularly scheduled time with their father, Tom, who had moved out about a year and a half earlier and lived nearby. Beth felt Tom would also like to be included in therapy, though she was concerned about whether they could be civil to each other in my office.

With Beth's permission, I called Tom to let him know I was seeing his daughters, and invited him to participate in our work. He was wary, but willing. At first I alternated meeting with the girls and each parent, helping everyone to express his or her grief at the separation and sorting out other feelings. I charged the parents to talk directly and respectfully to each other when issues arose, rather than sending messages through the girls. I credited Beth and Tom for being willing to hear their daughters' angry and sad feelings, and for curbing their negative comments about the other parent. Although some time was spent working on the presenting problems of school and sibling issues, we worked mostly on divorce issues.

As frequently happens, Tom and Beth were having a hard time sharing their Quaker Meeting, too. Although both had been active and valued members when they were together, it had become difficult for them to attend the same Meeting. Each parent brought the girls to Meeting when it was their turn to be with them, but felt awkward in the Meeting house when they were not "on duty." Tom expressed a feeling of distance from members who either didn't know what to say to him or perhaps disapproved. Beth had more emotional support from the Meeting, but felt uncomfortable that some members seemed to be "siding" with her against Tom.

The couple had utilized a clearness committee briefly just prior to their separation. Using silent worship and asking for spiritual guidance, the committee had helped them to clarify their feelings and decision and to keep Anna and May in mind as they moved forward. Beth and Tom worked out a visiting schedule that allowed each of them to continue to be involved in the girls' lives, and agreed to share responsibility for major decisions regarding the children. Neither parent kept in touch with members of their clearness committee for a year.

Then, with my encouragement, Beth and Tom reconvened their committee. They discussed their worry about the girls' behavior and the dilemma of how to continue to be part of the Meeting themselves. Although Beth and Tom initially felt uncomfortable asking for more help, they were warmly received by all but one member of their committee. Several expressed relief to be asked, since they had felt things hadn't been going well for the family, and were uncertain how to help. Some members felt led to meet with the girls in an informal setting to see how they could support them. Two men met with Tom separately, concerned that the Meeting may be losing him. After several separate gatherings, the committee met formally with all four family members in quiet worship, seeking divine guidance for them.

Meanwhile, more traditional therapy continued. I attended a school meeting with Beth, Tom, and both girls' teachers in an effort to understand how their academic work was being affected. Anna and May met together with me, and they talked and colored and played their way to a clearer picture of their feelings about each other, their parents, and the separation. They both expressed the wish that their parents would get back together, and they wept about how unlikely that seemed. They spoke about how hard it was to like their father's new girlfriend, Diane, although she treated them well. We worked together to figure how they could both express their feelings to their mother and father, a difficult task since they didn't want to hurt either one. Although Anna felt too shy to talk to any adult Meeting members, May was happy to talk to her First Day school teacher about some of her problems. She sometimes sat with this teacher and her family during worship. Since both girls had learned some conflict resolution skills in school and First Day school, they readily agreed to try some "fair fighting" approaches, like trying to find consensual agreements, banning name-calling and put-downs, and expressing feelings directly to each other. They seemed happy to be more affectionate.

After several months, Beth and Tom met together with me without the girls for a series of six sessions. They spent several hours clearing the air, yelling and crying about some of the painful events before and since their separation. Eventually they got down to the difficult work of redefining their responsibility to their daughters and each other as co-parents. They recognized that Anna and May needed both parents to consider their needs as children, and to keep working toward a civil relationship. We discussed the Peace Testimony (a basic Quaker tenet) as it applies to families and their commitment to work through conflict rather than getting stuck in it.

As I often do with client families, I asked Beth and Tom how their spiritual and religious beliefs influenced their daily life, and specifically how they were using their time for worship. Beth and Tom, like many families, found it difficult to attend Meeting for Worship during times of intense stress and confusion, and sometimes got there but were unable to center. We discussed alternatives to Sunday Meeting, and they liked the idea of a smaller gathering for worship, perhaps at their children's school or an evening Meeting for Worship. I gently encouraged shorter quiet times on a daily basis, and asked about readings and music that might help them to be in touch with the Spirit for comfort and guidance. For Tom, time out of doors was spiritually renewing and healing, and he made time for walks alone and with the girls. Beth began to sing more and to be more aware of how she was responding to music. I asked about prayers, hymns, and Bible readings that comforted them in their childhood, and encouraged both Tom and Beth to share them with Anna and May as well as revisit them now for themselves.

In a final session, all five of us agreed that divorce stinks. Tom and Beth reminded the girls that although they could no longer live together, they intended to work together to be the best parents they could be for Anna and May's sake. Anna and May agreed that life after their parents' divorce seemed more okay now, and that they were happier and doing better in school. We agreed that any member of the family could call me for a consultation. As I said good-bye, I thanked each person for letting me into their lives.

My work with this family was in some ways indistinguishable from any therapist's, or from my work with any non-Quaker family. And sometimes my work with a Quaker family is different because the Meeting or the parents are unable to respond as well as they did in this case. An important Friendly element for me is respect for each individual and my belief that they are capable of making changes on their own. I saw Tom and Beth at an impasse in their discord, but wanting to do what their daughters needed. Anna and May were stuck, too. When I reminded the girls of some tools they already had, and helped them develop some new ones, they were free to act more lovingly toward each other and to operate more freely in school and other places in their world. Their Meeting also needed a few reminders. But like the individuals involved, that community also moved toward health and inclusion.

Not surprisingly, I have chosen an example with an outcome that met all parties' goals fairly well. In other instances therapy did not accomplish what the family needed. Then I need to re-member that we are called to be present and centered, and to hold on to the faith that the healing force at work is the Spirit.

Just as I cannot imagine my life without my three children and husband, I cannot imagine being without my Quaker faith and my work as a family therapist. My experiences in all of these realms challenge me to grow and develop in similar directions. I end up with a deeper belief in God, a sense of "that of God" within me and all people, a commitment to be respectful to myself and others, and a knowledge of the importance of community.

Notes

1. Daniel Gottlieb, *Family Matters; Healing in the Heart of the Family* (New York, Penguin Books, 1991).

2. Gottlieb, *Family Matters*, 244-245, 248.

3. Mary Pipher, *The Shelter of Each Other, Rebuilding our Families* (New York: Random House, Inc., 1996).

4. William J. Doherty, *Psychotherapy and Moral Responsibility.* Address given at Allegheny University, International Conference on Contextual Therapy, Philadelphia, PA, November 7, 1997.

5. William J. Doherty, *Soul Searching, Why Psychotherapy Must Promote Moral Responsibility* (New York: Perseus Books, 1995).

6. Harry J. Aponte, *Bread and Spirit, Therapy with the New Poor* (New York: W.W. Norton & Co., 1994).

VIII. Worship with Children:
Openings for Pastoral Care

Keith Maddock

C HILDREN IN WORSHIP ARE A GIFT to their faith community. Although their presence may expose the raw edges of the generation gap, raising emotional issues for adult members of religious gatherings, children in worship can also heal some of the anxieties that we bring with us into worship.

Pastoral care, the broad ministry of mutual healing and growth within a Meeting, is most effective when it is developmentally-oriented. Each stage of human growth, with its moments of crisis and celebration, offers abundant opportunities for mutual support.[1] Such opportunities, in the context of a Quaker community, are consistent with the belief that we are all ministers to one another, regardless of age, education, or background.[2]

Part one of this essay focuses on potential conflict. When a restless child taxed my patience during worship, I began to reflect on our expectations of children and how we might offer them a more engaging vision of our spiritual life together. Part two reflects on building community through the revitalizing influence of children. It focuses on the ministry of, rather than to, children. While this perspective may lead to romanticizing their gifts, we need to take this risk in order to appreciate the healing power they offer. Children are often the embodiment of grace in the minds of adults who are struggling to realize a more holistic vision of their own. Finally, I will discuss the integration of children into the worshipping community and the sensitive issue of religious abuse, drawing upon traditional Quaker testimonies and other resources for mutual care.

Centering Amidst the Distractions

I was fidgeting in my chair, wondering when the Meeting for Worship would be over and I could leave the room. The problem was that, as an adult, I was expected to stay put and listen for the Spirit—regardless of any distractions the Spirit (or my own mind) might throw in the way. During this particular meeting, people were sharing stories about the Spirit moving in their everyday lives, and many spoke eloquently of their faith-journeys through periods of conflict and doubt. Listening attentively to each story, I was also cherishing the intervals of silence when I could gather memories from my own experience.

But those moments became increasingly rare as a young child in the row immediately behind me became restless. At first she poked her little head around the foot of my chair and gave me one of those disarming smiles that small children seem born with. I smiled back, repressing a temptation to play peek-a-boo. Then I simply tried to ignore her.

Silence can be terribly oppressive for children (as it can be for us all) when they're tired or needing attention. Over the course of a half-hour or so, she went from being playful to complaining. To make matters worse, her mother was also becoming frustrated as she tried to distract the child with crayons and frantic whispers. I was no longer settled into the spirit of the evening and the stories of hope and renewal were lost amidst childish whines. Becoming more and more impatient, I wondered if I was the only one in the room who minded.

Finally, I turned around and asked the mother if she would take the child outside for a while. I thought it was a polite request. But the look I got from the mother in response was enough to burn a hole through me. After a furious scrutiny of my nametag, she picked

137

up her little girl and walked out of the room. I was soon to learn that I had ventured into that dangerous space between a mother and her child where few people dare to tread.

Later, the woman cornered me in the hall, saying that we needed to talk. Without further discussion, she insisted that she had a right to bring her child to Meeting. She was trying to teach her to appreciate the silence and no one could deny her that. And worse, because I asked her to take the child out of the room, *both of them* now felt unwelcome.

It never occurred to me to apologize for what I felt was a reasonable request. But I suggested she take her concern to Ministry and Council if she wanted to pursue the issue further. It seemed a wiser course than to risk further confrontation. Apparently she did just that, and a few days later I was approached discreetly by one of the committee members. While they appreciated my concern, they had listened to the mother's grievance as well. I'm not sure, however, that the mother *felt* she had been heard. Later in the week she spoke up in Meeting for business as an advocate for the inclusion of children in worship, mentioning offhand that someone had turned her child away. When the gathered Friends applauded her position, I could not help feeling resentful about the misinterpretation of what had happened.

In retrospect, I have tried to appreciate the merits of the woman's argument. When I told a teacher friend about the incident, she suggested an alternative response that might have avoided conflict and frustration. Since I was probably more disturbed by the mother's restlessness than the child's, I could have simply told the mother not to worry, that her daughter was fine. With the relief of parental anxiety, the child might have felt more comfortable. Another possibility was to ask the child if she wanted to go outside and play. This sounded like a more risky alternative for a middle-aged man like myself, but it might have drawn the mother's attention to the child's needs rather than to her own. Whatever response I may have adopted, the primary concern was to allow the Meeting to be gathered, to foster a sense of gathered community in the Meeting without making anyone of any age feel excluded.

It is ironic that I've always been an advocate for children in religious communities. When adults complained about distractions, I was one of those who quoted the words of Jesus, saying, "Let the little children come to me," and "Unless we become like one of them, we will not enter the Kingdom of Heaven." If the complainers didn't understand that, it was sometimes all I could do to keep my cool. It was as though every child were my own.

Before becoming a Quaker, I worked for several years as a youth minister in Protestant congregations. The full inclusion of children and youth in the community was one of my favorite themes, and on occasion I even tried to include young people in communion services. In churches where outward sacraments are regarded as the exclusive privilege of adults, I was testing the limits. Nevertheless, when children appeared in the sanctuary, they generally won the hearts of most of the opposition. On one occasion, however, I was to be disappointed. After preaching a lively sermon about the inclusion of children and waiting for the pre-arranged return of the children from Sunday school, only one child appeared on cue—and his mother led him in by the hand. Later, I learned that the Sunday school superintendent had reservations at the last minute, and held the children back. At that point I realized that teaching children about communion—or *community*—was hopeless unless adults understood and lived the meaning of it themselves.

Years later, I fear that a role-reversal may have taken place. During a Quaker Meeting, I asked a mother quietly if she would mind taking her restless child outside for a while. At that time I was reflecting on my own need for rest and silence, and on my *inner* child who was enjoying a well-deserved rest after a busy day. While indulging the need of my exterior grown-up for stillness and recovery, I could imagine taking *my* child in my arms, thanking

God for the joy of play and discovery that this part of me continued to offer. And I prayed for his safety and future happiness.

When a real child peeked around the foot of my chair and smiled up at me during these reflections, I felt that the inward and the outward Light had become one. Later, when I heard the same child squirming and complaining, my heart went out to her. I waited for what seemed an eternity before turning to speak to the mother. And when I did, it was with a good deal of discomfort that I asked the mother to take the child outside.

What I felt toward the child was a form of empathy, understanding the child's point-of-view because there is still something of the child's playfulness and vulnerability alive in myself. Such empathy can be infectious, creating a bond of instant communication between adults and children. This bond can be recognized and cultivated in each of us, especially during a silent Meeting when we are invited to let our everyday inhibitions fall away.

I suspect that the woman who confronted me was on the right track, trying to expose her child to the Quaker silence at an early stage in her development. At the same time, however, I wonder if she neglected her own need for solitude in her concern to educate her daughter. She may also have forgotten the strength of her own influence in the child's world. Regardless of how gathered the Meeting may have been, the child was more likely to be tuned in to her mother's distress than to anything else that was happening.

Although we speak of *being gathered* in a silent Meeting, we continue to be alone in our personal encounters with God. Elise Boulding, the author of *Children and Solitude*, has explored how this experience, which she calls *creative solitude*, can be made available to children. She suggests we begin by finding meaning in it for ourselves. "Adults who seek it do not need to explain it to children,"[3] she writes.

There's also something to be said for letting children explore their surroundings and discover what other limits there are to bump up against, besides parental authority. In our Meeting there has been a small baby boom in the past few years, and it is not unusual to emerge from deep contemplation to find a small face gazing up at you from below. A smile of acknowledgment seems to go a long way toward making that child feel safe and accepted. Once the novelty of exploration wears off, the child looks around for parental security. And, if the parent is attentive, the need is satisfied without any disturbance at all.

In this way, both the boundaries and the satisfaction of belonging materialize for the child out of personal encounter. Harold Loukes, the author of *Friends and their Children*, writes:

> Quakers . . . have tried to expose their children to religious experience without the distortions of their own errors; to awaken their sensitiveness and to encourage them to see and to choose and to respond for themselves.[4]

He relates this observation to the experiential nature of Quaker faith. The search for religious experience is a search for the whole meaning of any experience, beginning with the world as-it-is— open for discovery and safeguarded, but not anxiously constrained by parental concern.

My actual response to a restless child brought other issues to the surface. Assuming that children are accepted as part of the worshipping community, how can we communicate that acceptance to them as well as to other adults? In an active Meeting, with singing and movement, adaptations can be made to encourage their participation. In a silent Meeting, the possibilities may be less evident.

Today, many unprogrammed Meetings include children for fifteen minutes either at the beginning or at the end of worship. But it is not always certain that they are adequately prepared to participate meaningfully in the experience. Loukes confirms the difficulty of offering children an experience of silent worship without gradually introducing them to it through music and liturgy. Yet he adds that the worst thing that can happen to them in silence is boredom, while the risk of grappling with adult religious expressions may be more bewildering. He writes:

> In the silence the child is at least safely left to himself, and if religious ideas begin to stir, they arise from his inward life.[5]

Healing Community

This is how one worshipping community recovered a sense of compassionate unity through the presence of a child in its midst.

One morning as the Meeting was being gathered, our thoughts were suddenly interrupted by the sound of moving furniture. A fifteen-month-old boy, testing the strength of his limbs, was pushing a chair across the front of the Meeting room. While his mother and father weighed parental anxiety against glowing pride, other Friends looked on in wonder.

After Meeting concluded, a white-haired woman inched her way over to the father and said with a twinkle in her eye, "If anyone complains about the noise, I want you to know that I'm on the child's side."

Many Friends who knew the family were aware that a miracle was taking place in their midst. A year and a half earlier, that same child had been born premature and was not expected to survive. As the days and weeks passed and he continued to fight for life, a number of members and attenders of the Meeting gathered each day in the hospital quiet room for a silent vigil. The family members were convinced that their consistent show of support had a direct effect upon the boy's ultimate survival.

Eventually he was strong enough to be taken out of the hospital, and brought home. His first appearance in the Meeting was a triumph when his father held him high during the introduction of new attenders. Each time I saw the child after that, he seemed wide-eyed with wonder. People who didn't know this child's story may have found his presence distracting, or a charming diversion at the most. But the warmth of the members' response could not go unnoticed.

The story also has a sequel in the life of the Meeting. His grandmother first told me of the comment made by the older woman after the distraction with the chair. It was an important statement of support for the family, for this elder was one of our most senior and respected members. Only a few days after her expression of support, she suffered a heart attack and died in hospital.

Her memorial was one of the best-attended events ever seen in the Toronto Friends' House. So many people came that three Meetings had to take place simultaneously in different parts of the building. All generations were represented, from Friends' Meetings and from the wider community. As a doorkeeper, one of my tasks was to seat latecomers and help avert distractions during vocal ministries. Although there were a few restless infants present, their parents managed to keep them content. After the first half-hour, however, some older children came into the building through a side door and were milling about in the hall, waiting to stampede for the stairs leading to the upper floors. Taking my role seriously, I held my finger to my lips and mimed tiptoeing through the hall. As they imitated my action, I began to realize how silly I must have looked.

Then I imagined I could hear our departed friend's voice in my ear, saying, "If anyone complains about the noise, I want you to know that I'm on the children's side." She reminded me that a memorial Meeting is actually the celebration of a life. Even in this context, there is a place for the nurture of children. Harold Loukes has pointed out that while children may grieve, they need to be assured that the world still goes on with their own place in it assured. He continues:

> We can give them this reassurance better by the quality of our own emotional acceptance than by attempting to introduce a puzzling set of new concepts: we need to convey to them the sense that though we are troubled we

are not overwhelmed; that though a tree has been uprooted the garden is alive with growth.[6]

In the Religious Society of Friends, pastoral care is not necessarily the role of special ministers. It may be overseen by committees, like Ministry and Counsel, but essentially all members—including children—are called to participate. The inclusion of children in worship has been recognized as so important to the healthy growth of our communities, that most yearly Meetings have included an article on the subject in their *Advices and Queries*, general guidelines for pastoral care. As a member of Canadian Yearly Meeting, I am most familiar with the one expressed in the new British discipline:

> Rejoice in the presence of children and young people in your Meeting and recognise the gifts they bring. Remember that the Meeting as a whole share a responsibility for every child in its care. Seek for them as for yourself a full development of God's gifts and the abundant life Jesus tells us can be ours.[7]

The queries, suggestions for reflection included with this statement, draw attention to how we share our deepest gifts with them, while leaving them free to develop as the Spirit of God leads. More specifically, we ask if we encourage children to share their insights with us, and whether we are ready to learn from and be cared for by them as well as to accept our responsibilities for their spiritual growth.

Pastoral care is brought into a clearer focus when we consider how children can be included more fully in the life of the Meeting and educated in the religious, social, and moral values that we all cherish. Pastoral care extends to concern for whole families and extended families that are struggling with a host of problems in the modern world. Conventional marriages may be less common than they used to be, and relationships often suffer from emotional breakdown and financial hardship. Children are most vulnerable in such circumstances, and must not be over-looked simply because they are below eye-level during occasions of adult interaction and dialogue.

Our frequently romanticized view of childhood and our general lack of attention to their life situations easily lead us to overlook the fact that they also have crises. These may not always be re-lated to abuse or exceptional events in their lives, but simply to the day-to-day changes which they have not yet learned to cope with on their own. It is important to be aware of and to respond to the life-changes of children, because the way they experience and interpret such changes will affect every part of their developing sense of selfhood.[8]

While Quaker children today may no longer grow up in close-knit religious communities as in days gone by, they may benefit from the attention provided by an extended family. People bring their children to Meeting, often expressing a need to introduce them to spiritual and moral values that are not introduced any-where else in this competitive and troubled world. Acknowledg-ing God's presence in each individual, the Meeting is responsible for making them feel welcome. "Making friends with children is the first step to making Friends of them," writes Loukes.[9] There are many opportunities to welcome and encourage their active participation, from interacting with older adults in worship to enjoying their own activities in nursery and First Day school.

It is a mistake to regard children solely as the objects of care and concern. Throughout their lives they continue to be dynamic individuals, responding to the world around them and offering to share their love and enjoyment with other people they encounter. Pastoral care involves the ministry *of*, as well as ministry *to* chil-dren. In the broader understanding of ministry that Quakers main-tain, even the simple act of a child pushing a chair across the room can, in the language of our testimonies, *speak to our condition.*

Through the spontaneous outreach of the young, we learn to be open and receptive to the unexpected ministrations of the Spirit in our lives. I was reminded of this while standing in the crowded dining room one day around Christmas, suffering from the seasonal depression that often afflicts single people. As my mind was drifting off in the din of voices, I felt a sudden tug at my belt. A young girl was looking up at me with a solemn expression in her eyes. "Merry Christmas," she said, before disappearing into the forest of trousers and stockings below. "Thank you," I whispered, almost buckling at the knees with the sudden release of emotional tension. I felt cared for.

The visible presence of children in Meeting for Worship is most deeply felt when they file out of the room. While it may be a relief for some adults to see them go, it should not be the sole responsibility of parents to accompany them. Adults with children, and whose children have grown up, often need quiet and mental freedom to nurture their own interior space. What an opportunity it is for those without children to share in the spiritual development of young people. Later, the serious work of committee meetings, social activism, fund-raising, and other activities may seem unrelated to the presence of young children. But the exuberance of children's activity nearby, rather than being distractions, may be appreciated as sources of energy and hope for the challenges that lie ahead.

Through the experience of feeling loved and encouraged to share their gifts in an extended family, the quality of their first experience in a religious gathering is of vital importance. If there is an atmosphere of acceptance, joy, and radiating warmth, the worshippers create an impression of strength, virtue, and acceptance that will remain with the children throughout their lives.

Children of the Light

One contemporary theorist of pastoral care has written, "The key to human flowering is an open, trustful, nourishing, joyful relationship with the loving Spirit who is the source of all life, all healing, all growth."[10] It is this form of relationship that young children may experience in a Meeting that is centered in worship. And it is this vision of community that can enable adults to focus on the life-giving Spirit in their midst.

While reflecting on the experiences from my own Meeting, I began to realize that they reflected a tension between the socialization of children and faith in their potential for individual growth. Enabling children to explore the worship environment, through interaction with adults or through a deeper appreciation of solitude in the gathered silence, is both a responsibility and an opportunity to expand our awareness of mutual pastoral care. When we come to Meeting, it may be as isolated individuals, busy social activists, or family units in search of a wider connection. Considering the strain on families, and the widening gap between generations in our society, how can we cultivate a sense of inclusive relationship within our Meetings? How can we encourage a spirituality of trust and respect that may open the way to mutual understanding and care?

These and similar questions may have less to do with instruction and training than with creating the right conditions for growth in which pastoral care can be most effective.[11] Spiritual development depends on an emerging sense of identity, an inward consciousness of being a person. It involves nurturing an ability to sort out what comes in through sensation and experience with what is already active within. Furthermore, it is inseparable from the process of socialization within a gathered community. Boulding observes, "Aloneness is essential because this is an experience of separating out from the world in order to integrate with it."[12]

Our Quaker tradition has valuable resources for the care of children. The early Quaker community found it important to provide ample opportunity for religious experience within the family circle *as well as* in the gathered Meeting. They set aside a special time in the daily routine for reading the Bible and waiting for the Spirit of God to touch their inner lives. Today we would include more intellectual synthesis, aesthetic experience, and social concern. "But," adds Boulding, "we easily overlook that critical ingredient of solitude, without which the identity of the seeking soul remains forever undifferentiated from the smorgasbord of experience on which it feeds." [13]

This continually expanding awareness of spiritual reality, a potential in all children from a very young age, takes different forms depending on environment and teaching. Rufus Jones wrote beautifully about his experience as a young child among adults in silent worship. While almost nothing was said to him in the way of instruction, adults and children joined together in listening to God. He wrote:

> In these simple ways my religious disposition was being formed and the roots of my faith in unseen realities were reaching down far below my crude and childish surface thinking.[14]

Though unaware of the significance of what was taking place, he intuited something of the mystery of faith.

But then, this seed was planted in the home, where silence was an element in the daily family routine. In such ideal circumstances, the child finds it natural and easy to trust in silence. Boulding comments, "in a family where inward solitude is highly prized, individuals may slip easily into and out of each others' solitude."[15]

Communities of early Friends considered domestic stability to be a primary influence on moral culture. Children knew life, love, and fun as well as the somber realities of pain and loss first hand through close relationships. Again, Boulding reminds us:

> In the long stretches of solitude open to the young of that less cluttered age, they worked out their own solutions to the conflicting inward and outward pulls they felt.[16]

Solutions did not come in ready-made scriptural formulas or solely through verbal admonitions, though these were among many seeds planted in their hearts. Each child brought forth his or her own individual fruit.

Transplanting a child's faith to a larger gathering is a much more complex operation today. An experience of being in an unfamiliar environment dominated by adults does not necessarily lead to an experience of God's love. It cannot be taken for granted that the Meeting for Worship will have the desired influence on a child unless the child's mind and heart have been prepared with experiences of warm and imaginative interaction in the family and in a wider community, without the need for outward stimulation.

Quaker journalists who recorded their early childhood revelations were often exceptional in their later dedication and sensitivity to the Inward Light. One of them, John Comly, wrote about the incalculable advantages of taking little children to Meeting and getting them accustomed to the discipline of stillness. In 1853 he wrote:

> It may be the means of laying a foundation, very early in life, for the most exalted virtues. The seeds of Divine goodness thus planted, or that germinate in good wishes and good desires, when the infant mind is thus retired, may take deep root and bring forth early fruits of genuine religion . . . Under these solemnizing, tender feelings, the pure, innocent, uncontaminated infant mind worships in spirit and in truth. It learns to love such opportunities—delights to feel such a calmness and quietude . . . and enjoys a heaven within.[17]

How do adults make creative solitude available to children? This is an issue that embraces religious education and nurture as well as ongoing pastoral care through the various stages of life. Adults set the example as they seek truth through reflection, prayer, service, and imaginative interaction with the Spirit. Adults who seek a more holistic experience of God and support one another through their life crises and stages of growth do not need to explain it to children. In an environment where the gathered silence is fully lived, a child finds it easy and comfortable.

As a last resort, there may be ways to encourage this shared experience. The chair of a yearly Meeting program committee recently made a confession to me. As an experiment in non-verbal, creative worship, members were expected to bring creative projects to the opening intergenerational gathering. But the committee had neglected to inform them of this. A last minute panic was averted only when the chair remembered a recipe for play-dough, and provided an ample supply of it for all generations to indulge in during the silence. Later, many reported that they had experienced a warmer and more profound gathering in that worship than they had known before.

In the long run, play-dough may be a wonderful community-building device, but is not enough to nurture a lasting sense of gathered worship. With or without helps, the silence *and stillness* of Meeting can open a unique door into spiritual life for children as well as for adults. Rufus Jones wrote the following:

> It does not seem necessary to explain Quaker silence to children . . . they feel what it means. They do not know how to use very long periods of hush, but there is something in short, living, throbbing times of silence which finds the child's submerged life and steers it to nobler living and holier aspiration. I doubt if there is any method of worship which works with a subtler power or which brings into operation in the interior life a more effective moral and spiritual culture. Sometimes a real spiritual wave would sweep over the Meeting in these silent hushes, which made me feel very solemn and which carried me . . . down into something which was deeper than my own thoughts.[18]

Quaker testimonies seem to be on solid ground concerning the spiritual nurture of children. This is very reassuring in these times as we become more sensitized to the religious abuse of children *and adults.* During the past few decades, the Religious Society of Friends has seen an influx of new members from other denominations, many of them fleeing from negative experiences of religious training and discipline in their own childhood. As a result, pastoral care among Friends is increasingly sensitized to religious abuses in their own history. Helping members and newcomers recover trust, Meetings find it important to ensure their children a safe and positive environment for growth.

According to Donald Capps, author of *The Child's Song: The Religious Abuse of Children,* abuse may take a variety of forms, including theological justification for physical punishment and the promotion of ideas and beliefs that instill feelings of shame and fear in children.[19] Andrew Lester, the author of *Pastoral Care with Children in Crisis,* also observes that when children do not receive appropriate pastoral care during a stressful event, the meaning of the event may be distorted. The child may conclude that God is angry, uncaring, or even mean-spirited.[20]

What aspects of our tradition stand in the way of nurturing the emotional and spiritual health of children? Which resources help us to develop our own healthy and nurturing responses? If you are from a group other than the Quakers, you can reflect on these questions from your own faith perspective. Yet, for the Quaker, the traditional peace testimony is crucial in its rejection of *all* forms of physical—and perhaps even *emotional*—violence. The thoughtful teaching of this testimony in words and daily behavior can help to create a comforting environment for all generations. In the second case, belief in the revelation of a loving God through every human being, of any age, may defend against the manipulation and repression of the most vulnerable. The need for reflection and clearness in every interaction and teaching leads us to question the most deeply entrenched theological ideas—including the concept of original sin.

All good parents are anxious not to make mistakes in the care and nurture of their children, and especially to avoid making the same mistakes their own parents may have made with them. For such reasons, adult anxiety is often most apparent to the child in spiritual training. The great decline in numbers of children in religious communities over the past several decades may be partly the result of such stifling concern. Loukes reminds us that, "Any parent knows that the care of children is a perpetual reminder of his own need for forgiveness."[21] Yet we must not lose sight of the fact that children are forgiving by nature, as long as they feel safe and wanted.

Quaker instruction has traditionally been designed to prepare young people for the choices they will need to make when they grow into adulthood. Hopefully, they learn to question all forms of teaching and discipline that do not confirm their first experience of spiritual reality, which Loukes refers to as "the dawning of love."[22] Such a discretionary discipline is grounded in the belief that "there is Truth to be found, indescribable and incommunicable but waiting to be discovered in the mystery of personal encounter."[23]

Pressed for time and opportunity for religious nurture in the home, parents may find support in the extended family that Meetings and congregations have to offer. From my own perspective, as a single adult, the presence of children in Meetings for Worship is a profound opening to inward peace. As I grow older and less confident of my tolerance for distractions, it becomes increasingly important for me to recover my inner child and nurture it. My experience of worship is in this way enhanced by the presence of real children, interacting with adults in the worship setting. They remind me of the child who was born to reconcile the world with its creator. Sharing the experience of worship with children reminds us that we are all—from new-born infants to the aged and infirm—children of the Light.

Notes

1. Howard Clinebell, *Basic Types of Pastoral Care and Counselling: Resources for the Ministry of Healing and Growth* (Burlington, Ontario: Welch Publishing, 1984), 26.

2. Clinebell, *Basic Types of Pastoral Care and Counselling*, 26.

3. Elise Boulding, *Children and Solitude*, Pendle Hill Pamphlet 125, (Wallingford, PA:Pendle Hill Publications, 1983), 21.

4. Harold Loukes, *Friends and their Children* (London: George G. Harrap & Co. Ltd., 1958), 14.

5. Loukes, *Friends and their Children*, 24.

6. Loukes, *Friends and their Children*, 47.

7. *Quaker Faith and Practice : The Book of Christian Discipline of the Yearly Meeting of the Religious Society of Friends in Britain*, 1995, 1.02, 19.

8. Andrew D. Lester, *Pastoral Care with Children in Crisis* (Philadelphia: The Westminster Press, 1985), 48.

9. Loukes, *Friends and their Children*, 62.

10. Clinebell, *Basic Types of Pastoral Care and Counselling*, 3.

11. Loukes, *Friends and their Children*, 27.

12. Boulding, *Children and Solitude*, 13.

13. Boulding, *Children and Solitude*, 18.

14. Rufus Jones, *Finding the Trail of Life* (N.Y.: The MacMillan Company, 1926), 22.

15. Boulding, *Children and Solitude*, 21.

16. Boulding, *Children and Solitude*, 15.

17. John Comly, quoted in Howard H. Brinton, *Quaker Journals: Varieties of Religious Experience Among Friends* (Wallingford, PA: Pendle Hill Publications, 1972), 13.

18. Jones, *Finding the Trail of Life*, 89.

19. Donald Capps, *The Child's Song: The Religious Abuse of Children* (Louisville, KN: Westminster John Knox Press: 1995), xii.

20. Lester, *Pastoral Care with Children in Crisis,* 49.

21. Loukes, *Friends and their Children,* 44.

22. Loukes, *Friends and their Children,* 113.

23. Loukes, *Friends and their Children,* 127.

IX. Violence and Nonviolence:
Quaker Spirituality and
the Treatment of
Domestic Violence Offenders

Dan Snyder

A STORY IN THE NINETEENTH CHAPTER OF ACTS tells of the seven sons of Sceva who, after hearing about all the wonders Paul was performing in the name of Jesus, went out and attempted to exorcise demons saying, "In the name of Jesus whom Paul preaches, I command you to come out." The demons answer saying, "Jesus we know, Paul we know, but who are you?" Then the man who was possessed attacked them, and the scripture says, "they fled out of the house naked and wounded."[1]

Several years ago, when I was offering a treatment program for domestic violence offenders, I often felt as if I were up against forces whose depths I couldn't fathom and whose pathology was beyond what psychology can understand and treat. It was as if these forces were confronting me saying, "Freud we know, Jung we know, but who are you?" My desire to work in this field was in part a calling to face the challenge of this question. If my advocacy of the Quaker pacifist vision was ever going to be anything more than a philosophical or political stance, it would have to be tested and deepened in the face of these violent forces. The Friends' peace testimony is anchored in the life of the Holy Spirit, and is effective only to the extent that we live "in the virtue of that life and power that [takes] away the occasion of all wars."[2] I knew this work would challenge me to pray more deeply and more urgently than work with a more comfortable set of clients, although the fact that I worked within a context of legal leverage and sanctions probably saved me from suffering the same fate as the sons of Sceva.

The apparent reformation in behavior that such leverage produces, however, is not evidence of inward healing. Coerced behavior usually lasts only as long as the coercion. The healing of domestic violence will not come from forces of external control, but from the genuine inner transformation of men who batter. During the course of this work, I witnessed a number of such transformations. I also encountered men for whom no transformation seemed possible in spite of my best efforts, and like the sons of Sceva, I confronted forces which seemed to have nothing but contempt for the more tender things in life. These forces required me to examine deeply the roots of my spirituality. No borrowed authority would do.

While I brought my psychological training to this task, it was my spirituality that was ultimately challenged. When these men became threatening or defiant, and I found myself wanting to retreat in fear, prayer gave me the courage to stay connected. Certainly I could speak of my internal states as countertransference. Certainly one must be aware of countertransference events and make use of them in an ongoing understanding of unconscious relational dynamics with clients. I came to believe, however, that an exclusive focus on the clinical language of psychology obscures the deeper spiritual issues. The men who came to me for treatment required me to go beyond psychology to an ever-deepening search for a centeredness in God which is the surest antidote to countertransference there is. A radical spirituality, when allowed to shape and guide the work of psychology, will end up revolutionizing it.

This chapter, therefore, will consist in an exploration of five themes within Quaker thought and practice as they inform and ground a spirituality of nonviolence. The challenge to learn about the treatment of domestic violence offenders matched the challenge to re-examine some of my basic assumptions about Quakerism. First, I found I needed to examine the nature of confrontation, power, and authority. Quakers tend to be very reluctant to confront boldly, directly, and with authority. We are suspicious of those who exercise power. Yet confrontation, backed up by legal leverage, is essential in the treatment of domestic violence. A second issue, closely related to problems with confrontation and power, is that of prophetic judgment. Many of us have been wounded by the condemning and self-righteous attitudes of those who claim to speak for God, so we embrace an ethic of tolerance that can leave us open to an abuse of our good will. We must re-vision our understanding of judgment from an attitude of condemnation to one of discernment. These considerations then lead me to the third issue which is a re-examination of the meaning of forgiveness. When is forgiveness more codependent than healing? Fourth, I found I needed to wonder more deeply about what is meant by the popular Quaker advice that one should seek to speak to "that of God in everyone." It was more the language of profound sinfulness than godliness that was descriptive of many of the men I saw. Yet the language of sin is not often found in the modern Quaker vocabulary. Finally, I was challenged to look more deeply into the meaning and practice of prayer. If I was to be a truly nonviolent influence in these men's lives, it would not be because of any personal philosophical or political convictions. Rather, it could arise only out of the virtue of the Life and Power of God.

Confrontation: From Power to Authority

All clinicians are faced with the necessity to confront their clients with the ways in which they are hurtful to themselves or others. Nowhere is this necessity more evident or more urgent than in clinical work with men who batter. Confrontation inevitably stiffens resistance, however, unless there is a relational context within which it takes place. Clients who are not a threat to themselves or others present less of a problem. Therapy involves the gradual building up over time of a relational space that invites trust. Confrontation can safely be postponed until the relationship is strong enough to sustain it. This is a luxury, however, which is not permitted in work with batterers. The clinician who seeks to join these men in a therapeutic relationship is inviting trust on the one hand, and is responsible for enforcing compliance on the other. Most of the therapy consists of showing them the ways in which they are destructive in their relationships, and on how they insist on seeing the world in terms that avoid responsibility for change.

Given the need for this type of confrontation, many approaches to treatment fail to consider the dynamics of power that are inevitably present in mandated programs. Some of these confrontational approaches to treatment re-create a scenario of intimidation and control which repeats, in more subtle form, the same violence for which the offender is being held accountable. In these programs, the offender, whose very pathology centers around issues of power and control, constantly assesses the balance of power. Consequently, he responds to highly confrontive therapy by becoming either aggresively defiant, or passively compliant, depending upon whether he considers himself in a one-up or a one-down position. It's a difficult issue. On the one hand, if we fail to confront clearly, directly, and consistently, what happens to the issue of accountability for the very real harm done, the terrible wounds, both physical and emotional, that are left in the wake of domestic violence? There can be no healing where there is no accountability. Put in more spiritual terms, there can be no healing where there is no confession. On the other hand, since genuine confession cannot be coerced; confrontation alone is not enough and may even deepen the resistance to change. In sorting through this dilemma, it is important to make a distinction between power and authority.

Batterers are confronted with power when the legal system intervenes, arrests, and confines them. This is overt, coercive power, and it is essential where a man lacks the internal structures necessary for self-containment. Like a broken arm, which requires a cast to immobilize and contain it until it can heal, these men need external containment. The arm lacks the internal integrity necessary to function. It requires an external skeleton to immobilize it and contain it until it can heal. A delicate balance, however, is at work. Too much external control can lead to either dependence, a deepening bitterness, and a failure to develop internal responsibility. On the other hand, too little external control not only fails to provide the structure necessary for healing but also puts victims at risk. Clinicians stand at the fulcrum of this balance. While we use the power of our association with the legal system to provide structure for clients and protection for victims, our real authority only emerges gradually as we seek to find and speak to "that of God" in our clients and thereby nurture their healing.

Quakers believe that it is out of one's sensitivity to the reality and presence of God that one's authority emerges. True authority, as its obvious relation to the word "author" suggests, is a creative voice that emerges from within. Power has strictly to do with our command of resources that enable us to coerce the behavior of others. The British had power; Gandhi had authority. Bull Connor had power; Martin Luther King had authority. The Romans, Herod, Pontius Pilate had power; Jesus had authority. When we speak with authority, we speak with a passion that rises out of the Spirit; we issue an invitation to share a vision, to join in a community of Spirit. Authority is persuasive and inspiring. It is passionate in its willingness to take off its shoes and stand on holy ground. Confronting with authority is an act of intimacy that is possible only when we have first made peace with the terrors of our own aggression and pain. When we have not made this journey into our own souls, we will confront out of our power rather than our authority, because we can't bear to look into the mirror that our clients present. The clinician who works with batterers must move from power to authority, from enforcer to therapist, from one who denies their own potential for violence and condemns it in others, to one who has discovered the depths of their own brokenness, and has learned the path to healing.

One who has made this journey knows how to balance power and authority in treatment, and the shift from power to authority begins almost immediately. While many clients come to the assessment saying that they are there only because they are required to be, the appropriate clinical response is that they in fact have a choice. It is a limited one, treatment or jail, but it is still a choice. The reality and importance of internal freedom is very strongly emphasized at this point, since their acceptance of responsibility is essential to healing. A genuine feeling of responsibility, however, is very difficult without an equal feeling for personal freedom. This first encounter, therefore, is the batterer's first crisis of accountability. It is the first of many opportunities to accept responsibility, and he must do so in order to be accepted into the program. Once accepted, he signs a detailed behavioral contract, and the cast is in place.

At the beginning, clients behave as if they are responsible, even though an internal sense of responsibility is still very fragile. At this point, the structure of the program, backed up by the power of the court, provides the ongoing containment needed. Consequences for noncompliance are built into the contract. Because this is established and agreed upon at the beginning of treatment, the therapist is free to stay related and compassionate. This process of depersonalizing power by building it into the structure of the program creates a space for the emergence of a genuine authority which addresses and nurtures the child of God. True servant leadership means that we not abandon leadership in order to be a servant, nor abandon service in order to be a leader, but that we exercise a responsible stewardship of the very real power that we have in the service of healing. As Paul Lacey puts it:

> Leadership is not a matter of being a servant or wielding power; it is learning to wield power as a servant. Leaders must inevitably wield some power or see it wielded by someone else, perhaps someone without any responsibility for its effects. A sober knowledge of power—like a respectful knowledge of electricity—can lead to its effective and appropriate use.[3]

Clinicians who work with batterers must have a clear-minded awareness of their power, and the conditions for its use must be plainly spelled out in the contract. This "effective and appropriate use" of power sets the stage for the emergence of genuine authority. This shift from power to authority is paralleled by a shift from condemnation to discernment.

Judgment: From Condemnation to Discernment

The effectiveness of therapists working in this field depends greatly upon how well we get ourselves out of power struggles, and into a relationship based upon real trust. Our responsibilities are not unlike the tasks and responsibilities of the prophet. The prophet, of course, proclaims judgment, which is certainly an act of confrontation. To some, prophetic judgment means condemnation and rejection. But what does the notion of prophetic judgment mean when interpreted relationally?

The word "judgment," while meaning "condemnation," also means "discernment." Where condemnation is an act of separation through censure, disapproval, and blame, discernment is profoundly relational. Discernment suggests a deep knowing of the other. It implies clarity of insight, the ability to search out and know that which is hidden, to sort out and bring to light the secrets and hidden sins that we carry within. Discernment is sometimes painful but ultimately healing, whereas condemnation is just painful. Discernment is "tough love," clearly setting limits while offering the possibility of ongoing relationship on new terms with a new sense of both responsibility and freedom.

Discernment, like authority, rises out of one's relationship to God. Condemnation, like the abuse of power, rises out of fear and alienation. Where condemnation distances, isolates, and rejects further relationship, discernment implies the possibility of a new relationship, standing on new ground, and offering new hope. While the prophets spoke in anger, and portrayed themselves as giving voice to the wrath of God, over and over they repent of their wrath, and present a picture of God's repentance from wrath. The central message of the prophets is not one of condemnation, but one of God's yearning tenderness, abiding love, and relentless pursuit of connection and intimacy.

Therapeutic confrontation can be no less than this kind of prophetic judgment. In giving up judgment-as-condemnation, and embracing judgment-as-discernment, it becomes possible to maintain a relatedness with violent men, and reject dualistic and polarizing attitudes about personal worth, good versus bad, approval versus disapproval, acceptance versus rejection. For all of us, if we look for self esteem in assessments of relative goodness, then it is always up for auction in the marketplace of our own or other peoples' opinions, to be gained or lost in one moment's success and another moment's failure. We become caught in a dynamic of endlessly comparing ourselves against the successes and failures of others, and we either envy them or despise them depending upon how well our stock is trading against theirs. But if self esteem has nothing to do with being good, if instead it is solely a matter of being loved, and of returning again and again to Love as the source and center of our being, then we are free to come clean about our badness. We are free frankly to acknowledge it and to offer it up for healing. This is the sacrament of confession, neither a false humility nor a devastated self-esteem, but frank, honest confession. When I am centered in Love, I need not fear the truth.

Those who work with batterers need to be very clear about this distinction. Condemnation is ubiquitous in our culture. Couples do it. Televangelists do it. Liberals blame conservatives. Conservatives blame liberals. But blame is nothing more than a game of hot potato. In the absence of love, everyone scrambles for the high moral ground claiming goodness for themselves while seeking to throw badness off onto someone else. As long as everyone shares the assumption that the sinfulness implicit in domestic violence must be carried by someone, it is, of course, the perpetrator who carries it. No one can bear the burden of their sinfulness alone, however. Behind the batter's denial, minimization, projection, and manipulation, lies the desperate attempt to avoid confirmation of a secret fear that he is truly deserving of utter condemnation.

With victims of domestic violence, considerations about the dynamics of blame, of course, are of small importance compared to the need to support and hear their outrage and pain. The full expression of anger is an important first step toward claiming a greater sense of empowerment. Only later will a challenge to blaming behavior be valuable in order to foster healthier ways to bring anger into a relationship. When therapists who work with batterers have an unconscious and unhealed identification with the victim, this aspect of their countertransference tempts them to engage in blaming and impedes successful treatment. Therapists who cannot separate blame from responsibility should not see these clients for the simple reason that blame reinforces the unconscious dynamics that manifest in abuse in the first place. Condemnation ultimately serves no one. Even perpetrators whose sociopathy prevents them from accepting any kind of responsibility need containment rather than punishment, and their incarceration should be framed as such. Indeed Quakers originally conceived of "penitentiaries" as places of self-examination rather than prisons of condemnation. This shift from condemnation to discernment calls for a new look at the meaning of forgiveness.

Forgiveness from Codependence to Healing

As a student in clinical chaplaincy at a large urban mental hospital, I was seeing patients one day on one of the adult psychiatric wards when I was asked by a nurse to visit with a young man in an active phase of schizophrenia. He had asked to see the chaplain, and when I found him on the unit and told him who I was and why I had come to see him, he came right to the point: He wanted to know if God would forgive him for murder. Whether he had actually committed a murder or whether his belief that he had was part of his delusion was unknown to me, nor did it seem immediately relevant. He clearly believed that he had, and he was somewhat nervously asking me if he could be forgiven. Avoiding his anxiety, I quickly told him that I was sure he could be forgiven and immediately regretted it. As soon as the words were out of my mouth, I could see the doubt in his eyes and then the hopelessness. I felt as if, in the space of a few moments, I had joined the ranks of all those well-meaning pastors in his life who had tried to give him hope instead of being willing to accompany him into his fear and hopelessness. Rather than offer him the companionship of a fellow traveler, I abandoned him at the very beginning of his journey. It is not, finally, our emptiness and hopelessness that is so terrifying, but our isolation.

In time it became clear to me that the real issue was not whether God would forgive him, but whether he would commit himself to the difficult task of facing the reality of his illness and the necessity for treatment. The men who came into our program also wanted forgiveness, but they wanted the kind I tried to offer the young man in the hospital. They wanted rescuing rather than healing. Many of them would go to great lengths to avoid an honest look at the harm they had caused. They sought to surround themselves with those who are willing to rescue them from the consequences of their actions, and they longed to believe in a God who would do the same. But God is not codependent, and the forgiveness that God offers is not a Divine rescue. What God does offer, however, is the restoration of a relationship. I eventually learned to tell them "no, you cannot be forgiven, if forgiveness means wiping the slate clean, denial, forgetting, rescue, or if it means there is no need for reparation."

But, fortunately, forgiveness does not mean those things. It is something far more difficult than mere escape or reprieve. Forgiveness and healing are exactly the same thing. There is not one without the other. So yes, they can be forgiven, but only if they are willing to set out on a journey that will require them to face the stark reality of their violence, the pain and suffering it has caused, and the necessity for reparation and for genuine transformation.

George Fox's exhortation to Friends in the ministry quoted in the introduction to this volume presents this issue very clearly. He states that we must:

> be a terror to all the adversaries of God, and a dread, answering that of God in them all, spreading the Truth abroad, awakening the witness, confounding deceit, gathering up out of transgression into the life, the covenant of light and peace with God.[4]

There is very close tension in this statement between being a terror and answering; between awakening the witness and confounding deceit. When forgiveness means the restoration of a relationship and the giving up of alienation from God, one then faces the alchemy of Love, with all of its joys and terrors, its requirements for truth and humility, and its call to a radical new life. This movement toward healing is the essence of forgiveness. The prophet brings to light all that keeps us alienated from God; the pastor points the way to forgiveness through healing.

In our program there were many who responded to the call, who did the work that was necessary and began to discover a new life, based in a new center of their being with new vision and new priorities. These men helped me to believe there is that of God in us all. Those who accepted the invitation came home to a new truth and freedom, and, therefore, to a new awareness of both their freedom and responsibility to build trust rather than fear, healing rather than hatred, life rather than death. Unfortunately, there were also those men who seemed completely inaccessible, hardened against the most discerning confrontation and the most comforting pastoral care. With them there could be no therapy in the traditional sense; there was no shared search for healing. These were the men who forced me to examine more deeply my assumptions about the meaning of our Quaker conviction that there is that of God in everyone.

That of God Within:
From Inner Light to Inner Relatedness

Throughout my work in the domestic violence program I sought to "speak to that of God" in my clients. I eventually became clear, however, that, at least with some clients, I was not speaking to any goodness that was psychologically accessible. This program taught me the danger of assuming that everyone is basically good. I believe I have met some people who have centered their lives in profoundly evil purposes. Although I believe that we are all created in the image and likeness of God, and that none of us is essentially bad, my difficulty with a discussion of human essences is that, whether I say I'm essentially good or bad, I'm saying nothing at all about my relatedness. Whether I consider myself essentially a god or a devil, this type of language does not address my isolation; it seems to presume that I am essentially alone.

Our Quaker language about "that of God in everyone," "the inward Light," and "the Seed," are all metaphors that can be in-

terpreted in ways that fail to challenge our notions of aloneness.
Never mind that these phrases were originally used in profoundly
relational contexts. Modern Quakers sometimes pay no attention
to historical context, and many are entirely ignorant of it. Since
we live in a culture that takes essential aloneness for granted, these
popular Quaker phrases, divorced from their original relational
contexts, are simply assimilated into a modern worldview that
scripts us to look for divinity hidden somewhere in our
isolated and individualized interiority. It's not there.

Disputations over the meanings of these phrases have run
throughout Quaker history and have even contributed to the
separations. Wilmer Cooper writes that:

> much modern Quaker thought, especially that which has
> been influenced by Jungian psychology, sees the divine
> image, the Light Within, as an essential aspect of the hu-
> man unconscious. This would suggest that the religious
> dimension of the self is part and parcel of the human self,
> rather than being derived from a source of spiritual reality
> that transcends humanity.[4]

While Jung actually does write about a "transcendent function,"
and while he also makes a distinction between the human self
and the larger archetypal Self, these points are often lost in
popular interpretations of his ideas. The resulting view, in which
divinity is seen as part of our human equipment, constellates what
Jung called a "shadow," or that part of the personality that inevitably contains all the disowned elements that cannot be integrated
into such an elevated understanding of who we are.

For Quakers, the view that we are essentially good, and that
our innate goodness empowers our pacifism leads to massive
repression of our potential for hatred and violence. Thus we
observe the paradoxical phenomena of Quaker pacifists
engaging in an unconscious passive aggression. Cooper goes on to
say that:

if the Light Within is no more than ourselves or no more than a level of the unconscious, then it will have little redemptive power; and if the distinction between the divine and human is thereby lost, then the transforming power of the Light will have no effect.[5]

Transforming and redemptive power is restored, however, when these Quaker phrases are re-interpreted in a relational context. What we discover in the center of our being is not a Divine Spark or a piece of God, but a meeting place, or as Thomas Kelly called it, "an amazing inner sanctuary,"[6] where we are called into a profound and transforming relationship. The central truth about our essence is that, whether we are mostly good or mostly bad, we are infinitely and passionately loved. When I seek to speak to "that of God" in my clients, I am not speaking to their essential goodness, but to their essential longing to know God.

Men who batter have lived their lives in the belief that there is no one who can love them. They are profoundly narcissistically wounded. They are sinful, not primarily because of their behavior, but because they are alienated. They are exemplars of the real meaning of original sin, which is that we are born into a world that has forgotten its essential relatedness to God. It is the batter's longing to be loved that is behind his attempts to create the illusion of being good. Only when he can come to see himself as loved, in spite of being responsible for considerable suffering and, therefore, not particularly good, can he discover a relationship that neither shames him nor condemns him but invites him to confession, and from confession, to forgiveness and healing.

This longing to be loved is touched when we speak to that of God in another. We are not attempting to deny the reality of our sinfulness, or theirs. Rather, we take a sober look at it, acknowledge it and then bring it to the inward sanctuary where we wait quietly for the still, small voice. Of course we all fight against our inner emptiness and powerlessness. We resist it and deny it. But when we are finally brought to an acceptance of the fact that we can't possibly be good, right, or whole within ourselves, that God intends for us to be empty because the soul is a space in the human heart that God has created for Him\Herself, then we come to the realization that nothing can satisfy our longing except an immediate and intimate relationship with God. Our brokenness causes us to cry out to God. Our poverty and powerlessness brings us to the threshold of prayer.

Prayer: From "Spiritual Warefare" to "Resist Not Evil"

One study found that, while most offenders show dramatic increases in blood pressure and pulse in situations of conflict, for a minority of offenders, about 20%, the heart rate actually goes down. As conflict intensifies, this type of batterer enters a state of inner calm and focused attention. For them, violence is not a problem of poor impulse control, low frustration tolerance, or poor conflict management skills. They appear to choose violence. The author of the article in which this study is cited says that, "it's possible that these men are so deeply, irrevocably, wounded . . . that they are beyond the help of therapy."[7] This is pretty scary. They seem possessed by forces so oppressive that no light is left in their eyes. When there is no way of getting connected, there is no place, no meeting ground upon which healing work can begin. They have often been battering for a long time and with a number of different partners. These men stalk, intimidate, threaten, and, all too often, carry out their threats. Their violence is severe, and they are unmoved by the suffering they cause. They are possessed, whether one understands that literally or metaphorically, by forces that issue a challenge to whoever takes it upon themselves to offer help. They say, in effect, "Who are you and what sort of light do you seek to shine in my darkness; by what power do you presume to cast me out?"

Shortly after we started our program, a man who seemed hardened and defiant came to me for a court-ordered assessment. Like most of our clients, he was evasive when asked about his violence, but what little he told me sent chills down my spine. He clearly was not appropriate for our program, and I recommended a more intensive process, even though I knew he wouldn't follow up. I ended the session, and since he had made thinly veiled threats, I then had an ethical and legal obligation commonly referred to as a "duty to protect." I had been unable to get any of the information I needed to contact his wife, so I called the police and was told that he would be picked up. I managed to put him out of my mind long enough to finish my work for the day, but as soon I was home and ready to relax, my restlessness increased until I was genuinely frightened. I went to bed, but not being able to sleep, I prayed.

My reaching out for God seems to deepen when I am confronted with such hopelessness. Maybe it is nothing more than the prayer of desperation, the kind of prayer one prays in a burning plane. But I think there's more to it than that. I simply can't believe that God abandons anyone, no matter how tormented and wounded they may be. So, while I sometimes pray in fear, I have also prayed in anger. I know it's not my authority that brings healing; I know that God has called me to this work, so my prayer was an anguished "Where are you? This man is being tortured by his rage and violence; he is wreaking havoc in the lives of his wife and children. Be with him. Be with them. Be with me in the midst of this fear."

My prayer wasn't more than that, but in the silence that followed, I began to feel a very tender Presence, and then the words of Psalm 139 came to mind: "Even the darkness is not dark to thee, the night is bright as the day; for darkness is as light with thee."[8] In other words, let go. Wait in the shadows for the light that is already there. These were hard instructions. But, having come to the limits of my own ability to shape the course of events, surrender was the only choice I had left. I slept, and the next morning I awoke with no more concern. Several months went by and I had forgotten all about him when one day I was surprised to see that he had called the center to make another appointment. When he came in, he told me that the police had picked him up and held him but that he had later been released, and was now coming back to me because he realized he needed help. Even more surprised, I asked him what had caused such a dramatic change. He told me that not long after his first visit, before the police could pick him up, he had made up his mind that he was going to kill his wife. He had gotten into his car and was driving around looking for her when a very strong thought came into his head saying something like, "You make the choices that affect your future, choose life, not death." Needless to say, I accepted him into our program. He finished his mandated counseling and then continued to come voluntarily for family counseling to work on his relationship with his daughter.

Whatever happened was clearly not of my doing. When he first came to see me, he was far beyond whatever resources I had to offer. When he came back, the difference was dramatic ,and the terrible oppression that had hung over him was gone. His demons, so to speak, had been cast out. But is this an appropriate metaphor for what happened? When we speak of "casting out demons," we have already bought into a way of understanding spiritual dynamics that employs metaphors of conflict. When I speak of spiritual responses to evil in this way, I find myself exploring images of coercive power. For example, I might "cast out" an intruder, or garbage, or old clothes. When I was a teenager, I "cast out" manure from the barn. But if that is what I'm supposed to do with demons, I've lost the battle before it has even begun, since I can find within myself no leverage, no native force with which I can serve an eviction notice on my own demons, let alone anyone else's. But what if the "power" that is needed to cast out demons isn't what we usually think of as "power" anyway? Images of exorcisms and "spiritual warfare," with convulsing children and sweating priests, only take violence into the sanctuary of the Spirit. A spirituality of nonviolence would view the whole concept of spiritual warfare as an oxymoron. There is nothing spiritual about warfare. A spirituality of nonviolence is rooted in "the virtue of that life and power that [takes] away the occasion of all wars."

James Nayler, a contemporary of George Fox, spoke of having found near the end of his life, "a spirit . . . that delights to do no evil." Nayler spoke of a spirit that "takes its kingdom with entreaty and not with contention," a spirit whose "ground and spring is the mercies and forgiveness of God."[9] We have no spiritual power, no contrary force, no leverage with which to drive out the forces of evil. But if we find our center in that Spirit of which James Nayler speaks, "As it bears no evil in itself, so it conceives none in the other," we awaken not to some new kind of coercive power, but to what can only be called spiritual authority. We have come finally to Jesus' command to "resist not evil."[10]

This command is truly at the heart of a spirituality of nonviolence. It also generates considerable confusion. Jesus' command is not a recommendation that we allow ourselves to be run over by evil, and indeed, nonviolent action is a profound resistance to evil; it merely shifts the means of conflict from violent to nonviolent alternatives. Thus, it is important to distinguish between practical nonviolent resistance as a moral alternative to violent conflict, and the spirituality that underlies it. When we fail to make this distinction, we can lose the spirituality of nonviolence in an exclusive focus on its political or philosophical aspects. The truly profound work of nonviolence ultimately rises out of the Light that comes in the darkest part of the night; it is the work of that Spirit that takes away the occasion of all wars. Jesus' command directs us to a most extraordinary spiritual reorienting of our lives, for it is impossible to obey unless we ground ourselves wholly and without reserve in "the mercies and forgiveness of God." There is no middle ground.

In the end, a pacifism rooted solely in political or ethical considerations, without being grounded in the Spirit, will be unable to stand. Nonviolent action that is truly led, as opposed to being merely calculated, will be rightly placed, timed, and spoken. Nonviolent action that rises out of nonviolent Presence will speak to the seed of violence in the ourselves and others. I am convinced that Friends must return to the radical spirituality of our roots, a spirituality of nonviolence that is the true source of our pacifism. In the absence of regular disciplines of prayer, and the profound transformations that result from it, we will ultimately be no better off than the sons of Sceva.

Conclusion

The batterers who came to me for treatment ultimately taught me as much about my Quakerism as I taught them about their violence. For over 300 years Quakers have sought to be faithful to a call to nonviolence as well as a call to direct confrontation of oppression. This involves us in an inherent tension, since the first calls for meekness and humility, and the second boldness and courage. The former easily falls into passivity, and the latter into passive aggression. Some modern Friends may fail to set limits at all out of a misguided sense of tolerance or sensitivity, while others battle oppression with a nonviolence that merely masks the anger and control that has accrued within the Quaker shadow. Only the humility born of looking deeply into the subtleties of our own capacity for violence has any hope of healing the violence we see in others. The central Quaker witness is that only nonviolence has any hope of healing violence; only Love has any hope of healing fear. Put simply, the radical spirituality witnessed to by George Fox, James Nayler, Catherine Phillips, Elizabeth Fry, Thomas Kelly, and many others is the only sure source of a genuinely nonviolent response to violence at all levels. Only a life centered in the Holy Spirit can speak directly and powerfully to the condition of violent men.

So when the demons confront us saying "Jesus we know and Paul we know, but who are you?" we can answer simply by trusting our heart's understanding of scripture's teaching:

> I'm certainly not Jesus nor am I Paul, but I am someone who will stand with you and relentlessly bear witness that you are created for dignity and purity of heart. When I speak to that of God within you, I am not uttering cliches, nor do I deny the real destructiveness and harm that you have caused and are capable of causing further. You have been an occasion for the expression of real evil. But your life isn't over, and as long as you live, I will continue to bear witness, if not to you directly, then in the privacy of my own prayer, that you are a child of God. That witness has not ceased since Christ's resurrection. It will not cease with you. Whether you choose the peace of intimacy with God or continue to hide in the shadows, two paths have been set before you: the way of life and the way of death. Choose, therefore, Life.[11]

Notes

1. Acts 19: 13-16.

2. John L. Nickalls, ed., *The Journal of George Fox* (Philadelphia, PA: Philadelphia Yearly Meeting, 1997), 65.

3. Paul Lacey, *Quakers and the Use of Power*, Pendle Hill Pamphlet 241 (Wallingford, PA: Pendle Hill Publications, 1982), 28.

4. Nickells, ed., *The Journal of George Fox*, 263.

5. Wilmer A. Cooper, *A Living Faith: An Historical Study of Quaker Beliefs* (Richmond, IN: Friends United Press, 1990), 15.

6. Cooper, *A Living Faith*, 16.

7. Thomas R. Kelly, A *Testament of Devotion* (NY: Harper and Row, 1941), 29.

8. Hara Estroff Marano, "Inside the Heart of Marital Violence," *Psychology Today* (November - December 1993): 77.

9. Psalm 139:12.

10. Kenneth Boulding, *There is a Spirit: The Nayler Sonnets* (Nyack, NY: Fellowship publications, 1979), xi.

11. Matthew: 5:39.

X. The Journey Home

Carolyn Treadway

WHO CAN BEAR TO LIVE, WHO CAN CHOOSE LIFE, when there is no one who cares whether they live or die? Who can do the deep work of healing past wounds if there is no one to companion them on their journey? Theologian Henri Nouwen tells the story of Mr. Harrison, a forty-eight-year-old farm laborer, isolated, alienated, and ill who fears both death and life.[1] Mr. Harrison dies during surgery since there is no reason to live if there is nobody to live for, and no man can stay alive when nobody is waiting for him.[2] Nouwen describes ways the chaplain might have saved Mr. Harrison's life by becoming his tomorrow, waiting for him in life and death, and helping him to realize that returning to life is a gift to him who is waiting.[3]

Since reading the moving story of Mr. Harrison years ago, it has haunted me. The story has also informed my definitions of who I am to be as a pastoral counselor, and what I am to do. My definitions are not confined by diagnostic categorizing or clinical interventions. Far more than this, as a pastoral counselor I am privileged to enter the depths of life and death with my clients, and I await their safe returns. I am a companion on their journeys into the issues and the realms of life, of self and relationship, and of spiritual unfolding. I am a midwife to their journeys home, to their journeys away from alienation and separation, and home to themselves, to their relationships with others, and to their relationships with God.

176

Pastoral Counseling and Quaker Beliefs

Pastoral counseling is, hopefully, rooted in the Spirit and constantly open to the leading of the Spirit. This differentiates pastoral from secular counseling. Before, during, and after each counseling session I try to be mindful of the Spirit and to invite God's presence. Every part of the work I do with clients is informed by spirituality and by Quaker beliefs and practices. For many years as a therapist I neither understood nor named this basic truth, although I lived it unaware. Then theological and pastoral counseling studies awakened me to the realization that we cannot separate ourselves (who we are as persons) from our beliefs and the way those beliefs are expressed in our lives and our practices, whatever our practices are. Self, faith, and practice are integrally related. For me, my work *is* the practice of my beliefs. My life *is* my practice; it *is* my beliefs made manifest, however well or poorly I may live out at any particular time what I profess to believe. My beliefs, my spirituality, and my inner theology shape my self concept, my relationships, my perceptions of my place in the Universe, my life, and my work.

One way or another, any person's belief system shapes and is shaped by the world, that person's self concept, and his or her relationship to the Universe. That belief system may be guided by Jesus Christ, or Buddha, or Higher Power, or Cosmic Force. Or guided by Wall Street, the Mafia, family, school, tribe, or nation. What a person believes guides how he or she lives and shapes what gives meaning to life. As I more fully realized this, I understood that the core or essence of counseling is to addres the client's belief system, context of meaning, and relationship to the Universe. These are theological and spiritual issues. Whether or not this larger context is ever mentioned or spiritual terms are ever used with the client, this context provides the lens through which I have come to perceive and address any issues presented by the client. My perception of this essential core of counseling has changed me from a secular to a pastoral counselor.

All of us develop a basic inner theology before we can walk or talk, as John Gleason describes in *Growing Up To God*.[4] Our first "gods"—having omnipotent power over our life and death—are our parents or earliest care givers. They teach us the nature of our universe and our place in it. They welcome us into, or cast us out from, our first home. They create the model for the belief system that shapes our life. This first inner theology may come into real conflict with what we are later taught. For example, the idea of God as a loving Father may only strike disbelief and terror in the heart of an incest survivor who was abused for years by her own male parent. The more discrepancy there is between a person's first inner theology and later spiritual teachings, or between that first theology and what a person *wants* to believe, the more difficult the journey of spiritual development may be. For some clients, the core issue, deeply buried under a myriad of "presenting problems," is to relearn the nature of the Universe and their place in it. Put differently, the core issue is to come to see oneself as a child of a loving God, and to come home to a loving God. For many clients, this is a key issue in their therapeutic journey, though not at all in their minds when they seek therapy.

In this chapter, I will describe the process of pastoral counseling with two clients, Mary and Susan (whose identities and stories of course have been disguised), on their very different journeys homeward. I do so to illustrate the pastoral dimension of this therapy and some of the ways this process is rooted in and reflects Quaker belief and practice.

Mary

Healing the Pain

Mary returned to counseling at the age of forty-eight, the same age as Mr. Harrison. Like him she was isolated and alienated and, as it was later revealed, like him "caught in a terrible trap, a psychic paralysis, wanting neither to live nor die."[5] She was also extremely angry, extremely depressed, and extremely anxious. Many times previously over the years she had been in counseling and/or received medication. Nothing had worked to help her heal the core of her pain. The event that precipitated her coming for counseling at this particular time was an episode of intense rage during a holiday dinner with her extended family in which she had splattered the turkey all over the festive table, frightening everyone including herself.

Mary had a lot to be enraged about. Born the middle child of three to alcoholic, abusive parents, she had experienced and witnessed incredible abuse and neglect throughout the years of her growing up. In essence she had no "childhood" and had to raise herself. Always a sensitive child, the fear and pain she experienced wounded her to the core. No caring person in her life mediated the effects of her home environment. Consistently, she was treated as if she did not matter, thus she learned to regard herself as "worthless, absolutely worthless." Early in her teen years, very hungry for attention, she went out with a man she scarcely knew. He raped her, which added intense shame to her "rotten" self concept, and her fear and mistrust of people increased. She kept herself at a distance from others, and assuaged her pain through years of heavy alcohol use. When she drank, she could become the life of the party, and thus find some connection with people, yet over the years her isolation, shame, rage, anxiety, and despair only increased. Mary did not marry. She filled her time with hard work at her technical job, for which she received little appreciation or reward. She developed few outside interests. She felt that she was missing out on life.

To get the attention and care she needed, Mary endlessly attempted to please others. After her mother's death, true to her own and her family patterns, Mary became the only child willing to care for her ill and demented father. She took him into her home and spent enormous energy and time caring for him.

Unfortunately, her father was even less able than he had been during her childhood to give her any appreciation or attention in return. He trashed both her and her house for a number of years. Her siblings refused to help or to give her respite care. Furthermore, the siblings received the major part of the father's inheritance, even though she alone had taken care of him. Her rage over being treated this way by her family, combined with her fury from her view of herself as "worthless," resulted in her smashing the turkey that fateful holiday, and catapulted her back into therapy.

Welcoming into therapy a person who has been in this degree of pain for so long means that I, as therapist, must be willing to enter *with her* into the territory of the deepest rage and pain and despair that she may present. If I am afraid and hold back, or if I enter too deeply too soon, the person will likely flee from therapy or there will be no sustaining connection to help them stay. If I *join* the client too completely in this territory, or if I too become overwhelmed with strong emotions, I then cannot pose a difference in order to help her change. In such delicate and humbling work, I need to know my limitations. The ability to welcome the client in ways that can lead toward new life comes only from the Source of Life, from God. God resides with me, as She resides with the client. There is *no way* to be apart from God, as the psalmist reminds us:

> Whither shall I go from thy Spirit? Or whither shall I flee from thy presence? If I ascend to heaven, thou art there! If I make my bed in Sheol, thou art there! If I take the wings of the morning and dwell in the uttermost parts of the sea, even there thy hand shall lead me, and thy right hand shall hold me.[6]

Whether or not the client is aware of this, I am. I call upon the Spirit to be present for the client and for me, to guide me, and to sustain me as I endeavor to be a calm and sustaining presence for my client. The miracle is that again and again, it works! Not inevitably, but often! Again and again—each time miraculous—something happens between the client and me which allows us to connect, to embark on the journey together. This "something" is not of me, but through me. *I* don't know how to do this, nor even what it is that happens. The totality of what the client may present can easily be "beyond *me*." But I need not fear, because:

> Yea, though I walk through the valley of the shadow of death, I fear no evil, for thou art with me; thy rod and thy staff, they comfort me.[7]

Drawing on my Quaker beliefs, I can turn to God, seek that of God within myself, and reach out to that of God in my client, knowing that it is God who provides for our connection with each other.

Listening With Ears of Faith

Months after our first session, Mary told me of its impact on her. She remembered I had said: "You have a *lot* on your plate," and that I had *wanted* to help her with it. She felt heard, understood, and supported. Rarely in her life had she felt this, and she wanted more of it. So she returned, and has returned for more than two years. Long-term therapy such as this is a luxury now rarely allowed by insurance stipulations, but Mary has been fortunate to be able to continue to come. (Her insurance pays some, and she pays some.) She is committed not to end therapy too soon this time around. Over the months, I have been privileged to join Mary in exploring the farthest realms of the Dark and the Light in her life. Like her, I have been touched and changed by her journey and our journey together. As we began together, I first listened, " just listened" and bore witness to her great anger and alienation and to the injustice of all that she had endured and had been done to her. But my listening was grounded in my belief in her as a human being and child of God, grounded in these basic Quaker beliefs which apply to her as much as everyone else, even though *she* would not have agreed. I listened with ears of faith, faith in who she is, no matter what she had lived through or done, and faith in who she can yet become. After the rage came months of Mary's expression of the pain that fueled her rage: the heartrending isolation, the decimated sense of self, the hopelessness, the unending anxiety, and the total despair.

Who can endure, or even witness, this degree of pain if it is not held by love? Without the transforming container of love, *everything* would shatter or fly apart. At least this is how it feels. We *need* to know love will never leave us, no matter what. We need Divine Love, and we need human love, especially if we do not experience God's love. Yet when we are so wounded, we cannot believe in and cannot trust either human or Divine Love. *Nothing* in our life offers an experiential basis for believing Isaiah's affirmation: "I will not forget you. . . . I have held you in the palm of my hand."[8] Through the deep and sacred relationship of pastoral counseling, perhaps a crack in the client's perception can open, or a glimmer of hope arise that *perhaps* love could be possible "even for a worthless person like me." Sustained herself by God's love, the pastoral counselor hopefully can become an expression of that love incarnate and can demonstrate that another way, another belief system, *is* possible.

The Transforming Power of Love

Both Maureen Graham and Dan Snyder in this volume speak of the transforming power of love.[9] Love is the core of caring, of counseling, of healing, of faith. Bill Oglesby, in his *Biblical Themes for Pastoral Care*,[10] powerfully describes the movement in counseling from the words of judgment— "there you are" and "here I am"—to the words of forgiveness and reconciliation *when connected by* "I love you" (italics mine). It is the "I *know* you," "I am *still* here," and "I *do* love you" *lived out over time* with the client which heals.

For Mary, one of her first moments to feel loved and capable of being loved occurred some months into therapy. She revealed a very vulnerable "here I am," and was met by my "I hear/love/understand you." Riddled with the pain of a memory long repressed, and cringing with shame, Mary described an incident as a young teen when, mimicking the cruelty all around her, she had been cruel to her small pet. She had immediately realized that her behavior had actually harmed and frightened her pet; her devastation and self-recrimination were then complete. She had *become* her abusive parents. Feeling terrible about what she had done that one time, it had become a dark secret, festering in her without a ray of light all these years. This was the first time she had ever told anyone about the incident. I waited with her and shared her pain. Then I asked: "If you could turn the clock back and go to that young teen just after she hurt her pet, what would you want to do with her?" Immediately, Mary burst into tears. Finally she said: "I'd hug her." This was the moment Mary began to have compassion toward herself, began to perceive herself as worthy and deserving of "being hugged." It was a powerful and transforming moment.

As Mary began to have glimmers that she *was* deserving of love, and that she *could* possibly hope to be loved, it only increased her rage and despair that she was *not*. She became angrier than ever at the ways others had hurt her and continued to mistreat her and at the ways she continued to be cruel toward herself. She became more suspicious of others, including me, and whether they would *really* care and stand by her. Like a caged wild creature, the more she tried to free herself, the more entrapped she became. Parts of herself were in a fundamental war with each other. "I deserve to be loved and respected" was in a deadly battle with "I deserve to be annihilated." The old familiar annihilation gained the upper hand, and Mary once again attempted suicide—yet in a way that allowed "I deserve to be cared for" as well. Mary swallowed a full bottle of pills on her way to my office, so that she was losing consciousness by the time she reached my parking lot. She knew I would be looking for her and would come to find her and get her into the hospital. She had to take the drastic step of attempting suicide to feel she *deserved* the care she knew she needed and to *make* others provide that care.

During and after Mary's hospitalization, I attempted to help her rename, and reconsider, her own story. I named her latest suicide attempt as her try not to end her life but to find new life. I called her attempt an absolute statement that her old ways of being in this world were not working, and invited her to find new ways to perceive who she is and what her life is all about. I named this as her continuing journey, and I reminded her I would continue to companion her on it, and that I would continue to believe in her and hold faith for her until she could hold it for herself. I reminded her that, at least for now (while hospitalized), she was safe and cared for. Mary began to hope and began to be more willing to *let* someone reach her. She *wanted* to hope, yet she mistrusted everybody. To realize that *anyone* would continue to find her worthy of care when she had been so "bad" or self-destructive was unbelievable. To believe it meant that Mary had to change her whole world view. Thus began an extended period of ups and downs in the dance between belief and doubt, hope and despair. Her emerging new, more positive beliefs and sense of herself were so fragile, so vulnerable. The slightest event, the slightest nuance, could send her into recurring rage or self-mutilation, extreme anxiety, or the pits of despair.

How can I, as therapist, *remain with* my client on this interminable roller coaster, on this seemingly endless journey of waiting and midwifing the client's safe return? At times for therapist as well as client, it seems too long, too hard, too much to bear. At such times, my turning to God is crucial: God's love *alone* can endure that which is beyond human capacity. Over and over again as a therapist I have experienced this. I have said: "OK, God, take this one *now*; it's beyond me; she's *Yours*." Over and over again, something beyond me is given to me or comes through me. I am sustained, and I can stay with the process and continue to offer sustenance to my client. I can draw not only upon my own relationship with God, but upon my faith community, denomination, and the entire history of the church (any church, any spiritual tradition). In the Third Century AD, Cyprian wrote an essay entitled "The Good of Patience."[11] Since reading it in 1983, I felt it had been written for me. It has helped me in many difficult times with clients, for it helps me know that all persons who have ever waited lovingly on behalf of another are with me as a cloud of witnesses, if I will learn to "see" them. Awareness of this cloud of witnesses helps me to be patient, and to remain present and loving.

Mary's journey homeward has continued. I am very grateful she is still here, ever growing and dealing with herself and her world. I am very grateful for all the wonderful qualities she has, for her depth of soul, and for the loving ways she contributes to our world despite her ups and downs, her struggles, and her hiding. Frequently, I tell Mary of the things I value so much about her, and she has begun at last to believe that she *does* have qualities to value. Over the months she has developed more understanding of the forces that led her to do what she did in life and to choose the paths she had chosen. She has developed more awareness of and empathy for herself and more belief in herself. She is grieving the childhood she never had and the years of her life she "lost" to alcoholism in her attempts to numb out her pain. She is continuing to work out the tangled snarls of the experiences and relationships which have limited her perceptions and beliefs and consequently her hopes, her opportunities, and her life. Courageously, she is seeking new and different ways to be in this world, to view and treat herself, to relate to others, and to find her relationship with God. Today, it could be said, Mary is trying to live out Rilke's words:

Toward all that is unsolved in your heart: Be patient; try
to love the questions. Do not seek the answers which
cannot be given. You would not be able to live them.
Live everything. Live the questions now. You will then,
gradually without noticing it, live into the answers some
distant day.[12]

The journey is Mary's, but we are living parts of it out together, for
I am still privileged to be her witness, companion, and midwife in
the pastoral counseling process which facilitates her coming home.

Choosing Life

It can be such a struggle to *choose life*, to choose self-affirmation
and caring instead of destruction and cruelty. Choosing life is such
a risk when the world is so scary. It is so much easier to hide in the
familiar darkness. What can possibly give us the courage to change
our perceptions and beliefs, or to frame our world in a radically
different way? I believe this courage comes from God, and God
alone—or, put differently, from that of God within each of us. I
believe the courage to change can start with the dim perception
that "maybe things could be different." Thomas Kelly describes
this so well, in words that have beckoned meaningfully to me for
many years:

Over the margins of life comes a whisper, a faint call, a
premonition of richer living which we know we are passing by. . . . We are further strained by an inward uneasi-
ness, because we have hints that there is a way of life vastly
richer and deeper than all this hurried existence . . . If only
we could slip over into that Center!"[13]

Although she would not realize it in these terms, Mary has begun to heed that "faint call." At times she can now see herself as
an "old soul," as one whose sensitivity and innate spiritual awareness were always deeper than those of others around her. She can

see that consequently she was more deeply wounded by the cruelty and abuse of her upbringing than were others in her family who were less aware. She can see the difference between her old and her new emerging beliefs and world view, and she longs for the new even as she fears it. This longing is testament to the power of the Spirit within each of us. Despite cruelty and neglect and abuse, despite being smashed and shattered and banished for decades, Mary's soul (or deeper being) is still within her, *longing to grow, longing to come fully into the Light,* and giving her tenacity to continue her journey toward home.

As therapist, I invite this "coming into the Light" however I can, as the following incident exemplifies. Recently, Mary was expressing anger and pain that she continues to slip back into feeling badly about herself, even into feeling that she's trash and should be trashed, or should hurt herself. I listened, then quietly replied:

> Mary, just stop. Just stop hurting yourself now. You do not need this anymore. Whenever you feel like hurting yourself or anything else—any time you feel this way—I will be with you in spirit. In spirit, I will take your hurtful hand and stroke it. I will, in spirit, be with you to say: Just stop. No more war. Be at peace.

Mary was stunned into silence. Then the tears came. Her reply was: "You have touched my heart. You have reminded me there is another way." So, in a moment of sacred therapeutic encounter, that of God in me—grounded in my peace church beliefs about no more war—reached out to connect in love with that of God in Mary, who responded from her deep self: "Yes, yes, I *want*, I *long for* another way to be." And so for us both, regardless of how we each would name it, the "faint call" of God became the Presence of the Spirit in the counseling room, holding us both, guiding us and transforming us moment by moment.

Mary's journey reminds me of what *I* too, and so many of us, need to learn and to remember. Mary's journey homeward calls for her to perceive some deeper meaning from the cruelty and injustice her life has held, and to transform her destructive experiences of the past into positive good for the future. Elisabeth Kubler-Ross teaches us: "Where there is no love, *put love*, then you will find love."[14] My Quaker heritage taught me to witness to injustice and to speak truth to power, with the necessity of coming from a loving and centered place inside myself when I do. Mary is slowly learning that there *is* a deep place inside herself that *can* have a loving response to injustice or mistreatment. As her world becomes safer and her fears lessen, she no longer needs to strike out immediately in defensive self-protection. *She* can be the one to bring calmness and restraint, love and depth to a difficult situation. It is so empowering to realize this! And is this not the journey homeward for *each* of us? Is it not difficult for each of us to respond lovingly and patiently in the face of mistreatment and injustice and cruelty? Is it not difficult for each of us to let the *Spirit* speak through us, through our behaviors, in the face of adversity? Yet are we not, *each of us, CALLED to do this?* I think we are, and I am grateful to Mary for reminding me of this call. I think this is what our Quakerism has called us to do, person to person and nation to nation, since Quakerism was born.

The New Marketplace

As a therapist, I am most aware of the spiritual grounding and dimensions of my work whenever I am doing long-term personality change work, or "soul work," as described with Mary. In today's marketplace, however, such work can be a rare and precious luxury. The field of counseling has changed greatly in the last few years and is now driven by insurance mandate rather than client choice. With the advent of managed care, "outsiders" have not only entered but also taken control of the formerly confidential and sacred domain between client and therapist. For many counselors, what we do and how well we do it is scrutinized by people we never meet, yet who have authority to determine whether or not the counseling will continue—at least whether insurance will pay for it. Such changes in the field have been difficult for both client and therapist, but like them or not, the changes are here and will not go away. The current emphasis on "cost effectiveness" and "positive outcomes" and consequent short-term therapy has led me to reconsider both how to do therapy and who I am as a therapist, especially as a *pastoral* therapist. The process of addressing these concerns has led me into some unexpected new learnings.

How can a client utilize or a therapist offer therapy in six or eight or twelve sessions? Thirty-nine years ago when I was trained, the very idea of this would have been unthinkable! But now, in many cases, managed care will allow no more than six or a dozen sessions, and clients are often unwilling or unable to pay out of pocket for additional sessions. Clients now seem to *come* to therapy with the idea that they will *finish* within the brief time limits mandated by managed care. It is indeed a different mind-set than even a few years ago. How can I *still* be pastoral as a counselor when there is so little time to establish a relationship, especially when relationship itself is no longer considered (by insurance companies) a significant variable in achieving successful outcomes in therapy? Under managed care, what will happen to the "soul work" that to me is the essence of therapy? Such questions have no easy answers, but they did lead me to explore different models of brief therapy, particularly Solution Focused Brief Therapy. To my great surprise, I found that doing therapy in this manner was entirely consistent with my most fundamental Quaker beliefs. It was like coming home!

Presentation of the Solution Focused Brief Therapy model is well beyond the scope of this chapter (but interested readers might like to read books and articles by Insoo Kim Berg, Patricia O'Hanlon Hudson, Scott Miller, William Hudson O'Hanlon, Steve de Shazer, or Michelle Weiner-Davis on this topic.) I will use one client's process of therapy to illustrate this model and some of the ways that using it are, for me, still very much grounded in my Quaker beliefs and practice.

Brief Therapy: Susan

Solution Focused Brief Therapy is geared toward client *strengths and abilities*. It is not interested in history, or in pathology, but in creating the changes the client wants now. The focus is upon things that are working *well*. Do more of what *is* working well, and less of what isn't. If nothing is working, do something different. Look for exceptions that allow new possibilities. Scott Miller describes a five step model of forming a cooperative working relationship *with* the client, negotiating well-formed goals, orienting the client toward change (or solutions), intervening in ways that facilitate change, and maintaining change.[15] This five-step model could apply for Quaker negotiation or Quaker peacemaking in any number of situations or settings! Gearing toward client strengths and abilities rests upon belief in the client as a person with inner resources, and upon calling forth "that of God" in the client. I have been doing this for years, but never called it solution focused therapy! It is refreshing to put the *client* in charge of the goals for therapy; after all it *is* the client's life. Treating clients in ways that convey our belief that *they* know what they want and how to get there, and that *they* have the resources to get there, is very em-powering for them. Clear, concrete, positive goals stated in specific terms can give complex issues a simple and direct focus that can facilitate rapid change. Above all, putting the emphasis back upon clients as creators of their own solutions is a way of calling forth all that is and can be in a person. Is that not "of God"? Is that not "Quakerly"? I think it is.

Let me now turn to the story of Susan, whose journey homeward (in therapy) was very different from that of Mary, but no less a "journey home." Literally, she came to therapy so that she could make her house into her home. Susan, in her late thirties, had remarried six months prior to starting therapy. The second marriage for both her husband and herself, they had three teenage children between them. There were many difficulties with ex-spouses, custody and co-parenting issues, and divided loyalties of the children. Susan was walking on eggshells in her own house. Afraid lest the slightest thing she did might cause reverberations with her stepchildren, thus evoking hostility from the children's mother and causing conflict between the ex-spouses (the stepchildren's parents), Susan interacted only minimally with her stepchildren. She felt ill at ease and personally responsible that the new family was not blending as well as it should. She wanted the five of them in the new, blended family to *become* a family. Her husband was supportive, but felt things were going alright, while Susan did not feel this way.

Susan was referred to counseling by managed care through her insurance company. Eight sessions were authorized, so we knew from the beginning that our process would be short-term. She described the concerns which brought her to counseling, and I soon asked her how things would be different at home if a miracle happened and these concerns were suddenly no longer there. What would be happening that was not happening now? Who would be doing what? How would she be acting differently? Gathering this information as specifically as possible, and brainstorming various possibilities, we quickly generated concrete ideas for things she might try to do. These became her specific goals for the next weeks, small goals but definitely aimed toward her desired solutions.

In subsequent sessions, I asked what was new or different, what had worked well, what the responses of others had been, and what she wanted to do next. I noted differences I saw and congratulated Susan on the changes, no matter how small. She gained more confidence and tried more. She figured out what *she* needed for herself in order to take more steps in the desired directions and then acted upon what she needed. An important part of this was working out with her husband more effective ways that he could support and encourage her and back her up with his children *if* she needed it. She became more interactive with all the children and less worried about her husband's ex-wife. Gradually, she held clearer boundaries with her stepchildren regarding their behavior. She reflected upon herself, decided what she valued and what she wanted to change about the ways she was being herself in her new family, and did more and more of what she wanted to be doing with them. As therapist, I frequently validated her continued progress toward the solutions she had created. For her eighth and final session, Susan brought her husband along. She used the session to review the changes she and the family had made and the ways they would keep those changes going. She and her husband also noted what they liked most about the differences, and generated new ideas for more changes they would like to see and how to accomplish these. Susan completed therapy by saying that she felt relaxed and comfortable in her new family now, and felt "at home." She had come home to her own home.

Coming Home: Mary and Susan

As described in the beginning of this chapter, I seek to invite persons to come home to themselves, others, and God through the process of pastoral counseling. Even though their therapeutic processes were very different, this invitation was as true for Susan as for Mary. While spirituality was never specifically mentioned in Susan's therapy, unlike Mary's, Susan's process was still fully grounded in spirituality and Quaker beliefs, at least for me as therapist. With both Susan and Mary I sought to express the Love of God through the ways I appreciated, valued, and respected them, and called forth their own abilities to be loving and centered (coming from their deep selves). Drawing from my Quaker beliefs, I viewed both Mary and Susan as children of God and treated them as persons of infinite possibility, able to overcome painful history and to find new views of self and world, and able to generate many fine solutions to the concerns that initiated counseling.

Like Mary and Susan, *each* of us is a child of God, *a person of infinite possibility*. Would that *each of us* could be called forth, as they were, to become more of the person we *were created to be*. With God's help, if we will be connected to Her through prayer and faith community, perhaps we can become loving, centered children of God who help to make this world a sacred home for all.

Notes

1. Henri J. M. Nouwen, *The Wounded Healer* (Garden City, NY: Image Books, 1972), 51-77.

2. Nouwen, *The Wounded Healer*, 66-67.

3. Nouwen, *The Wounded Healer*, 67-70.

4. John J. Gleason, Jr., *Growing Up To God: Eight Steps In Religious Development* (Nashville, TN: Abingdon Press, 1975), 26-37.

5. Nouwen, *The Wounded Healer*, 61.

6. Psalm 139:7-10.

7. Psalm 23:4.

8. Isaiah 49:15-16.

9. Maureen Graham, "Quaker Ministry and Pastoral Care: Centered Presence, Relational Engagement , Prophetic Witness," chapter I, and Dan Snyder, "Violence and Nonviolence: Quaker Spirituality and the Treatment of Domestic Violence Offenders," chapter IX.

10. William B. Oglesby, Jr., *Biblical Themes For Pastoral Care* (Nashville, TN: Abingdon Press, 1980), 84-86.

11. Cyprian, "The Good of Patience," translated by Sister George Edward Conway, *Fathers of the Church* 36 (June 1958): 257-287.

12. Ranier Maria Rilke, quotation, citation not noted.

13. Thomas R. Kelly, A *Testament of Devotion* (New York and London: Harper and Brothers, 1941), 115.

14. Elisabeth Kubler-Ross, workshop presentation, "Life, Death, and Transition Workshop," Glenview, IL, June 1983.

15. Adapted from copyright workshop handouts by Scott D. Miller, "From Problem to Solution: The Solution Focused Brief Therapy Approach" at a Solution Focused Brief Therapy Workshop held at the Brief Family Therapy Center, Milwaukee, WI, March 1993.

XI. Quakers and Complementary Medicine/Healing

Marthajane Robinson

DURING A HEALING TRAINING SESSION, I stand to the right of my client, who is lying face-up on the massage table; I am working with one of my fellow students. I know next to nothing about her since it is early in the training. I know her marital status, what sort of job she has and, in a very general way, what she hopes to get out of this training. It is her first training and my second in this particular modality, Well-Springs, a type of body work which uses music as a way of connecting mind, spirit, and the physical being.

I start by centering, going deep within to that place

> Where no storms come,
> Where the green swell is in the havens dumb,
> and out of the swing of the sea.[1]

This is a vital step, for if I do not center, I will be unable to open to the physical, emotional, and spiritual place in which my client finds herself. I then begin to assess her condition, a process analogous to an initial diagnosis in mainstream (allopathic) medicine, by passing my hands from her head down to her toes, keeping them steadily and gently moving about six inches above her. Her energy field is fairly consistent, somewhat passive, and withdrawn. As I reach her lower legs, about half way down her right shin, the

195

field changes dramatically. It is hard, intense, and feels almost as if there is something in the leg which is "not her." I ask, "Who is that living in your leg?" At first she does not understand, and I say, "There is something really stuck there, and it feels as if it comes from someone else. Who is it?" After a pause, she says, "That is where my father held me when he beat me." She begins to cry and scream, the music draws her further down in her body and being, the block begins to loosen. After the session, we talk about what happened, the events and the feelings and how they influence her life now.

What was going on in that session, and how does it relate to Quakerism and specifically to Quaker pastoral care? In the following sections of this chapter, I will define what I mean by healing, explain how those of us who do this work understand what is happening during a session, discuss problems associated with that understanding, and how the work relates to Quaker theology and practice and to pastoral care.

A Definition of Healing

The history of the healing arts is an ancient one, stretching far back into the mists of time. The use of healing herbs, touch or laying on of hands, rituals involving shamanic journeys, sand paintings, music, chanting, and dance have been part of human culture since we have been human. Although often associated with the feminine aspects of human personality, healing is certainly not exclusively the province of women. Because healing is intimately connected with religion, holistic healing practices thrived more in times when humanity envisioned the Divine to be female, or at least to have many female characteristics. Modern, scientific medicine is primarily symptom-based and began to develop after our cosmology changed from a belief in Goddess to God.[2] Modern medicine looks upon illness as a specific condition caused by a specific agent or combination of agents. Deal with the agent(s)—a bacterium, blood pressure, electrolyte imbalance, insulin levels, etc.—and the patient will get better.

Some physicians are healers as well as doctors. Dr. Guthrie, for example, founded a clinic in Sayre, PA, which drew patients because of his reputation for being able to help when all others had given up hope. Both homeopathic and osteopathic medicine were founded by physicians, although homeopathy is now regarded as outside mainstream medicine. Within the last 10 to 20 years, allopathic medicine has been moving toward a more holistic approach, treating patients within the context of their lives. These advances have also been facilitated by research in the relatively new field of psychoneuroimmunology, the study of the influence of the mind and emotions upon physical systems.

Healers draw upon older concepts of universal oneness, the Divine manifesting in all creation, connected spiritually more to earth than to sky. The direction of the spirit moves from immanence to transcendence, rather than the other way round.

In her book, *Woman as Healer*, Jeanne Achterberg states the following:

> Their [healers'] work is likely to reflect a broad sense of healing that aspires to wholeness or harmony within the self, the family, and the global community. They see body, mind, and spirit as the inseparable nature of humankind; they believe that any healing ministrations have an impact on each element of this triune nature. They regard sickness as a potential catalyst for both emotional and spiritual growth, among other things. These healers have chosen to accompany, help, lead, reach, and care for others who seek wholeness.[3]

Achterberg speaks of dealing with the whole individual, of not separating body, mind, psyche, emotion, and spirit. As a healer, I do indeed look at physical illness as a manifestation of imbalance in the whole and see it as a way into the deeper being. Physical illness is real. Of course it is. Bacteria, viruses, the aging process, and many other elements affect our bodies. If I have a sinus infection, I go see a doctor to get treatment of the physical causes for that infection; but when I come home, I look at why I got sick. What else is happening in my life right now? What is my body trying to tell me in the only way it has? What do I need to deal with so that I am not so vulnerable to whatever "bug" happens to be going around? What is the stress—anger, loneliness, sadness, just plain doing too much? Once I figure out—more like *feel out*—what is happening deep within me, I can thank my body for bringing it to my attention and deal with it directly through writing, prayer, and meditation, or maybe just a good cry or scream. In listening to my body, I am coming home in more ways than just walking in my front door.

Healing involves relationship with oneself, with others, and with the Divine. Healing uses a process of clearing, of discernment, and results in emotional and spiritual growth. As part of this growth and because we are of one piece, the physical being may also become stronger and healthier, although the damage to the body may have gone beyond healing. However, a physically ill person can still be well and whole.

Healing is about finding meaning in all of life's experiences, as Achterberg notes:

> Healing relates not so much to techniques as to philosophic and spiritual foundations. The bond that is established between the healer of this genre and the healee is life-giving and life-enriching for both. The relationship, itself, is held in reverence, with the awareness that it is made of trust, love, and hope. They [healers] aver that they are, indeed, working in sacred space.[4]

Soon after I began my practice, I had a client who was undergoing radiation treatments for a recurrence of breast cancer. The first time I saw Linda, she stated emphatically, "I don't want you messing with my head. I just want to have the side effects lessened." I could see that she was a very angry person, but I respected her wishes. As our relationship developed, she told me about her family, her job, her relationship with Betty. Linda was a chemist and scientifically minded. She came from a Jewish family, but had given up on religion and spirituality. She was cynical, tough, and had a sharp tongue. Although Linda loved her work, she hated her job. She had little use for her co-workers.

Linda was a lesbian, and her family, particularly her brother, had never accepted her sexual orientation. She didn't want to see him or speak to him. Fortunately, she did have a long-time relationship with Betty, who also came to the sessions and saw me to help her deal with her grief over her partner's impending death. Although Linda expected that she would again get better, Betty was more realistic.

As I worked with Linda and her partner, she gradually became more open to the idea that, in some ways, her cancer was an expression of her anger, and along with continuing to have bodywork, we began to talk about her family, her fears, and her losses. And, much to her surprise, she learned that spirituality was very important to her.

Linda came to see me for about a year and a half, finally becoming too ill to continue our sessions. She lived some distance away, so it was difficult for me to go to her, although I did a few times. The last time I saw Linda, she was very happy. She told me that she had had a wonderful visit with her brother in which they both had talked about their family and its troubles and then had lovingly forgiven each other for the pain they had inflicted through the years. She died a short time after that. Her funeral was joyous and spiritual, a sharp contrast to what she had originally envisioned. About a hundred people came, including some who had worked with her. Her brother gave a moving eulogy in which he talked about their relationship and how it had changed in the months before she died. Linda died healed and whole.

As a result of interactions with a healer, clients/patients can come to a new relationship with themselves, their condition, and others, helping them to become more centered and balanced and able to handle what happens in their lives with less stress. If the client has a chronic medical condition or is terminally ill, he or she can begin to see the situation with different eyes, enabling peaceful and constructive acceptance.

What's Going on Here?

There are many modalities used by contemporary healers: Therapeutic Touch, Well-springs, and Traeger (the three I practice), Reiki, Shiatsu, Acupressure, Reflexology, Mariel, Myofascial work, to mention only a few. Most healers choose a modality based on what they have found helpful in their own healing and/or appeals to their philosophical outlook.

Although the terms used to describe what happens during a healing interaction may differ, the basic concept is that the being—body, mind, spirit, psyche, emotions—is a field of energy and that, when the flow of the energy is disrupted or blocked, symptoms appear in some part of the being. By using the word "part," it may appear that I am separating different aspects of the being, but that is not the case. Rather it is that each "part" of the being is a hologram of the whole; the whole appears in each part, so that there is no separation.

The understanding of energy comes from quantum physics, which states that everything in the manifested universe is energy in different configurations and densities, constantly changing, ever moving. I see all "parts" of the being, not just the physical, as different layers (again think of holograms) of energy, all contributing to the wholeness of the person with whom I am working. Some scientists find the concept that quantum theory can be applied to feelings and thoughts utterly ridiculous; others feel that their work may have broader implications than only describing how the physical universe works. The difficulty lies, once again, in trying to explain a metaphysical, experiential process in terms of an empirical proof. In my view quantum theory is truly a holistic approach to the world. As I do my work, I can feel changes in the being as they occur, changes in what I call energy concentrations. People's physical health often improves; their way of being in the world changes. I personally see parallels in quantum theory which deepen my understanding of my work.[5]

How do I know that this energy is present? Of course, on the physical level, all life is electrical, getting the energy needed to perform life's functions from the chemical battery inside. Electrocardiograms (EKG) or electroencephalograms (EEG) measure this electrical energy in different parts of the body. Proper electrolyte balance is important because the battery can't function if the chemicals in it are not in proper proportion.

How do we sense the energy of the mind, the emotions, the psyche, and the spirit? People may be sensing this energy when they talk about the "vibes" of a room. A well-trained chaplain or therapist has a sense of the state of a patient/client as soon as he or she enters a room. Sometimes sensing a person's energy does not require their presence. (All my life I have able to know who is on the phone before I picked up the receiver, even predicting that someone I was close to was going to call before the phone rang. Somehow, I felt their energy.) Is the patient depressed, angry, withdrawn? A person who is sensitive to the state of others can "know" this and more. It is a part of good clinical/spiritual assessment.

This assessment, however, is more of general mood than of energy itself. How do I specifically evaluate the energy of a patient/client? Try an experiment. Gently rub your hands together a few times, then cup them slightly and slowly move them away from one another and then back again. Keep going in and out—and keep moving. You will probably begin to feel something between your hands. Sometimes it seems warm or tingly. To me, it feels as if there is a soft mass, like a Nerf ball, between my hands, which pushes back as I bring my hands together and resists slightly as I pull them apart. If you don't feel it right away, try again. It is important not to think while you are doing it. If you are concentrating on whether you really are feeling anything or not, you won't pick up the energy—it's subtle. Stay out of the rational. Just focus on what your hands feel. You may think that you are just sensing the friction from rubbing your hands together, but when you become more adept at sensing fields, this step becomes unnecessary. What you are feeling is your energy field. I sense the patient/client's field when I do healing treatments.

Next, invite someone to stand calmly with eyes closed. Again rub your hands gently together. Starting at the top of the head, run your hands slowly and evenly down the body, about six inches from the surface. Tune in to what your hands are feeling, not to whether you think you're feeling anything. Don't judge. If you feel something, it is not the breeze from the window or just your imagination. As you proceed down the body, you may begin to pick up differences in the way the field feels. In some spots, it may be warm/cold, slow/fast moving, light/dense. In others, the energy field may feel as if it disappears entirely. These differences are what you are looking for, because they signal changes or constrictions in the field.

When I do this, I usually pick up feelings as well: uncried tears, screams that have been suppressed and, of course, anger. These stuck feelings are generally in the areas of the body that have physical symptoms. Shoulders may hurt ("What are you carrying that is so heavy?"), the heart aches ("Has something or someone broken your heart?"), the lungs may be congested ("What keeps you from breathing freely?" "Why are you holding your breath?"), and stomachs feel upset ("What is it that you have swallowed and can't digest?"). These questions a pastoral counselor may ask in appropriate ways. Our feelings live in our bodies beyond words. Physical touch may access these feelings more powerfully than words might.

Our society values the intellect, and many of us intellectualize our feelings. We can talk about what it means to be angry, sad, rejected, etc., but we find it difficult to actually feel these emotions, especially since some of them, anger in particular, are considered "bad." Once we understand that physical symptoms are frequently an indication of emotional/psychological/spiritual dis-ease, we can begin to work at deeper levels, rather than using the body to store feelings. Stomachs, shoulders, and hearts were not designed with this purpose in mind. Our bodies lovingly keep these feelings from our consciousness until we are able to deal with them, but the price may be physical symptoms.

We need to understand that there is no reason for guilt. Most of us beat ourselves up already; it is not helpful to do so even more. The truth is that we do whatever we need to preserve our beings. Slow destruction is far better than quick. We do the best we can at the time, even though looking back, we might say that what we did was not ultimately healthy. One of my teachers, Dianne Woodruff, put it this way:

> When there is something that the being is unable to process, a group of cells steps up and chooses to go down in flames to preserve the whole. Cells voluntarily die. And if that is not enough, another group steps up. It is a loving thing, and we should thank our bodies because they care so much for us.

At the time, I was struggling with the thought that I was responsible for my cancer and lupus and found myself in tears because her words were so true and comforting. Instead of damning my body for getting sick, I was able to appreciate its loving strength.

I work by stroking, massaging, rocking the body, or just by laying my hands where I feel the constriction. I send energy to the field, envisioning the energy as a white light or water which gently fills the whole body. The healer does not send his or her own energy to the client. The energy passes from the Divine through me. I must be as clear as possible, so that I can be a channel, rather than the origin of the energy. If I send my own energy, it probably will feel invasive to the client—and I will become very tired.

With touch and music, both of which are processed by the right brain, the seat of image and metaphor, clients may experience emotionally charged memories, dreamlike images, and colors. They may cry or get very angry, even kicking and screaming; but at the end of the session, they are at the very least relaxed. They also often feel blissfully expanded and in touch with whatever they name as the Divine. Often this is a client's first sense of the Divine as a direct experience.

What evidence demonstrates the effectiveness of this approach? Studies have been done on patients who have undergone Therapeutic Touch which indicate that changes in EEG pattern[6] and in hemoglobin[7] occur during treatment. Like meditation or hypnosis, energy work seems to help clients enter an altered state of consciousness where there is wisdom usually unavailable to the conscious mind.

Most evidence of effectiveness is anecdotal. In the hospital, I have worked with patients who are in much pain; the pain decreases and so does their anxiety level. During my Clinical Pastoral Education residency at the Hospital of the University of Pennsylvania, a young man who had been shot in the eye was brought to the emergency room. The bullet had to be removed, but the surgeon could not give him a general anesthesia because of possible brain damage. Naturally the patient was quite agitated, as well as in pain. He was given Lidocaine and Versed as painkillers. I stood at his feet, putting my hands lightly on his ankles and occasionally reaching up to his knees, stroking down to his feet to ground him, keeping him present. As the surgeon probed for the bullet in his eye, I kept saying, "Keith, send your thoughts down here to me; feel how I am touching your feet. Come all the way down here where I am." When the procedure was over, the surgeon turned to me and said with a strange look on his face, "Wow! I've never seen Lidocaine work so well."

I have a client who has had trouble for years with excessive menstrual bleeding. Occasionally she has been hospitalized with bad hemorrhaging. She had weak personal boundaries, did not have many techniques for dealing with emotions, and had very little body awareness. As we worked together using both talk therapy and bodywork, her bleeding lessened and her periods became more regular. Her personal boundaries became stronger. She was able to see her bleeding as a bodily expression of her "bleeding" into all the people around her. After about a year of therapy, she is beginning a normal menopause. She has left a high-stress job and says she "feels at home in [her] skin." And she is discovering and exploring her spirituality.

Other patients and clients have experienced significant pain relief and greater range of motion. One patient had feeling return in her feet after sensing little or nothing for years as a result of numerous back surgeries. Wounds heal more quickly. As a personal example, I bruise easily, rapidly getting large black and blue marks after very slight bumps. If I immediately clear the area by stroking it gently and send it some energy by placing my hand on it with the intention to heal, I may not bruise at all, or the mark will be smaller and disappear within a day or so instead of lasting a week.

Recently I had a client in his eighties who had such terrible restless leg syndrome that his feet were never still. His feet were so painful that, when I first starting working with him, I could hardly pass my hands over them, let alone touch them, without making him jump. He also had many other physical problems which caused him a great deal of discomfort.

He felt he had to control his symptoms and his pain, which was part of the problem. He told me that it would be alright if I touched his feet as long as I told him first. He could then keep himself from wincing. While working on the physical problem, I also talked to him about his need to control, advising him to let his body do what it needed to do. By the end of the third treatment, his legs were perfectly still, and I could put my hands on his feet, even exerting a little pressure, without his having any pain. He was so relaxed that he didn't want to get up off the bed (I saw him in his home). He said that he felt wonderful and had no pain at all. A few weeks later, he went into the hospital and died peacefully. The work we did together certainly eased his discomfort; it may have eased his journey through death as well.

Problems

I cannot prove scientifically that what I have done with clients and with myself is actually effective. Healing is an experiential process, not easily amenable to controlled studies. The healing session starts as soon as the healer begins to interact with the client, from the moment they first meet—perhaps even before, as the healer senses the client's energy from afar and they both anticipate the session. All the variables in the situation are difficult, if not impossible, to control. Is the healing a placebo effect or the reaction people have because someone is paying attention to them, touching them? I believe there is much more to it, because I feel changes in the field as I work; but even if the healing is nothing more than placebo or attention, the method is effective. Prayer and a relationship with the Divine are equally hard to prove empirically, although Larry Dossey's scientific studies show that prayer makes a real difference in healing.[8] People have been doing healing work since people have been people. If it were not effective in some way, these practices would not have survived.

Does it work all the time? Of course not—but then, neither do mainstream medical techniques, and often no one is able to say why. A patient's basic physical condition, attitude and feelings, the relationship with the doctor, and variations in the physical agent causing the disease or condition impact the effectiveness of medical treatments. Patients/clients need to know that there are no guarantees. I know of one case in which a cancer patient went to a healer, who told her that she would be cured in six months. The so-called healer asked for a substantial sum of money up front, saw the patient once, and had some telephone conversations with her. At the end of six months, the patient was no better. When she called again, the healer wanted more money and would not see her unless she sent it. If anyone offers guarantees of cure, the healer should be avoided. As with the medical establishment, we need to be informed and alert consumers.

Before I actively work with someone, particularly in the hospital where this manner of treatment is not standard, I explain a bit about what I do and how it might be helpful. Most important, I ask permission to proceed. Touching is powerful and very intimate. Some people, especially survivors of physical or sexual abuse, are often uncomfortable with being touched—although ironically, undemanding touch may be one of the things they need the most. Breasts and genital areas, in both men and women, are obviously off-limits. As with any therapy, however, respecting people's defenses and boundaries is vital. I have one client who is quite ticklish. Ticklishness in adults can be a sign of held energy. At first, I only cleared her field without touching her, keeping my hands about six inches above her body, as I did with the elderly patient mentioned above. As she became more open, I could work gently on the area, although it was still sensitive. She had come to realize that this area was where she stored a lot of old anger and had begun to release it. Only when people's defenses are respected, can they begin to make a choice to change them.

Relationship to Quakerism

Healing has been part of Quakerism since the beginning of the Religious Society of Friends. George Fox, the founder of Quakerism, recorded many healings of himself and others in his *Journal*. In 1948, Henry J. Cadbury published George Fox's *Book of*

Miracles,[9] reconstructed from a long-lost manuscript which had not been published by Fox's executors. Accounts of healings by other early Friends are part of our history as well. Today many Quakers are involved in healing work, both as clients and as practitioners. What is the fit between Quakerism and healing, and why has healing found a compatible home in the Religious Society of Friends?

A healing session is much like a unprogrammed Meeting for Worship. Just as when Friends enter Meeting for Worship, the healer and client enter into a sacred space in which both are open to the movement of the Spirit; the focus is on the process, not on the outcome. The session is open-ended with no clearly defined goal.

Meeting for Worship is something that we and God do together. In the same vein, I tell the client that this is something we do together, rather than something I do to them. The power of Meeting for Worship lies in the community created by the attenders and the presence of God. Similarly, healing takes place in the "community" created by the healer, the client and the Divine.

The processes are also similar. Both begin with centering, seeking the quiet space within. As they continue, the communion among the participants and God deepens. During the session, clients may "speak"—have emotional experiences which carry a message for them and for the healer—or may remain silent, finding a deep inner peace. As the end draws near, there is a sense of coming back into the every day, of becoming grounded in the current world but of not losing the deeper reality. As the client/Meeting member undergoes more "sessions," that sense of the deeper reality becomes more real, changing the way the person is in the world. In a message during Meeting for Worship, a member of my home Meeting said that all Meetings should have a sign over the door which states, "Beware all ye who enter here; your life will change." The hope of the healer and client is that the work will enable the client to change positively the way he or she sees the world and how to interact with it.

In addition, Quaker beliefs and healing have much in common. After his revelation of Christ's relationship with humankind, George Fox said, ". . . and that I knew experimentally."[10] By this he meant that he came to his understanding through his own experience, without any intermediary. Catholics emphasize the Pope as the ultimate religious authority in certain areas; Protestants emphasize the Bible. Based on Fox's revelation, Quakers believe that the ultimate authority lies in one's own spiritual experience. This experience is grounded in the Meeting community which is a mirror, reflecting upon the individual's experience, offering support and clearness. The Religious Society of Friends stands against any one Quaker attempting to impose his or her beliefs (experience) upon another.

So it is with healing. It is a mystical experience in which the clients, if they can be open, receive what they need from the Divine. Their experience during the session, although similar in feeling to many others, is theirs alone. What they derive from the healing time, although reflected upon by the healer acting as facilitator, is directly theirs. They can choose to hear and act or not on the wisdom revealed to them. No one can heal anyone else any more than they can be the source of spiritual authority for anyone else. Just as in Meeting for Worship, clients participate in the process as much as they are able to—and that's good enough. There need be no guilt about not doing it right. To me, the most important message of healing is, "You are OK as you are. Not that there is no room for growth. We all have that, thank God. But you are starting from a sound base." As I understand it, this is the meaning of grace. As Paul says in Philippians:

> It is not to be thought that I have already achieved all this. I have not yet reached perfection, but I press on, hoping to take hold of that for which Christ once took hold for me. My friends, I do not reckon myself to have got hold of it yet. All I can say is this: forgetting what is behind me, and reaching out for that which lies ahead, I

press towards the goal to win the prize which is God's call to the life above, in Christ Jesus.[11]

Quakers believe in continuing revelation, which means that God still interacts directly with us. This ongoing revelation helps us grow and mature spiritually. Change and progress occur in this process; it is not static. Progress and change are possible with this point of view. As one works in the spiritual garden, the garden grows and becomes more varied; there is deeper understanding of the world of the spirit and a closer relationship with the Divine.

As a healer, I assume that clients are capable of rediscovering (revelation) their basic wholeness. I ask my clients two questions: "Can you see yourself as whole?" and "What are you willing to give up to be whole?" These are spiritual questions. Deep healing is a spiritual process, requiring people to give up (surrender) the safety of the way they are now, to step into the unknown, seek the unknowable, to find joy and safety in that place. Another way to pose the question is the following: "Do you believe you can and are you willing to walk through the fire back into Eden?" If sometime in the process, the client is able to answer these questions positively, then the possibility exists. The focusing of intent upon being whole begins the process.

What is this basic wholeness which lies within us all, even when we are sick or dying? Quakers believe in that of God in every person (the Inner Light, the Christ within). Is that not also our wholeness? When I was young, I thought of the Inner Light as something that was located somewhere around my heart, like a lamp. Now I realize that it pervades every part of me, every cell of my body, every atom that makes up those cells, as well as all other aspects of my being. As I continue to deepen and "walk in the Light," more is illumined for me and I heal on all levels.

For me, a strong connection exists between healing and the Quaker peace testimony. When one is, as one of my friends puts it, "among the walking healing," one becomes more centered and peaceful. Peace in society and the world begins inside each of us.

Peaceful, centered people make for a more peaceful world. As we clear stuck energy, we are less likely to be triggered by the anger, despair, and fear of those around us. We all have difficult people in our lives. How we are able to deal with them depends on where we live inside. And quite miraculously, our peaceful energy is contagious.

At one time, I was so angry that I didn't know how angry I was. My spirituality suffered greatly, primarily I think because I spent so much energy on judging myself and others. And I had a multitude of physical problems. I now realize that the main ones (cancer and lupus) were conditions in which I was eating myself up. I will never forget how my children began to change as I was able to release that stuck anger energy—and I wasn't doing anything to them; I was just working on me.

As Quakers have always valued simplicity, life also becomes more simple as the stresses of held energy are released. The perspective changes on what matters. I spend much less time worrying about money, wondering how I will get what I need, or thinking about experiences in the past which were difficult. I live in the present, where God lives, more of the time. Since that is the only time we have to live anyway, it makes life much simpler than running into the past or future. More energy for doing becomes available by focusing on being rather than on the doing itself—a spiritual posture.

Implications for Pastoral Care

As a chaplain and a pastoral counselor, I incorporate healing energy work in my practice. But how can this perspective be useful to someone who has not had specific training to do healing work?

During the time I worked as a chaplain, I led sessions on Therapeutic Touch and healing work for Clinical Pastoral Education (CPE) students, occupational and physical therapists, and other hospital staff. After I led them through a demonstration of the techniques described in this chapter, and they had a chance to work with one another, they realized that they were beginning to see a bit differently. Although they were not capable of doing a full treatment—indeed, it would not have been appropriate for them to do so—they felt that they were able to join more deeply with the patient. They became more aware of how important touching is and how doing it with a healing orientation could connect them more deeply. The focus of the interaction broadens, moving from just the patient's words to how feelings are being expressed in the patient's body. Where does the tension lie? The tension can be relieved just by gently focusing on it. The caring person can do this without the patient's being consciously aware of it.

As you hold someone's hand, see his or her energy, perhaps as light or water, flowing freely through the system and out the finger tips. Necks and shoulders, along with the lower back, are common places where tension and feelings are held and pain occurs. Focus on the sense of the field you get if you put your hand on the patient's shoulder. Since this is not an intellectual process, it does not interfere with listening to the patient's words or with verbal pastoral interventions.

I once visited a young man who was blind. As I spoke with him, I was holding his hand in mine and visualizing his energy flowing easily and clearly. After awhile, he said to me, "What are you doing?" and I explained. He was pleased and intrigued. I think that because he was blind, he was more sensitive to the flow of energy—and he was a Pentecostal Christian, so he was also comfortable with laying on of hands. Most patients won't be aware of what you are doing; however, it is still effective.

The healing orientation is important if you are a chaplain or pastoral counselor. You can become more aware of your issues and what blocks your own wholeness. What triggers you in encounters with patients/clients, and where do you feel that in your body? Go there, sit quietly with the feeling, ask it what it needs or wants to tell you. Remember that you are looking in a mirror when you interact with others. The result may surprise you and lead to greater understanding of self. You cannot help others to heal if you are not actively healing yourself.

Most of all, the healing orientation reminds us that our work is about being, not doing. Our society is so goal-oriented with treatment plans and outcome-based evaluations. Goals are appropriate for some fields, but to my mind, not to ours. Ours is the land of the spirit, where the outcome is not under our control, where we must be able to live without knowing the answers, learning to let go of our judgments and attachment to our expectations and desires. A wonderful button I got at Friends General Conference Gathering one year says, "[The] Way will open when I get out of the way." In healing we consciously, actively look for that way and join with the Divine to create fuller, more meaningful lives for ourselves, and help others to do the same.

Healing

I sing the body electric,
    the shape that lives beyond the flesh,
    the life that flows beyond the blood,
    the spark that binds ourselves in one.
I praise the touch that senses life,
    the sight that sees the power within,
    the holding that lets go,
    that knits the body, spirit, mind and heart
    into new birth of self.
There wellness lies, a peaceful spot,
    a shimmering golden circle
    of wholeness, health and life,
    even in the dying.[12]

Notes

1. Gerard Manley Hopkins, "A Nun Takes the Veil," in Samuel
    Barber; *Collected Songs for Low Voice* (New York: G. Schirmer,
    1980), 32.

2. Jeanne Achterberg, *Woman as Healer* (Boston: Shambala Publica-
    tions, Inc., 1990), 2.

3. Achterberg, *Woman as Healer,* 4.

4. Achterberg, *Woman as Healer,* 4.

5. Marthajane Robinson, "Suffering and God: How Can they Both
    Be? Or God as Strange Attractor, " unpublished paper, 1994.

6. Dolores Krieger, *The Therapeutic Touch: How to Use Your Hands to
    Heal* (New York: Fireside, 1979), 153-164.

7. Dolores Krieger, "Healing by the laying-on of hands as a facilita-
    tor of bioenergetic exchange: The response of in-vivo human
    hemoglobin," *International Journal for Psychoenergetic Systems* 2
    (1976).

8. Larry Dossey, MD, *Healing Words: the Power of Prayer and the
    Practice of Medicine.* (San Francisco, HarperCollins, 1993).

9. Henry J. Cadbury, *George Fox's Book of Miracles.* (Cambridge:
    The University Press, 1948).

10. George Fox, *Journal.* (London: J.M. Dent & Sons LTD, 1962), 9.

11. Philippians 3:12-16, *The New English Bible with the Apocrypha.*
    (New York: Oxford University Press, 1972), 254.

12. Marthajane Robinson, Unpublished poem, 1986.

XII. The Formation of a Quaker Chaplain's Identity:
Theological Reflections on Quaker Distinctives and Chaplaincy Training

Susanne Kromberg

Introduction

Two Clinical Pastoral Education (CPE) hospital sites accepted me for training, partly because I was a Quaker. Neither of the CPE supervisors had ever had a Quaker student before, and they wanted me for the religious diversity I would bring to the group and I was glad to bring it. The experience was more challenging than we perhaps anticipated. Historical disputes between Quakers and Protestant denominations date back to the seventeenth century.

Obvious and subtle issues spawned difficult differences. When both the supervisor and I knew that there might be difficulties, we faced them openly and directly: sacraments, unfamiliarity with Christian creeds, prayers, and practices. The others—for instance perfection and hierarchy—were issues we may have been aware of, but their effect on us took us unawares. How was I to know that my own struggles with pride would collide head-on with a Lutheran supervisor's deep-seated sense of everyone's sinfulness? How was I to know that my questions about my authority as a minister would make my Methodist supervisor feel uncertain about his authority in relationship to me?

215

On the surface, learning in CPE appears to be self-directed. Students formulate their own learning goals and decide how to measure their success in reaching those goals. Despite this, I would argue that the typical structure of CPE programs is hierarchical and the relationship between supervisor and student is not designed to be mutual. CPE programs do not allow time for supervisors to get to know their students' personalities or religious beliefs. Therefore supervisors take charge of the learning process based on limited knowledge of their students. Unfortunately, because of the hierarchical nature of CPE, many supervisors are unwilling or unable to adjust those first impressions. Paradoxically, the problems may be exacerbated if students try to explain their beliefs more fully or suggest that their supervisors' perceptions may be inaccurate. Supervisors will often feel their authority to be challenged and miss the substance of the discussion. Instead they may dismiss such statements as indicating a parental transference issue or as revealing students' problems with authority. Because Quakers value non-hierarchical relationships, the lack of mutuality and equality in the relationship between students and supervisors may lead Quakers to have a difficult time fitting into the model of chaplaincy training.

In most other respects, I believe Quakers are eminently suited to the philosophy of learning of Clinical Pastoral Education. Just as Quakers base their theology on personal experience, so does experience form the core of learning in CPE. Students learn first by interacting with patients and staff in the capacity of chaplain. Working as a hospital chaplain typically accounts for half the training time. The other half is spent in reflecting on those experiences with the peer group and supervisor. By reflecting on our own and others' actions, our identity as chaplains take shape, our vision of the role of a chaplain is formed, and chaplaincy behavior is modeled and taught.

An important facet of the CPE learning experience is modeling. I certainly learned from watching and hearing about what my supervisor and peers had done. But in addition to learning from modeled behavior, I know I learned about my own beliefs and practices when my instinct was to do something different from what others were doing. Those experiences made me examine why I do what I do and what I might have done instead of what others did. I am not sure whether learning by reacting against a situation is a particularly Quaker thing to do, but I do think Quaker students may feel more comfortable with that form of learning than others. After all, we have fewer prescribed beliefs and actions in our tradition and may feel freer to find our own way. That is sometimes a confusing way to learn, and a book and a chapter like this might have helped me to make sense of the experiences that formed the basis of my learning.

I have interpreted my experiences through the prism of a Christian Quaker from the unprogrammed tradition. Although some of my experiences may be specific to my own background, I draw on early Quakers George Fox and Robert Barclay to make these reflections useful to Friends with perspectives other than mine.

Obvious Issues

The obvious issues were less difficult to deal with than I had feared at first, with one exception. The struggle to become clear on whether or not to baptize was every bit as difficult as I had anticipated. I ended up deciding to do it, but not without great misgivings and soul searching. But I will write more about that later. First I want to address some of the advantages that being a Quaker CPE student provided.

Openness to Different Approaches

One of the objectives of chaplaincy training is to help students be available to patients from all kinds of backgrounds. The goal is to encourage us to learn about our limitations, to recognize the signs that indicate that our own prejudices might get in the way, and to learn when to refer a patient to someone else. At the same time, the students' prime goal is to learn to work not only with patients whose religious outlook we share, but to be able to work with all patients, whatever their spiritual and emotional needs might be and whatever their issues are. We were to learn to deal spiritually with a number of emotional and practical problems, even issues with which we had no prior familiarity. The aim is to learn openness and flexibility in handling unknown situations, and to be professional even in situations with which we might disagree or disapprove. This openness to diversity is a value that is embraced by most liberal Quakers. There are numerous non-traditional perspectives in our Meetings.

Many liberal Quakers have encountered other faiths within their own Meeting, especially Buddhist perspectives. Even those that may not have other faiths represented within their own Meeting express the desire to be inclusive of them. A strong emphasis on familiarity with international affairs and societal issues fosters a working knowledge of other cultures, religions, and lifestyles. Which liberal Quaker Meeting has not dealt with gay relationships and the issues of children and the non-traditional family patterns that are often associated with those relationships?

There were a number of situations when this diversity came into play in my CPE experience. On one occasion, a Buddhist patient died unexpectedly and the family members were in shock. I was called in to visit them, and I did my best to be supportive of them, including encouraging them to ask for a priest from their own faith tradition to come and be with them. When it turned out to be impossible to get the priest to come, the family turned to me and asked me to pray with them over the deceased. I believe that, thanks to Quaker openness, I was sufficiently conversant with their faith—and the faith of Hindu and Muslim families that I later ministered to— that I could minister to them effectively with words and concepts with which we all felt comfortable.

On another occasion I met a patient who had unique beliefs. The patient was a transsexual who had developed his/her own belief system, combining elements of several major faiths and some of his/her own ideas that were informed by his/her gender experiences. With genuine curiosity I engaged in conversation about how his/her faith supported him/her in the medical crisis.

In those situations, my Quaker experience of diversity was to my advantage. I had already begun to deal with my own judgmentalism in encounters within my own faith tradition, and I was therefore more easily able to focus on how the patients' faith systems worked for them in the current crisis. But many of my peers were coming face to face for the first time with religious views with which they disagreed. A number of my fellow students had to struggle not to judge.

A disadvantage usually accompanies every advantage: Chaplains are expected to lead patients in the common rituals and practices of mainline Christianity. Although I am a Christian, I am also a Quaker in the unprogrammed tradition, and as such I was unfamiliar with the traditional prayers and sacraments that I was expected to perform.

Unfamiliarity with Common Christian Prayers and Practices

When I began chaplaincy training, I had never witnessed a baptism or an anointing, and I had been to only one mainstream church funeral that I could remember. As a child in Botswana, I had to repeat the Lord's prayer at school assembly every day. But I had said the Lord's prayer out loud maybe ten times since I left grade school, and not once since I had become a Friend fifteen years ago. In chaplaincy training, I remember the first time I had to say the Lord's prayer with a patient. Since I knew I was on shaky ground, I invited the patient to join in with me, hoping that he might prompt me if I stumbled. No such luck. The patient remained silent, and I just did the best I could, scared that I would be exposed as a fraud as a chaplain. At the end, the patient gave me a funny look, and I suspect I did not get it right. After that visit, I went straight to the chaplain's office and memorized some of the key prayers and rituals of the Christian tradition.

A worse example came when I was asked to anoint a terminally ill patient. I was not sufficiently prepared for this eventuality because I had thought that I would be given the opportunity to refresh my memory when I went to the chaplain's office to get the chrism ring, which contained the oil I would use for the anointing. But this family had brought their own oil that had been blessed by their pastor before they left home for the hospital. I then thought this was my solution and asked how the anointing was done in their tradition, saying that I would be honored to do it with them in the fashion they were accustomed to. But the uncertainty must have been apparent on my face because the patient and his wife told me that I did not have to do it if it made me uncomfortable. We ended up praying together without the anointing. Even as I write about it now, I feel guilty about abandoning them in a time of need.

As part of our initial training in CPE, we watched a video showing a baptism, anointing, and examples of prayers. In retrospect, I think it would have been wise for me to practice them first, or at least accompany my supervisor or one of my peers to watch how they did it before I tried my hand at it. Although I had studied those videos and learned the technicalities, it was still not a substitute for actually doing the sacraments or being steeped in them by growing up in a culture where they are practiced. Becoming involved in those rituals is so much more than the words and actions of the ritual itself. It is also an attitude, a demeanor, and an exuding of an aura of confidence and being in charge. I was not familiar with any of those aspects of Christian practices, as I expect many Quakers would not be.

This was a particular problem since I had never been involved with other churches before I joined the Religious Society of

Friends. But the issue of sacraments may present a different set of difficulties to some Friends who have come from other denominations. They may have bad memories of practices and rituals from their years in other churches. The practices may evoke painful memories of being judged, excluded, or made to feel that there was something wrong with them. They may struggle to overcome their own antipathies in order to accept that those prayers, rituals, and practices can be comforting, healing, and spiritually nurturing to others.

Sacraments

My biggest struggle with the sacraments had to do with baptism. I will deal with baptism separately, because to me, baptism is in a category of its own in terms of the sacraments. For a non-denominational hospital chaplain, communion and anointing do not usually take place in emergency situations. Even when they do, the patient or family can often decide whether or not they consider a Quaker chaplain to have the authority to perform the ritual or sacrament, or whether they would prefer to wait for someone from their own denomination. Baptisms, however, usually are hurried. They have to be done before the infant dies, and they usually happen in situations of extreme emotional distress. In those situations it has not seemed right to me to present the family with my dilemma. So it has been something I have had to decide on their behalf.

My supervisor's policy was that he would not require me to do anything that was not in keeping with my faith tradition, so I could have chosen not to engage with the issue at all. But I felt challenged by the knowledge that, for many of the people I would be ministering to, the sacraments are experienced as opportunities to deepen one's relationship with God. How could I be a minister—open to the ways in which God can reveal Godself—and not wrestle with the issue?

Many liberal Friends say that we do not practice the sacraments; indeed, they almost think of it as taboo. A closer look at our tradition, however, tells me something different. Both George Fox and Robert Barclay declared that there is a true and spiritual baptism and communion that was instituted with Christ, the new covenant, based on Scripture. Just as the Law on stone tablets would be replaced with the law in our hearts, so the external rites would be replaced with inward, unmediated revelation—what can be called the baptism or communion of the Spirit. Fox confesses a "baptism that is in Christ;"[1] Barclay defines baptism as "an appeal to God for a clear conscience, through the resurrection of Jesus Christ."[2] About communion, Barclay says: "Eating the flesh and blood of Christ has a necessary relationship to life, because if we do not eat his flesh and drink his blood we cannot have life."[3]

Fox and Barclay, it is true, are scornful of those who practice external rites, such as baptism by water and ritualized communion. But they do not condemn them, because they see the external rites as a help for those who have not experienced God in the same direct fashion as they believed they had.[4] Fox denied that the Lord's supper and baptism were unlawful,[5] and Barclay said that the external rites were prescribed by God as "prototypes and shadows of the true substance that was to be revealed in time."[6] Barclay even goes so far as to concede that "if there are any . . . who practice this ceremony with a true tenderness of spirit, and with real conscience toward God . . . they may be indulged in it. The Lord may . . . appear to them for a time when they use these [external rites]."[7]

I decided to give communion once, and then see how it felt. It felt right, although a little bit strange. But one day I had an experience that made it clear to me that I had made the right decision. An elderly Catholic man asked me to commune him. Since I am a woman, it was of course obvious that I could not be a priest, but he also knew that I was not Catholic. He had the choice of having the Catholic chaplains bring him communion, but he asked me to give him communion every day while he was in the hospital. For him, I believe that the shared experience across the boundaries that our denominations erect was a tangible experience of the greatness of God, of the transcendence of God over human limitations. The fact that it so obviously was meaningful to him also had an effect on me. Since my role as chaplain is to help meet the spiritual needs of patients, family, and staff in the hospital, my beliefs are of secondary importance. What matters is what the patient deems to be helpful.

Baptism

Knowing that I would not have to break with my tradition was only the beginning of my process of considering baptism. I still had to become clear on what my conscience told me. Unfortunately, my conscience would not tell me ahead of time how I would feel about performing a baptism. I had to wait until the situation arose to become clear on what I would feel led to do. Initially in my training, I asked my supervisor to be there as back-up if a request for a baptism should come while I was on call.

For me, the problem was not so much whether or not I believe in the principle of baptism for other people. It was more of a question of whether I should be the one to perform it. The mainstream position on baptism is that it is preferable when it is done by an ordained minister or priest. When that is not possible, as is often the case in a hospital, the rule for most denominations is that anyone who is baptized has the authority to perform a baptism. This is the sticking point for me and many Quakers. I am not baptized, at least not with water, and I was not sure whether baptism of the Holy Spirit counts according to the hospital rules. It was not enough for me to find out what church policy on that is. It was a question of what the family expects of someone who baptizes. Would I be deceiving them if they assumed that I, as a chaplain, would be baptized myself?

I finally arrived at the position that I believe myself to be authorized to baptize by virtue of my relationship with God. To me, being baptized means acknowledging God's presence and vital importance in my life. In this sense, I have been and continue to be baptized. I also discovered that most family members seem not to care about formalities and technicalities in those situations—there is something far, far deeper at stake. The chaplain's presence and willingness to be God's human face on earth is what they are looking for in their crisis.

This has become my philosophy in encountering faith practices that are not part of my own tradition: it does not matter what I believe or do not believe at times like that. It is not about my beliefs. What matters is the beliefs of the patients, and how they believe God can be present to them in a time of need. Anything I can do to enhance God's presence at that time, unless it is harmful, is something I would do. I have since learned that this seems to be the position that most Quaker chaplains arrive at: What matters is being there for patients in the way that they deem helpful, it is not about the chaplain's beliefs—other than his or her basic trust in God to be present.

Some of the times when I have been most profoundly touched have been at moments like those. The event that moved me most deeply in my year of chaplaincy training was when I was called to baptize a dying newborn baby boy. His parents waited for me to arrive and baptize the baby before they took him off life support. After the baptism, I stayed with them as his parents said goodbye to him, talking about what they had hoped for and dreamed about for him, how much they would miss him, and promising to honor him by keeping his memory alive. At times like that, one wonders whether anything at all can bring comfort. But it seems that the touch of a human hand can make God's comfort and love seem a little more real. I didn't do much other than to be there with them and encourage them as they created their own leave-taking ceremony. I felt deeply honored to do anything, however small, that might help them feel God's presence. Hand in hand with the pain of loss, I felt deep spiritual fulfillment in doing something that was really worth doing.

The Role of the Minister

Graduating from the Earlham School of Religion, I had had opportunity to consider the role of the minister, and how I would define my own role. I resonated with Fox's conversion experience when he joyfully came to know that "There is one, even Christ Jesus, who can speak to thy condition."[8] I believed that Christ would teach his people himself,[9] and my approach as a chaplain was to see patients as the experts on their own spiritual condition. I wanted to empower the patients to hear and recognize Christ's voice leading them. I thought that, as a professional, my responsibility would be to help them to find direction and to discover what their needs are, rather than for me to decide what they needed and direct their actions. I wanted to look for clues that would tell me what *they* wanted to do and what the care receivers needed, so I could help them do it.

Full of theory but with no experience, this is what I believed. With many patients, this was quite appropriate. But I soon realized that a number of patients wanted something else from me. They expected of a chaplain that s/he would walk into a room and take charge. Sometimes they seemed to expect that the chaplain would have specific activities to perform during the visit and would tell them what to do. There may be many reasons why this is the case: patients are used to that behavior from their pastor/minister/priest; the medical crisis makes them confused and in need of guidance; or merely the hospital routine that has most hospital employees telling patients what to do. For whatever reason, I was often met with "Oh, finally, the chaplain is here. *She* will know what to do."

On one occasion I visited a young man who had a terminal illness. He asked me to give him suggestions on what he could do to grow spiritually in the time he had left. Before I felt able to make suggestions, I wanted to know what spiritual growth meant to him. Was he longing for a deeper relationship with God? Was he looking for new devotional practices? Did he want to find peace with his impending death? Did he want to restore his relationships with friends and family, some of whom he had harshly pushed away during his illness? Did he need to forgive or be forgiven? Did he need to hear that he did not need to do anything, but was loved and accepted just as he was? Or was there something else? I asked him to tell me more about what he was hoping for, and he merely repeated his original statement. The more I sought to understand him and his particular situation, the more bewildered and disappointed he looked, and he finally said with great frustration: "Just tell me what I need to do!" He was looking to me for an answer, but since I did not consider myself the authority on his spiritual condition, I did not have an answer to give. It is an ongoing struggle for me to find a balance between what I see as empowering the patient and meeting the patient's needs for an authority figure.

More Subtle Issues

More subtle issues often revolved around questions of theology and practice, but they may not be as apparent and on their face do not fall within the commonly held perceptions of the defining characteristics of Quakerism. The list is subjective and says as much about the writer as about Quaker theology, and it probably says a great deal about the issues that my supervisors and peers wrestled with. But there were a number of issues that arose in my CPE experience where differences in theology played a part. These were silence; institutional loyalty; perfection; sin as broken relationship; and authority.

Since our denomination is small in numbers, I did not expect that my supervisor and peers would be familiar with Quakerism or even that they would understand my beliefs as I explained them. But I had not expected that communication might break down and conflict would result. I suspect we believed ourselves to be similar enough to assume certain things about one another. This expectation made it hard to see issues from the other's perspective; we didn't even know there was an "other" perspective. This led my supervisor and peers to insist that, in many cases, my questions were not theological but personal. At the time, I was not always able to explain it well enough myself. It is only in writing about it now that the deeper theological foundation for some of those differences become apparent to me. For my part, I was blind to the fact I had entered into an arena in which my beliefs might not fit. Though my beliefs about theological issues need not intrude with a patient, I did need to wrestle with them among my peers and supervisors.

Silence

Carol, a name I will use for one of my peers, had a very strong reaction against Quaker worship when I introduced it to the group. My supervisor had encouraged me to lead worship in the style that my religious tradition uses. I introduced my peer group to worship-sharing, reading a Bible passage, and giving those present a few queries that they might ponder during the period of open worship. But Carol said, "You are hiding behind your religion." No amount of explaining the Quaker tradition would convince her that I was not intentionally using the silence to hide myself, to keep the group from knowing me, my theology, and beliefs. She also felt that I used silence to strategize on how to get what I wanted. In short, she felt I was being manipulative.

To me, silence comes naturally. The silence that is the starting point for business meetings and unprogrammed worship feels very comfortable, and I extend it into my own life. As an introvert, I am often silent unless I have something specific to say, and this is especially true when I am in large groups. But silence was clearly not comfortable to my supervisor and some of my peers, especially those who were unfamiliar with contemplative spirituality. In CPE, I learned that some people will feel deprived of my verbal contribution to the group and sometimes feel that I am withholding my thoughts and feelings. I discovered something valuable, namely that there will be others also, including those to whom I am called to minister, who will find silence uncomfortable. I now make an effort to be more verbal.

Although the situation I have described above gave me valuable insights into myself as a person and how I affect others, it seems to me that it was at heart a theological matter. I have come to recognize that not all theological differences have been overcome, even in our ecumenical times and in places that welcome diversity. Not all approaches are understood or appreciated. Whenever the Quaker perspective was not understood, I lost learning opportunities, and trust and communication suffered. Whether my peers from more mainline denominations experienced similar frustrations, I will probably never know.

Institutional loyalty

"Carol and I have been over this silence business over and over again. I'm not sure another angry encounter will help resolve the issue, and I wonder if it would not be better to let it rest for a while and see if time and prayer might help."

In saying this to my supervisor, I discovered that I was inadvertently questioning the CPE philosophy of confrontation. Most supervisors hold that, in our society, disagreement and feelings of anger are too often kept hidden. They believe that this leads to repression of feelings and passive-aggressive behavior. They feel that it is vital to make CPE students practice confrontation and the honest expression of feelings in the peer group. While I agree with the philosophy in general, I believe that there may be times when it might be better to try something other than confrontation. But this kind of statement did not endear me to my supervisors.

Quakers have often been experienced as arrogant, claiming as we do that we may experience and know the will of God. We typically do not commit to philosophies and principles unless we have experienced the Truth at work in them. Our loyalty is to God and to covenanted relationships. Institutions and principles do not command loyalty in and of themselves; we only commit to them when we recognize them to embody the principle of Truth. For Quakers, our commitment to worldly institutions is tentative, always subject to new experience. Quakers have resisted—again and again—swearing oaths of loyalty to any worldly power.

In this we are different from many denominations, which take for granted that certain institutions, primarily the church itself, represent God's presence in human affairs. For members of those denominations, commitment to the community of faith is taken for granted. Many people of faith are loyal to their denomination although they disagree on many points. For them, their commitment is often to bring the church back into the life of the Spirit. This is perhaps especially true of and admirable in Catholic women who struggle unrelentingly to get their church to recognize their ministry. In general, I believe Quakers are slower to commit and less loyal to institutions.

Secular institutions generally require the loyalty of their employees, and hospitals are not exempt. Neither are chaplaincy programs and supervisors, whose jobs and egos are often tied in with students' commitment to the philosophy of the program. I was committed to the program and respected my supervisors, but they sensed that they had to earn my trust and loyalty, which did not come automatically because of their position as supervisors. On a few occasions, I did question the program and the supervisors' decisions and insights. I was one of the most forceful people in the program to do so, and this affected my relationships with my supervisors. It may be attributed in part to my rebelliousness, but from what I hear, this kind of rebelliousness is a common characteristic in Friends, who often find themselves in similar situations.

Perfection

In my first CPE setting, I became involved in a conflict with the peer whom I have called Carol. The conflict continued for nine months, eventually becoming a very difficult situation, not only for the two of us, but also for the peer group. The reason that the relationship eventually became so troubled, I believe, had in part to do with our supervisor's definition of sin. He believed that sin is broken relationship, and he would not rest until Carol and I had resolved our difficulties and reconciled.

During the first few months of our conflict, I too believed that it might be possible to overcome our differences. But I gradually began to feel that the differences in personality, life history, theology, and chaplaincy style were too extensive and too deep-seated. As one issue was resolved, another would appear. In addition, there were major transference issues with each of us reminding the other of the most difficult person from our past.

About seven months into our conflict, something happened that allowed me to let go. It was one of those painful yet grace-filled moments in worship when I saw my own shortcomings very clearly and was convicted of my faults, and I recognized and experienced that I was not a better person than Carol. With the sense of being convicted came a deep sense of peace and forgiveness in my heart, and I was led to apologize to Carol for the places where I felt I had erred. I felt released from my anger and resentment, and I felt that I could move beyond confrontation to work more constructively with her. It was a moment of grace for which I can claim no credit. For me, this religious experience was a turning point in my relationship with Carol.

I believe that this was a classical Quaker experience. Many of us have had the experience, often in Meeting for Worship, of scales falling from our eyes. All of a sudden, we realize that pride has kept us from recognizing our own faults, and we become so ashamed by the experience that it comes as a relief when we can apologize and mend our ways. One of the tests of whether an experience is genuine is to see if I profit from it; if I do, it is good to be cautious about claiming it is God's will. But if the experience is humbling, there is a better chance that it is a genuine leading.

Paradoxically, at the heart of experiences like this is the Quaker belief in perfection. Quakers have traditionally believed that it is possible to know the will of God and change one's ways as a result. In writing about perfection, or spiritual maturity, Barclay describes a full rebirth in which "death and sin are crucified and removed . . . and [the] heart becomes united and obedient to truth . . . [One] is freed from sin and transgression of the law of God, and in that respect perfect."[10]

It is important not to misunderstand what early Quakers meant by perfection. Early Quakers acknowledged the human propensity to sin. Contrary to what many modern liberal Quakers believe, our tradition did not discard the concept of human sinfulness. Rather, early Quakers believed that the Light was more powerful than human sin. They believed that if people submit to the power of God and are obedient, the Light will burn up human faults and illumine the way to a life lived in accordance with the will of God.[11] Quakers were offended by Puritans and other Protestants' lack of belief in God's power over sin.

Puritans and other Protestants were equally provoked and deeply offended by the Quaker view of perfection. They hold that it is impossible for humans to rise above sin because sin is part of the human condition. Since humans cannot refrain from sin, they are entirely dependent on God's grace to protect them from the consequences of their sins. To claim anything else amounted to blasphemy.

Nowadays, I think it makes most modern Quakers, myself included, uncomfortable to talk about perfection. Our understanding of sin, which is a theological concept, has become modified or even replaced by psychological interpretations. But while we may want to explain away perfection, we cannot, because our belief in leadings and continuing revelation is inextricably tied to the concept of perfection. By this I mean the belief that all humans have the potential to unite with God's will, not through our own achievement, but by God's grace. Our modern understanding of family systems and other psychological patterns may make it hard to believe we can attain a state of perfection. But as long as Quakers believe we can know God's will and follow such a leading, we must necessarily believe that we can attain—at least temporarily—perfection by doing God's will when we follow a leading. It is probably good not to think about our own actions in terms of perfection, but merely in trying to follow leadings. Quaker belief in perfection—modified by modern psychology as it may be—focuses on potential. This focus can release us from preoccupation with sin and falling short of perfection. It can allow us to find some peace with living up to the Light we have been given and still strive to do what God wants. In this, we continue to be at odds with other theological approaches which focus more on sinfulness.

My Lutheran supervisor, for instance, was not impressed with the religious experience I had had that led me to apologize to Carol and be free of anger with her. His response echoed the Puritan reaction of the seventeenth century. Although my supervisor's definition of sin as broken relationship may not be the classical Lutheran definition, his seeming preoccupation with sin was more typically Lutheran. He felt it was presumptuous of me to claim that I had experienced God's presence in this vivid way. To say that my attitude and actions would change as a result of a divine experience only made matters worse, even if it did make me more humble and forgiving. Instead, he looked for psychological motivations.

My experience of release from anger did not lead me to desire friendship and companionship with Carol. I felt willing and able to work with her and be supportive of her in a practical and genuine way. But I preferred to keep some distance between us. Far from easing the tension, the change in me made Carol feel deprived of my friendship and the dance of anger and confrontation that had constituted our relationship until then. My supervisor encouraged us to keep at it. His view, which is reinforced by the philosophy of CPE, is that differences should be worked out by confrontation and the expression of emotions.

As I found myself caught up in this dialogue, I began to feel that my integrity was being compromised. Carol brought out the worst in me, and I did not like the angry, petty, and increasingly fumbling and self-doubting person I was. The religious experience I had gave me temporary relief from the Susanne I did not like. But all my efforts with Carol failed, and when my supervisor mistrusted my religious experience and pressured me into continued confrontation with Carol, I was at a total loss. I became unloving and unforgiving anew.

At this point, another facet of the Quaker belief in perfection began to come into play, namely the tendency to retreat when one feels that one's integrity is being compromised. In his study of Quaker Philadelphia, E. Digby Baltzell claims that belief in perfection makes it hard for Quakers to accept compromise, and since compromise is inevitable, it ultimately leads Quakers to withdraw.[12] While there is no general recommendation for Quakers to withdraw when they feel their integrity is being compromised, there are several examples of when that was the chosen course of action.

One of the more well-known instances of Quaker withdrawal was when Quakers in the Pennsylvania legislature gave up their seats in the 1750s. The King of England and the people of Pennsylvania were pressuring the ruling Quaker legislature to raise funds for and recruit militia for a war against France and the Native Americans. Rather than give in, Pennsylvania Friends pressured their legislators to give up their seats. From then on, the number of Quaker representatives dwindled and the Society of Friends began to operate as a pressure group from the outside, rather than as a political power within the assembly.[13]

If our tradition does not expressly encourage withdrawal in times of conflict, it does prescribe silence and prayer during the process. In the times of greatest confusion and disagreement, we tend to resort to silence and prayer. Those times of prayer could be described as retreat from one another in order to be better able to listen to the Holy Spirit and to seek to become aware of a new way forward. While clear communication is important to Quakers and we have a tradition of speaking truth to power, our method does not easily provide for confrontation and expression of feelings as a way to move beyond conflict.

It would be wrong to blame our supervisor for the conflict, because the conflict was between Carol and myself. But this situation is probably an extreme example of how the Quaker belief in perfection can aggravate those with a different focus. My supervisor doubted my religious experience and, because of it, he considered me arrogant. Because he was preoccupied with sin, that remained his focus. Since he believed that Carol and I were sinners until our relationship was healed, he encouraged Carol to continue to express her frustration and anger in the hopes that it would improve our relationship. He thought this would be healthy for me, but it was not.

Sin as broken relationship

In a hospital there is no shortage of sincere prayers for healing from the hearts of devout believers, and the Bible promises that we will receive that which we ask for in the Lord's name. Why then are physical healings so rare? Chaplains are frequently challenged to give good answers to this question. Based on my own fairly limited experience, it seems that chaplains tend to define healing more broadly than just the physical aspect. Healing, for most chaplains, includes repairing or improving relationships with significant persons in one's life and with God.

All supervisors may not define sin as broken relationship, but for most supervisors, healing does include improving relationships. As a Quaker, I define sin as anything that is away from the will and love of God. Just as Quakers do not like to pin down beliefs in creeds, I am reluctant to define what specifically constitutes a sin. Although human relationships are important to God, I am not sure that healing a relationship is always in accordance with God's will. As a Quaker, I also think I have fewer expectations and prescribed ways of how this healing might come about.

At any rate, I found that several of my peers and my supervisors were willing to go much further than I was in intervening in relationships. Again, I think it may be related to Quaker perfection. It makes it easier to let go of the paradigm of sin. I found fairly consistent differences in how far we would pursue a patient into reconciling with an estranged family member or how far we would go in trying to get patients to move beyond denial of the severity of their illness. Our views on sin affected the development of our identity as chaplains and what we perceived the role of the chaplain to be. I had to find my own way, which was not always in accord with the supervisors and my peers.

Authority

How can a supervisor who believes in hierarchical models help a Quaker develop her identity and authority as a chaplain?

One of my learning goals was to learn to claim my personal and professional authority. I can be insecure, and I wanted to address this in CPE. There was not much help from my own faith tradition because liberal Quakers are ambiguous about authority. On the one hand, we rely on people taking leadership positions and believe in the authority that accompanies the belief in "that of

God" in every person. On the other hand, we define our beliefs concerning authority in vague terms or we express ourselves in terms of what it is we do not believe in. Liberal Quakers are at a practical level often unsupportive of people in leadership positions. I knew I would have to find my own way based on my own experiences, and I hoped that my supervisors would be available to help me. As a Quaker, I struggled to formulate an understanding of authority which took my training and religious and life experience into account but left room for the Inward Teacher at work in the patient as the true authority.

In the end, I did not find the help I was looking for. My supervisors believed that chaplains have automatic trust and authority by virtue of their training and ordination. Because my faith leads me to deal with authority issues in a special way, I should have been more aware of the crosscurrents surrounding this issue. But it did take me by surprise when my supervisors had difficulties understanding the theological components of my struggle. My reluctance to embrace the conventional model of the chaplain as the person in charge of spiritual matters was primarily seen as a personal hang-up and an unwillingness to assert my authority.

In my own learning, it often helps me to have understood something intellectually. This helps me to formulate goals and become clear on how I can go about achieving them. But in this challenging area for me, my supervisors, limited by their own theological blind spots, could not help me to conceptualize and formulate my own goals and my own understanding of the role of the chaplain. They redirected me to the personal arena when, I believe, a major part of the struggle was in the theological arena.

Another difficulty I encountered was the way the CPE program encourages students to become dependent on the supervisor in working on our own interpersonal issues. It was hard enough to learn how to claim my own authority in ways that did not violate my Quaker beliefs. But to do so in a context that encourages dependence on an authority figure, with a person who has a vested interest in the students' dependence, was doubly hard. I found it challenging and confusing to learn about my own boundaries when others' boundaries were not clear. As so often happens, I was tempted to seek my way out of that state of confusion by accepting guidance from an authority figure. It was a very frustrating situation.

My second site was even harder because my supervisor seemed to feel that by questioning my own authority or the authority of the chaplain, I was also questioning his authority. Whenever I asked for his help or the group's help, our conversations invariably ended up with my supervisor becoming upset and feeling that I was not listening to what he had to say. I felt frustrated when the discussion took a turn that did not speak to my concerns and, try as I might, I could not bring the conversation back on track. This is perhaps the area of chaplaincy training where I feel I did not learn what I had hoped to learn. Theological differences seemed to get in the way.

Instant Gratification

One of the patients I got to know had a stubborn, potentially life-threatening infection that required her to be on intravenous antibiotics for six weeks. "Lisa" was very frustrated that she could not go home. One day Lisa declared that she was going to pull out the IV lines and go home. She told me that if the Lord had decided that this was the time to bring her to heaven, then she was ready to go.

Western society and perhaps American culture in particular espouse instant gratification. They also promote taking charge, being in control, making things happen. To me, the greatest cultural problem that television imposes on society is not violence, but the craving for instant gratification. In soap operas, talk shows, drama, films, and news, the idea is given that problems can be solved instantly and dramatically. The instant and dramatic solutions are presented as the norm and the desirable. This is perhaps the arena where Quakers bring the greatest gift to chaplaincy.

Quakers are used to letting things take their time. We espouse a spirituality of letting things unfold, waiting for signs, waiting for guidance, waiting upon the still, small voice of the Lord. While we believe in the transforming power of the Holy Spirit, we believe transformation takes time. We believe that change is something over which we do not and ought not have control. We do not try to predict the outcome. Similarly in our decision-making process, we move slowly. If there is disagreement or confusion, the passage of time is seen as the way to help a solution evolve.

Most healing takes time, too. Patients are required to be patient. It is hard to recommend patience to someone who is experiencing great pain. But medical problems are usually accompanied by socio-psychological issues. Frequently the medical problem creates a socio-psychological problem or makes interpersonal relationships seem worse. At those times, the Quaker chaplain may bring the gift of conveying, as Julian of Norwich did, that "all shall be well" some day.

I remember in particular the family of a patient whom I will call Jane who had an illness that I will call pneumonia. Jane was not in critical condition when she was admitted but took a sudden turn for the worse and had to be taken to the intensive care unit. Over the next few days, while Jane hovered between life and death, I visited with her parents, teenage daughter, and friends. Although they always clung to hope, they were realistic and knew that Jane would probably not survive. She did not live. One day just before Jane died, her daughter and friend took me aside and said "You're our guardian angel. Even when you just walk past our room on your way to someone else, we feel reassured that nothing can go wrong." I am not foolish enough to believe that I am a guardian angel, nor did they believe that I could keep Jane from dying. But I think they were saying that my presence gave God's love a human face and that I helped them feel peaceful with the future as it unfolded. I believe this form of ministry comes easily to Quakers.

Conclusion

Quakers have numerous advantages in chaplaincy training by virtue of our faith. But we can encounter difficulties peculiar to Quakers. Perhaps the greatest problems for Quakers are to fit into the hierarchical model of CPE, and to learn to sense when Quaker distinctives are going unrecognized or are being misunderstood. Even when we do not overtly challenge the structure, we may find it hard to accept that the supervisor knows best and disregards the influence of Quaker spirituality or theological heritage. My greatest difficulties arose when others defined my questions in ways that did not recognize the spiritual and theological issues that were the foundation for my personal choices. Struggling to define myself and my ministry in that setting was extraordinarily hard, and at times crazy-making.

On the whole, however, I look back on my training as invaluable, both in terms of what I have learned as chaplain and in terms of life skills. Perhaps one of the reasons that the experience was so transformative was that I had to work so hard to name what I believed and why, and to recognize how my faith tradition interacts with who I believe myself to be and who I would like to be as a person and as a chaplain. The experience of not always being understood or heard also gave me a firsthand lesson in the importance of meeting people where they are. All of these things helped me to gain a more mature perspective and take more responsibility for myself. Lest anyone believe that I only learned from adversity, I want to say that the CPE experience gave me confidence in my skills. I felt that chaplaincy is something I am called to do. Above all, I felt blessed by getting to know the patients, family members, and staff, and to be a part of their lives.

Looking back on my year of chaplaincy training, I believe it would have been an easier experience if I had been intentional about naming how I live my faith, and this is my final word of advice to any Quaker who is considering chaplaincy training.[14/15]

As Quakers, we are unused to naming and describing our faith, but those are skills that can be a great asset in chaplaincy training. The chaplain's ability to put words to his or her own faith experience can help patients discover the resources God has given them to help them through their time of crisis. The greatest resource, I believe, is the assurance that each person is loved by God. This is the essence of chaplaincy.

Notes

1.   John L. Nickalls, ed., *The Journal of George Fox* (Philadelphia, PA: Philadelphia Yearly Meeting, 1997), 134.

2.   Dean Freiday, ed., *Barclay's Apology in Modern English* (Newberg, OR: Barclay Press, 1991), 308.

3.   Freiday, *Barclay's Apology*, 338.

4.   Freiday, *Barclay's Apology*, 327.

5.   Nickalls, *The Journal of George Fox*, 134.

6.   Freiday, *Barclay's Apology*, 301.

7.   Freiday, *Barclay's Apology*, 361.

8.   Nickalls, *The Journal of George Fox*, 11.

9.   Nickalls, *The Journal of George Fox*, 9.

10. Freiday, *Barclay's Apology*, 154.

11. Douglas Gwyn, *Apocalypse of the Word: The Life and Message of George Fox* (Richmond, IN: Friends United Press, 1984), 60-65.

12. E. Digby Baltzell, *Puritan Boston and Quaker Philadelphia* (Boston, MA: Beacon Press, 1979), 101.

13. Peter Brock, *Pioneers of the Peaceable Kingdom* (Princeton, NJ: Princeton University Press, 1968), 115-140.

Stories
Out of the Silence

The Hidden Treasure

The Parable of the Hidden Treasure.

THE kingdom of heaven is like unto treaſure hid in a field; the which when a man hath found, he hideth, and for ioy thereof goeth and ſelleth all that he hath, and buyeth that field.

Matthew, Chap. xiii.
v. xliv.

XIII. Where Two or Three are Gathered . . .

Jane Brown

> For where two or three are gathered in my name,
> there I am in the midst of them.
> Matthew 18:20

*I*n this expectancy we come together in silent worship, knowing that God is with us and can speak to us-even today! In this spirit we welcome all persons—of any faith or of none—to join with us.

Thus begins the invitation to worship with the Abington Friends Meeting of Jenkintown, Pennsylvania. The inviting statement reflects two basic tenets of the Quaker faith. One is that there is "that of God" with each person including those of differing faiths and those of no professed faith. The second tenet is that God's loving spirit is universally available to give direct guidance and comfort. These tenets form the underlying assumptions of this chapter and, I believe, of Quaker pastoral care giving.

Not so long ago, one of my favorite Jewish doctors came hurriedly into the pastoral care office. "Do you know the prayers of Yizkor?" he asked. When I acknowledged no knowledge of the prayers of which he spoke, he said, "Then let me teach you." He explained that there was a patient in the hospital emergency room who for the first time in 70 years was missing Yom Kippur services at his temple and that, according to Jewish law, he still needed to say these prayers to his God before the sun set. The physician then taught me the essence of the desired prayers.

This day was the tenth day of Rosh Hashanna, a time of penitence and atonement for one's sins against God and persons in one's life. On this day God's book would be sealed. According to

243

the Jewish tradition, if one's name was inscribed in the sealed book of life then one would have another year to live. The Yizkor prayer of repentance puts one's name in that book.

Leaving the doctor I hurried to the emergency room and found a very frightened man. I told him that I had come to say the prayers of Yom Kippur with him, but that he knew them much better than I so that together we would approach God. He seemed much relieved to know that he could do his duty on this holy day, even if it was with this one who simply, faithfully stumbled along beside him. Relying on my hastily tutored knowledge and his faithful history, we joined hands and faiths before a receptive God who, I was thankful, asks of us a willing spirit rather than exact correctness. A few days later when I saw this patient in his hospital room, he told me that his orthodox rabbi (who could not travel on Yom Kippur) had said that in that emergency room, I had become his Rabbi. I knew that in that shared moment, I had been gifted in being allowed to join him in a holy place.

This experience models a way to bring Quaker presence to a pastoral moment. The caring, Jewish doctor and the patient guided me to the God that they knew. Their words and history informed me of their ways of relating to that God. As a trustworthy friend, grounded in my own faith, I joined them on their journey. With a little knowledge we entered the holy space where the Spirit could receive and care for us.

Quakers speak of "that of God" within each person. I want to address "that of God" within the pastoral care giver, "that of God" within the care receiver and "that of God" within the relationship that is created when two or more come together. Each will be illustrated by a vignette out of my pastoral care giving experiences. This chapter would be neater if "that of God" were so easily contained. In reality, the Spirit of God doesn't fit so neatly into my three boxes. In life, the Spirit tends to spill out of what one thought was the original container and encounters itself in the other.

That of God Within the Pastoral Care giver

Using the language of his time, Quaker writer and theologian Elton Trueblood wrote:

> The man who supposes that he has no time to pray or to reflect, because the social tasks are numerous and urgent, will soon find that he has become fundamentally unproductive because he has separated his life from its root.[1]

This need for rooting in faith is even more true for the pastoral care giver. Before the care giver courageously walks into unfamiliar places or relationships and before the care giver reaches to "that of God" within another, she or he must have relationship with the Spirit.

So how do we prepare our selves to incarnate the Spirit in the time of care giving? The simple answer is to put our selves in a state of awareness of the presence of the Spirit as often in the day as possible. This allows the Spirit to be an integral, active part of our being and changes how we live in the world.

We can relate to both the biblical and the Living Christ. Reading biblical accounts of how the incarnated Christ related to others gives direction. If Jesus models for us how to be spiritually present, then we, too, are called to be not prideful and legalistic but understanding, accepting, and forgiving. Besides his heart going out to the helpless, diseased, and oppressed poor, it also went out to the rich and the self-righteous who were separated from God by the hardness of their hearts. Knowing the biblical Jesus informs us how to walk beside our neighbor in need.

In addition we need to put our selves in the presence of the Living Christ. Quaker author Thomas Kelly says:

> Inside of us there ought to go on a steady, daily, hourly process of relating ourselves to the Divine Goodness, of opening our lives to His warmth and love.[2]

From the 1800s a Philadelphia Quaker, Hannah Whitall Smith, writes in her autobiography of her journey to this relationship:

> By the discovery of God . . . I do not mean anything mysterious, or mystical, or unattainable. I simply mean becoming acquainted with Him as one becomes acquainted with a human friend; that is, finding out what is His nature, and His character, and coming to understand His Ways. . . . My own experience has been something like this. My knowledge of God, beginning on a very low plane, and in the midst of the greatest darkness and ignorance, advanced slowly through many stages, and with a vast amount of useless conflict and wrestling, to the place where I learned at last that Christ was the "express image" of God, and where I became, therefore, in a measure acquainted with Him, and discovered to my amazement and delight His utter unselfishness, and saw that it was safe to trust Him.[3]

Being nurtured by the Spirit leads to a different experience of existing in the world. This existence allows us to be companioned in our decisions or our actions. In the first unit of my training as a chaplain, long before I knew the "right" things to do with a patient, I was sent to a family because they said that they wanted a Quaker minister. Upon entering the hospital room I was struck by the skeleton-like figure of a woman lying unconscious on the bed. Standing around the head of the bed, emphasizing her slightness with their healthfulness, were three young men who were her sons. Seated in a chair to her left was her grieving husband. I was a part-time student in seminary and my livelihood was still in teaching high school math. But when the husband asked if I was a Quaker minister, I quickly searched my soul and answered, "Yes." I knew and still know that the Spirit uses each of us to minister to another. I answered out of that knowing.

In response to my affirmation, the husband said, "Then please pray with us." What followed was of the Spirit's doing because, as I passed by the end of the dying woman's bed, I prayed silently, "You'd better take over because I don't know what they want and I don't know what I'm doing." Today I would gently ask them what they wanted me to bring to the Spirit. Then, not knowing if they wanted Quaker silence or a verbal prayer, I simply took the woman's hand in mine and waited.

With this Quaker family, I was comfortable in the silence that followed. I felt an energy travel up my arm from the woman's hand that I held. Out of my mouth came a most beautiful, peaceful prayer whose words were as new to me as to the others. Never did it seem that the words passed through my mind or consciousness. Silence again followed the prayer, and we all sensed that the prayer was to be ended. I was disoriented by the experience and recall stumbling out of the room and immediately going to the nursery to be in touch with new life.

The following day, I was surprised to see the patient's name still listed. I had been told during my visit that she had less than four hours to live. To everyone's amazement, however, she later came back to consciousness and ate a final meal with her loving family while sharing her goodbyes. The family told me of this as she again lay unconscious in what was to be her final day. I celebrated their joy with them, and as I left the room the youngest of the sons followed me. He said that he wanted to tell me in private that he wasn't sure what had happened the day before but it felt as if we had been part of something holy. I heartily agreed and appreciated his affirmation of my experience.

Quakers believe that all moments and places are holy. The Spirit does not remain behind when we leave the Quaker meetinghouse. But the question is: How do we bring awareness of that holiness into the rooms of the world? How do we ourselves stay open to it so that it might flow through us?

In a peace lecture at Antioch University where I presently teach,

a visiting Catholic priest said he thought that a young unrecognized Dali Lama would have great difficulty coming to awareness
of his holiness if he were born in the United States today. The
reasoning of the priest was that the young priest would be so
bombarded by advertising, stimulating entertainment, and television that it would take a long time for the young Dali to come to
his holy awareness.[4] In that thought, I believe, lies the answer to
the previous question: How do we stay open to the Spirit? We
must create and enter the silence to meet the Spirit, to be fed, led,
and nurtured by the One who loves us.

When I worked in a Quaker hospital one of the nurses in the
Intensive Care Unit said that everyone gave a sigh of relief as
soon as I walked onto the floor. Rationally that made no sense
because they were the ones who knew how to give excellent professional care. Yet, my understanding is that I brought to them
something they had no time for. They had no time to simply be
quiet. To work within the demands of that hospital I had to take
time out during almost every hour to meditate. I believe what
that nurse experienced was the fruit of that meditative time.

Out of that belief, I worked with the supervisors to teach the
nurses to meditate and to give them the needed time. In meeting
for unprogrammed worship, Friends sit in silence together in the
presence of the Spirit. I understand this as one form of communion. Yet Friends also spend quiet time alone. This is the piece of
Quaker understanding that I attempted to teach the nurses.

Quiet time by itself is not necessarily quieting. Often when I
teach others to meditate, when I ask them just to see what happens when they are quiet, a thousand thoughts suddenly demand
their attention. To change quiet time to centering meditation, we
need to focus. I have found in my work that what one focuses on
varies with the make-up and experience of the individual.

Some major spiritual traditions focus on following the breath.
Thich Nhat Hanh, a well-known Vietnamese Buddhist priest,
has a simple meditation that adds words to that focus. It goes,

"Breathing in I calm my body, breathing out I smile."[5] Others focus on a spiritual word or phrase such as the Jesus prayer. Often the longer form—"Lord, Jesus Christ, Son of God, have mercy on me a sinner"—is used as a mantra to turn one's thoughts toward the Christ.[6] The repeated words of a familiar psalm can also be calming. For others, a walk in nature or soothing music are most effective. My own beginning attempts with meditation were with a flickering candle flame.

One of the physicians of our hospital asked me to teach him to meditate. I tried to teach him my way of simply entering into the stillness. But he had a brilliant mind that was constantly active, and it soon became apparent that simply sitting in silence was not going to work for him. After months of trial and error we found that the most effective way for him to meditate was to listen through earphones to his beloved classical music while he actually rode a bicycle up the coastal mountains. At that time, it was the only way he could find to calm his demanding mind. Meditation for him was active rest.

These various methods are not the final destination, but doors into the presence of the Spirit. The Holy Spirit is the source of both calmness and energy. But first the noise of the world and the mind must be silenced. Then the quieter voice within might be heard.

While doing research for my doctorate, I found that persons who learned to meditate to diminish their physical pain often also experienced life-changing, psychospiritual shifts as a result of simply entering the silence. Within the silence they came to deeper understandings and clarity. As a result of the internal shifts their relationships with the external world also shifted. Life was lived at a different pace, friends and family were more highly valued. The need to control diminished and the awareness of the beauty in the world increased.[7]

For the subjects in my research, this all happened without a goal. Meditation teachers often emphasize that there should not be a goal for any meditation beyond meditation itself. Those of us involved in care giving must meditate, in part, to cultivate the fruits of the Spirit. Then through us, hopefully, the Spirit can come into the lives of others.

The nurses that I taught were given permission to take quiet breaks of only a few minutes in the stairwell next to the intensive care unit as they needed it. Many found that a few minutes of meditation can have a powerful impact on their way of being in the world. My own hunger for meditative time requires that I have more extensive meditation. But if I can find this extended time in the early hours of the day then the brief moments of pulling out of the external world can be quite effective.

In time we become more like those with whom we associate. Time spent with the Spirit allows us to have more of the qualities of the Spirit. As it is written of Friends in the first chapter of the London Book of Discipline (1960), "they might be the prisms through which the Divine Light passes."[8] Relying more on the Spirit, they might relinquish that which they formerly tried to control. More in touch with the rhythms of life, they might be less hurried and delight in more beauty. That which has fallen into empty ritual might again be spirit-filled. What William Penn wrote of early Friends might it be said of each pastoral care giver, "They were changed men [and women] themselves before they went out to change others."[9]

That of God Within the Care Receiver

One expects to find the Spirit of God in the crashing of the ocean's wave against the rocks, in beautiful music, in grand cathedrals, or rolling wooded hills. But I smile with delight when I remember also finding the Wisdom of the Spirit in young, sexually active adolescents who sought help in the Adolescent Clinics of Indianapolis, Indiana. Without a doubt, they have been the most influential teachers of my life.

In her leadership in work with women in prisons in the 1800s, Elizabeth Fry wrote the following:

> Much depends on the spirit in which the visitor enters upon her work. It must be the spirit, not of judgment, but of mercy. She must not say in her heart, I am more holy than thou; but must rather keep in perpetual remembrance that "all have sinned, and come short of the glory of God" —that, therefore, great pity is due from us even to the greatest transgressors among our fellow-creatures. . . . The good principle in the hearts of many abandoned persons may be compared to the few remaining sparks of a nearly extinguished fire. By means of the utmost care and attention, united with the most gentle treatment, these may yet be fanned into a flame, but under the operation of a rough and violent hand, they will presently disappear, and may be lost forever. . . .[10]

The remaining sparks that Elizabeth Fry found in the imprisoned women, I also found in the young women of the adolescent clinics. I called those sparks "the Wisdom within."

What often brought the adolescents to the clinics, where I got to meet them as counselor, was that they were using sexual intercourse as a means of seeking intimacy and identity without much thought being given to the future costs. I did not see that choice to be of the Spirit. But often God uses our weaknesses and vulnerabilities to help us see greater possibilities for our lives. I saw this happen for these young ones.

I met them just as I was entering the world of pastoral counseling. Quite honestly, the difficulties of the lives of these inner-city teenagers initially overwhelmed me. With them I learned that there isn't always a choice in life between good and bad decisions, but sometimes between decisions that are the best that the circumstances allow.

As I realized that I did not have clear answers for the complex dilemmas of their lives, I relied on the advice of my supervisor who suggested that I just listen very closely and let them teach me. As far as I could see, that is all that I did for months. Then the director of the clinic asked what I was doing that was so effective. She said that she noticed that a high number of clients that I was working with were getting themselves back in school (a number were junior high drop-outs) and actively making healthier sexual choices. I remember shrugging my shoulders and replying with a confused smile that these must be "minor miracles."

As I was completing my degree in pastoral counseling, I chose to focus my master's thesis on exploring why these young people had started to make wiser choices for their lives. My understanding follows.

The wisdom was always available to them as it is to each of us. God's Spirit cares for the well being of each human being, but as individuals we have to be quiet long enough to hear the still, small voice. These children in adult bodies lived lives of overwhelming difficulties and little silence. As all sentient beings do, they longed for intimacy, a caring presence, and a loving touch. They didn't know how to satisfy these longings in healthy ways, nor did they know how to access the loving guidance they carried within them. Some combination of pain and courage caused them to seek external help. When they came to me and momentarily overwhelmed me, I thought all I did was listen. But now I understand that in quietly listening I allowed them enough silence to access the Wisdom within them as Fox wrote, "confounding deceit" and "awakening the witness" referred to in the Introduction.

First, I went into their individual hells with them. Carl Rogers (1961) writes of this experience in male terms:

> I would like him to know that I stand with him in this tight, constricted little world, and that I can look upon it relatively unafraid. Perhaps I can make it a safer world for him. . . . I would like to go with him on the fearful journey into himself, into the buried fear, and hate, and love which has never been able to flow in him. . . .[12]

To join the other person requires a real faith in the Spirit and in the other person's ability to work his or her own way toward the Light. A brother or sister of Spirit who is willing to join the estranged one on this journey incarnates the redemptive love of the Spirit of Christ. The freedom from bondage begins when they who are in bondage perceive the presence of one who is willing to join them in their world and hold them in unconditional positive regard. If the care giver embraces this acceptance, then growth toward fuller human functioning occurs. Wayne Oates refers to the fuller human functioning as "maturity" brought about through the nourishment of love and acceptance.[13]

With Rogers, I found that if the care giver is genuine, accepts the adolescents as persons of unconditional self-worth, is able to feel what it is like to be in the others' world and is able to convey this to the young people, then gradually the adolescents are able to explore and accept the totality of themselves. Persons in such intensely personal relationships, even for a relatively limited amount of hours, show significant changes in personality, attitudes, and behavior.

When another, especially significant other, listens with acceptance to the persons in need, then it is easier for them to listen to themselves. They can begin to accept the parts of themselves that have been rejected in the past as too awful to name or to face. They can listen to their anger, their shame, and their guilt. As they listen to these negative parts of themselves and express them to one who doesn't reject them but rather holds them in unconditional positive regard, then they become more accepting of themselves. They come to know more who they are, and they are open to change. In the presence of an accepting other, they can begin to feel joy in who they experience themselves to be rather than to feel fear.

Acceptance does not mean much unless there is also understanding. Empathic understanding is seeing the world as the other sees it while still keeping one's boundaries. It is allowing adolescents to be the guides in their world, their internal frame of reference, so that the care giver is able to know through them what seems so fearful, bizarre, or horrible. To be accepting is to fully receive them. It is to be sensitive to their shared experience so that one doesn't trample on sensitive ground. This may open up the pastoral care giver to new experiences so her understanding may also change. To journey into the other's world in such a nonjudgmental manner allows the care receiver to have the freedom to look into the nooks and crannies of his or her often buried experience. As the adolescent's world becomes understandable to the care giver, he or she can reflectively comment on what the care receiver already knows, thus assuring the other of mutual understanding.

Furthermore, the care giver can also give meaning to a teenager's experience. This again allows adolescents to explore the reality of themselves in their world and to make choices and changes with a supportive, caring presence, trusting positive judgments that arise in the counseling process.. The care giver can help care receivers identify blind spots, achieve new, different perspectives and become aware of unused opportunities. To be accepted in such a manner acknowledges the receiver of the care giving as a person of worth.

In the atmosphere of unconditional acceptance, teenagers move away from feeling unacceptable to themselves and undeserving of respect. They move toward conceiving themselves to be persons of worth, capable of self-direction. Their sense of self-esteem and self-efficacy increase.

As self-esteem increases, they find themselves to be more trustworthy. Before therapy they would ask themselves what others think they should do in a given situation. They would wonder what their parents or teacher would have them do. They would act in response to others' expectations. During this counseling process they begin to trust their own experience and begin to make decisions based on that experience. Therefore their behavioral options were increased to include their own possibilities in determining the most satisfying behavior.

In his book *Reaching Out*, Henri Nouwen names this open acceptance as hospitality:

> Hospitality means the creation of a free space where the stranger can enter and become a friend. Hospitality is not to change people, but to offer them space where change can take place . . . to open a wide spectrum of options for choice and commitment . . . where strangers can discover themselves as created free; free to sing their own songs, speak their own languages, dance their own dances. Hospitality is an attitude, one that offers a space where people are encouraged to listen with attention and care to the voices speaking in their own center.[14]

To gain understanding of my experience with adolescents, I relied heavily on the theory of Carl Rogers. Care giving based on Rogers is much more comparable to the interactions of Jesus in his ministry than to his death on the cross. In the biblical stories of Zacchaeus, Nicodemus, Peter, the woman caught in adultery, the woman at the well, and even Judas, Jesus portrays the love of God in relationship to persons. In his chapter on "Guilt and Forgiveness" (1956), Carroll Wise wrote of Jesus,

> He could offer a relationship which might help them to respond with acceptance and love, rather than hostility. Because he did not fear being hurt he could be compassionate, understanding, accepting and self-giving. The Cross is the supreme demonstration of this redemptive attitude.[15]

If we enter the session with compassion and concern, the care receiver can see in us the reflection of God's love and compassion. If we enter to listen and to hear, the care receiver can see reflected in us a God who listens. If we enter the room with acceptance and understanding, the person no longer has to defend herself and in the space provided can begin to hear and trust the gift of wisdom within. Nurturing and opening "that of God" within ourselves allows us to recognize, meet, and nurture "that of God" within the other.

That of God in the Relationship

Forty plus years of living had not prepared me for life in the big city. When I was considering leaving my little village of Yellow Springs, Ohio, to develop a pastoral care department in a Quaker-run hospital in Philadelphia, a friend asked me, "How do you have that much courage?" I appreciate his question now, but at the time I did not know how much courage it would take.

Many unexpected changes occurred for me, but one of the major changes concerned divisions of class. I found that economic and social classes which had mingled together in my village were almost totally separated financially, geographically, and educationally in the larger city. As I walked among people at both ends of the spectrum in the city, I found fear and anger. In the gulf between, I felt pain.

With the encouragement of a tiny ecumenical group that had gathered to study Job, I chose to walk directly into that pain. A Quaker friend in the Job group, who was on his way to Somalia with the American Friends Service Committee, told me that several times he had found people creating meaningful lives in the midst of what appeared to be overwhelming chaos. Believing him, I determined to find such people.

That night I wrote the following in my journal:

> Oh wonder of wonders—absolutely precious time with the Job group. I see that I go into the pain of Philly the way one goes into the pain of the body—be present—take the creative, healing energy—see the wonder of the people—

listen to them—as one goes into the experience of the
dying—those people tonight—especially David, think
your way is the hope of the world—you felt the pain of
Philadelphia, you cry, you cannot tolerate it so you
retreat to the Spirit . . . I felt whole tonight . . . the moon
is beautiful—I have found people who understood of what
I speak and who help me understand me.

The stage was set for the next event. Just as I began meeting with
the Job group, the Vice President of Development at Jeanes Hospital arranged a lunch for me for the following week with the
Quaker director of the new Lucretia Mott Center (Lucretia Mott
was a nineteenth century Quaker abolitionist and feminist). This
center is in the portion of north Philadelphia known as "the Badlands," an area where most of the young men don't live beyond
their teenage years. The director said that he was able to determine the needs of the young men, but that he feared the women
of the area weren't able to trust him enough to share. Energized by
the experience of the Job group and informed by my earlier work
with the inner city adolescents, I quickly offered to meet with the
women.

My expectations, my prejudiced expectations, were that I had
offered to enter into a group of thirty angry, Afro-American
women. Instead I walked into a room of wonderfully open women,
mostly of Spanish descent. I had a Spanish interpreter with me.
The one black woman who was there was stunning in her beauty
and part of the Women's Revitalization Project (WRP) that had
just built a housing unit in the area to provide quality living space
for single women who were drug free.

The women of this neighborhood group amazed me. They were
like flowers that break through the asphalt in the early spring.
Eight women gathered. Three were in education beyond high
school. They told me stories of their lives. I learned that residents
in the "Badlands" watch television in an upstairs bedroom
because if they watch it in the more exposed downstairs family

room, a bullet might come through the window and hit them. The mothers in the room only had daughters. They said that they were glad because sons didn't have a chance. The boys got caught up so early in the drug trade that they didn't survive. The woman from the Women's Revitalization Organization told me that the neighborhood was seventy percent female.

When I had walked the streets of that neighborhood at four in the afternoon, drugs were being sold openly on the streets. In response to this situation, these women referred to evening meetings they would have on the street corners. They explained that they would gather 30 to 75 women to just be together on the street corner at night and by doing that they interrupted the drug trade. It's difficult to sell drugs with 75 women in your way. The woman from the WRP said that by doing this in conjunction with the police and Temple University, the women of her community were able to reclaim the neighborhood where she lived. She offered to teach the women at the Lucretia Mott Center how to work with the police and other groups to increase their own power.

I was impressed with the hope that these women had in a situation that I had seen as painful and hopeless when I had stood too far away. When I asked them where their ability to survive and to move into their future came from, they said, with only one exception, it was from their mothers. This was a powerful statement on the effect of good parenting in even the most difficult situations. And the woman who was the exception said that it was her grandmother who had empowered her because her mother had become an addict.

I went into North Philly and found these amazing women. They preserved hope and life in the midst of that which overwhelmed me. These people were fruits of the poverty of North Philadelphia and believed that they had the power to change things. In the heart of the danger and the poverty, I found such strong evidence of life. I drove out that night, down the selected streets these women told me were the safest, with their infectious hope replacing my pain. The Spirit was in me and clearly already in them.

A massage therapist in my village of Yellow Springs taught me once how to go into painful places in my body. She taught me that when I fear the pain and isolate it by tightening up around it, the pain only increases. But when I enter the pain and soften the boundaries, then the pain loses its power and simply becomes a sensation.

As long as I tightened around the fear of the pain of the big city, the pain became worse for me. When I finally entered into the pain, crossed the boundaries, the pain within me turned into something productive and was able to meet and empower their hope while being empowered myself.

After two hours of listening to these women we moved toward closure. One of them said, "It seems like it would help us a lot, if someone came in and just listened, just understood." Another said as we closed, "At least we're not alone anymore." And it struck me how alone it must feel when most of us, myself included, stay out of the world of those who are marginal, whether it be through the message of poverty, mental illness, handicaps, or imprisonment. When we stay out we leave them to preserve the hope alone when we may have the means of empowering the hope. And I didn't want to leave them alone anymore.

I get to do the same thing when people die. Some of the most wonderful, meaningful times of a person's life occur as they approach death. The roles fall away, the masks are lifted, and who a person is and what he or she most values become evident both to the patient and the ones who journey with them. There is pain and sorrow but if one tightens up and avoids being present because of the fear of the pain and sorrow, then the rare opportunities of grace, hope, and love are lost for everyone involved. North Philly still has poverty, still has violence. But I also know wonderful people with hope and possibilities. I see the world differently because I now know them.

Walking into these situations can at first appear fearful, awful, unchangeable, threatening. We are sadly most limited when we don't walk into the marginal situations because of fear, because of a need to protect ourselves. People who are unfamiliar, speak another language, have another color, wear a different type of clothes, and live a life style different from ours, sometimes make us afraid and even hostile.

Our Biblical heritage teaches us that sometimes these guests may be carrying precious gifts with them which they are eager to reveal to a receptive one. When Abraham received three strangers at Mamre and offered them water, bread, and a fine tender calf, they revealed themselves to him as the Lord announcing that Sarah, his wife, would give birth to a son (Genesis 18:1-15). When the widow of Zarephath offered food and shelter to Elijah, he revealed himself as a man of God offering her an abundance of oil and meal and raising her son from the dead. When the two travelers of Emmaus invited the stranger, who had joined them on the road, to stay with them for the night, he made himself known in the breaking of the bread as the Lord and Savior (Luke 24:13-35).[16]

By turning away from the suffering and struggle of the poor and marginal, we may have shut the door on the stranger who is our means to grace. Then we miss the God-experiencing opportunity. The distinction between the host and guest proves to be artificial and evaporates in the recognition of the new found unity. Those who share the lot of the poor, and with them struggle for justice, may be discovering something about what it means to be a human being that others of us have largely lost in our obsession with competition, personal advancement, and consumerism. Through their eyes we are able to see that there is another way which leads to life. In their struggle, their hopefulness may convince us that change is possible and necessary in our society. And they, by their striving, set in motion a process by which not only their world, but ours can be transformed. We need to listen to Matthew 10:39, that "those who would save their lives by living to self will lose them."

On my bulletin board I keep an unreferenced quote of Rufus Jones. He wrote:

> A new way must be found and it must be a way that over-comes evil with good, that conquers darkness with light, that defeats error with truth and that achieves its gains and advances by the mighty co-operative power of love.[17]

What I experienced that evening, in North Philadelphia, was the "mighty co-operative power of love." Joining those women in their struggle brought the Spirit in new ways to us all.

Years ago, John Woolman, a well-known Quaker, had been drawn to enter the world of the Native Americans of the Delaware nation. He was drawn in love to them as he recognized that their ancestors had been the original owners of the land which the Europeans were now claiming. Across the language barrier he believed that some of them were acquainted with the Divine power. One night he chose to pray without the aid of an interpreter. When one of the Indians was asked if he understood the words, he replied that he didn't but that he "loved to feel where the words come from."[18] When, in our care giving role, we enter a world different than ours, though we can't know everything about the language or the culture, we can take into that world our faith in the source of love and acceptance. Quakers believe that we can listen and speak out of that place within ourselves and thus reach "that of God" within them too. Wherever we are, in the emergency room, in pain, in clinics, even in "the Badlands," we gather together in a holy place in God's presence, "answering to that of God," as Fox would put it..

In a book of daily readings for Quakers, *Daily Readings*, Janet Scott has written:

> As we act in obedience to the Light Within, we may become mediators through whom God's love is known.

We are called to share the task of God, to share the grief
and the joy, the sorrow, the self-giving, and the reconciliation. . . . To do God's work we do not have to be good
people. . . . Our hope and confidence is not in ourselves
but in God whose grace is sufficient to complete the
work . . . we find that at the heart of the darkness, at the
profoundest depths of the human anguish, God is already
present, already strengthening and comforting. . . .[19]

Another doctor whom I worked with observed how natural it
was for a Quaker to give care in an ecumenical setting. I believe
that hers was an excellent observation. Believing in "the God
within," we have fewer barrier to hearing the other's words, wisdom, and faith. The Quaker emphasis on the continued presence
of the Spirit allows us to know that we do not walk into new
difficulties alone, but that God will already be there. There is "God
within" the situation. And our tradition has taught us that to walk
in this Light we must continually return to its source. To be the
efficacious mediator of the Spirit's wisdom and love, we must be
mindful to access the "God within" ourselves.

Living in the Spirit, as the Abington Friends Meeting's invitation states, we as Quaker care givers can welcome all persons of
any faith or of none. We can walk with each, faithfully trusting
"that of God" will be in us, in the other, and in the relationship.

The words of a Quaker friend of mine, who trained for chaplaincy at another Philadelphia hospital, speak of this experientially. She wrote:

This work forces me to cross all boundaries—racial,
social, religious. . . . I have to see myself and the patient
as belonging to One People. Pastoral Care begins in the
recognition of the One Circle of the People of God. In
crisis, our theological differences fade to insignificance. In
the end it is only our shared humanity that counts—a common life, and death.[20]

To that description I would add a loving Spirit who is present to the one who cares, the one who receives, and those who seek together.

Notes

1. Elton Trueblood, *The New Man for Our Time* (New York: Harper and Row, 1970), 60.

2. Thomas Kelly, *Reality of the Spirit World*, Pendle Hill Pamphlet 21 (Wallingford, PA: Pendle Hill Publications, 1942), 41.

3. Hannah Whitall Smith, "The Unselfishness of God," #77 *Christian Faith and Practice of the London Yearly Meeting of the Religious Society of Friends* (London: Headley Brothers Ltd.,1960).

4. Wayne Teasdale, Antioch College Summer Peace Institute at Yellow Springs, Ohio: August 1998.

5. Thich Nhat Hanh, *The Miracle of Mindfulness: A Manual on Meditation* (Boston: Beacon Press, 1976), 16.

6. Morton Kelsey, *The Other Side of Silence: A Guide to Christian Meditation* (New York: The Missionary Society of St. Paul the Apostle, 1976), 114.

7. Jane Brown, "Psychospiritual Openings of Meditating Pain Patients: A Phenomenological Study" (Unpublished doctoral dissertation, 1996).

8. *Christian Faith and Practice of the London Yearly Meeting of the Religious Society of Friends* (London: Headley Brother Ltd, 1960), Introduction to Chapter 1.

9. William Penn, *William Penn's Preface to Fox's Journal* (1964) in *Christian Faith and Practice*, #16.

10. Elizabeth Fry, in Linda Hill Renfer, *Daily Readings from Quaker Writings Ancient and Modern* (Grants Pass, OR: Serenity Press, 1988), 71.

11. Jane Brown, "The Impact of the Counseling Relationship on Self Efficacy, Self Esteem and the Sexual Choices of Early Adolescents" (Unpublished master's thesis, 1988).

12. Carl Rogers, *On Becoming a Person* (Boston: Houghton Mifflin, 1961), 66-67.

13. Wayne Oates, quoted by E. Glenn Hinson, *Seekers after Mature Faith* (Waco, TX: Word Books, 1968), 177.

14. Henri Nouwen, *Reaching Out* (New York: Doubleday & Co. Inc., 1975), 51.

15. Carroll Wise, Psychiatry & the Bible (New York: Harper and Brothers, 1956), 83.

16. Nouwen, *Reaching Out,* 47.

17. Attributed to Rufus Jones.

18. John Woolman, *Journal* (Philadelphia: Friends' Book Association, 1892), 170-172.

19. Janet Scott in Renfer, *Daily Readings,* 83.

20. Zoe White, *A Quaker Theology of Pastoral Care,* Pendle Hill Pamphlet 281 (Wallingford, PA: Pendle Hill Publications, 1988), 7.

XIV. Gleanings from a Quaker Chaplain's Stories

Worth Hartman

The Day My Daddy Died

I T'S 6:30 A.M. ON SUNDAY MORNING and I'm at my usual spot. I'm bent over a note book surrounded by books, loose sheets, and open file folders, trying to decide what to say when I stand up to preach in four hours. I'm really behind this morning. Let's see: the body, Christ's church, and we all have gifts. Then the phone rings. That's really strange, so early. In a couple of minutes Nancy comes in the study and tries to tell me something in a quavering, emotional, strained voice, "Worth, Elden just called. Sad news. Your Dad has died. They think he had a sudden heart attack."

"What! Come on. This is some kind of practical joke. Very funny," I think to myself.

This nightmare doesn't seem to be going away. Nancy hasn't flip-flopped in peals of laughter yet. This is a pretty sick joke. I'd think she would have better taste. Come on. Come on. Somebody tell me the joke is over.

My Dad can't be dead. A heart attack? His heart is fine. He doesn't have any problems. This is some mistake. Heart attacks happen to old guys with bad hearts. My dad is fine. He's never been sick. This can't be. I'm going to call and find out for myself. I don't know why Nancy wouldn't let me talk to them. This must be a joke.

"Hello Elden. What is this stuff about Dad dying?" He tells me about it. Dad was lying in bed early this morning and just made a strange noise. Mom thought he was sick to his stomach but he didn't respond when shaken. Cousin Darrell happened to be staying the night. He gave Dad CPR but it didn't work. They took him to Community South Hospital and tried more CPR on the way.

"Mom, what is this. What's going on?"

She answers me in a voice filled with emotion, overcome, in shock. She's not quite making sense.

"You stay there and preach. You have your duty there. We're OK here." No way I'm going to preach this morning. I'm getting over there.

"We're coming, Mom. I'll be there in a little bit."

I call up Bill Taylor, a leader at the church, to tell him my Dad has died and I need to be with my family.

"I'm so sorry Worth. No problem. We'll take care of it this morning. Go ahead and be with your family. That's where you need to be now."

"Thanks. Yes. I'll be in touch as I learn more."

It seemed to take forever to get ready to go. I quickly threw some stuff together. With my family in tow I took the forty-minute journey that seemed like years.

When I walked through the door into the place I've known as home since I was six, I knew this was for real. The tears, weightiness, gravity, numbness, sense of crisis, panic, raw emotion. Oh dear God, it must be real. I go back to my parent's bedroom. Dad's not here, he's not around. This is strange.

He's always here when Mom is. When I come to this house they are both around. They are always together. Where's Dad? He must be dead. This nightmare is real.

Who do we call? What do we do? What are the plans? The calls start pouring in as the word spreads. Grover's dead. Could this be? "We're so sorry." "How did it happen?" The tears, shock, and disbelief wash over me every time I share this news, yet the telling makes it all the more real and true.

Then I start hearing the lines that would begin to drive me nuts. The more I hear them the more I'm filled with anger and bitterness.

"If you have to go that's the way to do it, all at once, not know what hit you."

"He died with his boots on."

"He went out active and busy as ever."

"None of this slow, debilitating illness. That 's how I'd want to go."

"No long, drawn out suffering."

"Out in a blaze of glory after a long, good life."

That's fine for all of you to say but I didn't get to say good-bye. Come on. Is there really some good way to die? You may want to go that way. What about me? This isn't fair, this is too abrupt. I had no warning. Go die yourself if it's so great. What the hell do you know about my grief?

"Yes. Thank You. Uh huh. Yes, it was very sudden, very unexpected. No warning, no previous problems, a shock to us. Yes, he was a wonderful man. Yes, he'll be missed."

I remember my parents' pastor coming to the house after he finished the church service. We formed a circle of prayer. I was really comforted by his words. He offered a healing prayer about Dad and eternal life and Dad teaching us something about bringing God's kingdom here on earth. What ever it was, it felt good.

It's time to make arrangements. This is a big deal. My Mom is going on in a pretty stream-of-consciousness way about honoring his greatness and that his spirit is still with us. The United Methodist Church press agent is handling the information and press release. He seems to have that pretty well together. He's got the time, place, who's involved, how to honor this big, influential, well-loved man who also happens to be my father. There is a public, state-event, side to this. How do we figure everything out?

Folks started coming by the house. The word is spreading. We're already having the visitation. One friend seemed to stay all afternoon. The food is pouring in as well as the flowers.

Then comes the visit to the funeral home. Mom says to the guy, "You didn't know my husband. He's to be cremated. It's life in the spirit that matters. We're planning something simple, a memorial service, a celebration of his life, honoring his greatness."

This somber, suited guy sat a mile across the room behind his fortress desk. "You don't want to get contaminated by our grief?" I fume to myself.

"No, Mrs. Hartman, I didn't know your husband personally." Bla bla blaa . . .

Come on out and be real, buddy. Come out from behind your fortress and be human, you cardboard character.

"Would you like to see the body?" asks the guy behind the desk.

Brother Elden—no; Brother Lowell—no; Mom—no; Worth—mumble, mumble. I'm weighing this inside for many minutes. What meaningless small talk this guy can make.

"YES I DO!!!" I must be different but yes, give me my Daddy. Did he really die? I wait a while for them to get him ready and bring him. They are wheeling him toward me. No, not in the office. My family doesn't want to see him. Just me. There, that's better.

Daddy, is that really you? It sort of looks like you and yet it doesn't. Your mouth looks strange, open like that. It's like when we used to catch you napping in the big chair, even snoring, and then you wouldn't admit it. You said you were just resting your eyes. You're so still, pale, and white. You're naked under that sheet. Should I look? There was so much more to say, so much more to do. There is so much you're going to miss. Julian was just born ten weeks ago. I'm going to miss you. I still need you. I was just starting to try to know you in some deeper way. This is too sudden, too soon, too abrupt. If you'd been sick a while maybe I could have cared for you some. You could have received some tender care. Like the night you were visiting, you were tired and I tucked you in my bed for a nap. Why did you go so quickly? I want to stroke you and hold you. Good-bye Daddy. I'm wiggling your toe as I go, a kind of funny, silly thing to do now. Not too dignified. You really were mortal. We feel more even now. You really are dead. Good-bye Daddy.

Gleanings

"The Day My Daddy Died" is my foundational grief story. I find this experience colors and shapes my work as a hospital chaplain. My ministry, at its core, is being witness, companion, friend, and interpreter to patients, families, staff, and the community. I stand with people as they live through or recall grief experiences. I witness grief ranging from the most extreme form, such as parents identifying their teenager daughter's body after a car accident, to more subtle forms of grief, such as the elderly grieving loss of their own independence and mobility. I can recognize aspects of grief: denial, anger, and depression, bargaining, and acceptance because I felt them all November 13, 1988, the day my father died. As I live and work out of that experience I carry inner knowledge of disbelief at sudden unexpected death. I remember my need to see my father's dead body. I recall the minister's comforting ritual and words of prayer and presence. I know the sadness of unfulfilled longings, unfinished business, and unspoken good-byes.

I relive my anger at stupid remarks uttered by well-meaning visitors. My grief experience gifts me with empathy for those I serve as chaplain. My caring comes from identification and a sense of connection. The grief of each individual I see is unique and their own, yet I know its outline, its flavor, its form. We have something in common. Although I have not felt the pain of losing a child, I have two children and know how precious and vulnerable they are. I have not had a spouse of fifty years die but I watched my mother's life change after she lost her husband of forty-six years of marriage.

The art of chaplaincy is to witness grief, empathize with those who grieve, but not absorb the grief. I have been asked how I sustain my energy and my call as I daily witness tragedy and loss. My response is threefold:

1. The grief I witness is not my grief. I may recall my own grief, cry with people but in that moment it is someone else who has lost a loved one, not I. My father died eleven years ago.
2. I share my responses, needs, and tough situations with colleagues, friends, and co-workers. In my openness and vulnerability I can find support, encouragement, and, if needed, correction. I was not alone when my father died.
3. God stands with me. I am a sign of God's caring and love. God knows this grief and pain through the death of his own child, Jesus. God and the body of Christ were present for me when my father died. "Come to me, all who labor and are heavy laden, and I will give you rest." (Matthew 11:28)

My own experience of grief is my best teacher and guide as I minister to others. I remember going to my first grief workshop. I was a brand new pastor, I had already done several funerals and now I was filled with new insight and information on the grieving process. I had heard from the experts, including Chaplains Dick Bailey and Bev Faulk from Methodist Hospital. (Five years later they both would become my mentors and teachers in chaplaincy training.) Returning to my church I was eager to share this newfound knowledge. The daytime women's circle indulged me and let me "take over" two of their regular meeting times to offer a two-part grief workshop. I would only have a few hours, no time to share all the information I had gleaned during my day-long workshop. I would have to give them a condensed version.

When the day came, we placed the tables in a large horseshoe and the women arrived and some even brought their friends. I am the young paster, filled with workshop knowledge surrounded by women in their seventies and eighties. These women had lost their spouses, children, babies. These wise women began to teach me, when I learned to be quiet and ask for their stories and experience. My father died the end of that year. My head and book learning became seasoned and challenged in the shattering, sobering, deepening experience of my own father's death. My head knowledge became heart wisdom through my father's death. As I recalled my efforts to teach about death and grief I felt chastened and humbled by my own grief experience. My own loss opened my heart and mind to new wisdom. This was the wisdom of hard experience and the wisdom of the church full of teachers that surrounded me. They initiated me into the mysteries of grief and survival.

I recall another occasion of coming to the women's group to introduce a new member-based pastoral care program. I would organize, teach, and support these women as they went forth to visit the sick and the shut-ins. They would come to meetings and share their experiences of their visiting and thereby deepen their skills. After politely listening to my persuasive and comprehensive presentation, the group leader emphatically reported that during the previous month the group sent twenty-five cards, made ten visits, sent numerous flower arrangements, and served a funeral dinner. And besides, she added, these ladies don't like to go to night meetings. There went my grand plan, my vision for a member-based pastoral care program. It was already going on right underneath my nose. These women were caring for others out of their own deep experience of loss, grief, and community. I just needed to see it, bless it and become a part of it.

A Quaker understanding of pastoral care is grounded in experience, direct, in a personal transforming experience of self and God. This guides and reflects my own testimony to the primacy of my own grief experience as I do chaplaincy. It also echoes my strong sense of God's call and God's guiding and equipping presence in my life and ministry. George Fox, the founder of the Religious Society of Friends, speaks in his journal of the realization that knowledge obtained from books and intellectual discourse is not adequate preparation for ministry. Only the direct, transforming, equipping light of Christ Jesus can answer our needs and ready us for our call and ministry in the world. Fox proclaimed he knew this "experimentally," from his own experience.[1]

One of the people George Fox witnessed to in 1652 was Margaret Fell, who later became his wife. Amidst the contradictory, competing faiths, sects, and creeds of the day, George Fox called Margaret Fell to heed her own direct, inward experience of God. He challenged her:

> You will say, "Christ saith this, the apostles say this"; but what cans't thou say? Art thou a child of Light and hast thou walked in the Light, and what thou speakest is it inwardly from God?[2]

Robert Barclay wrote Quaker's foundational theological work, *Apology*. Even this well educated, intellectual, systematic theologian and writer affirms the centrality of direct experience:

> . . . for what I have written comes more from my heart than from my head; what I have heard with the ears of my soul, and seen with my inward eyes and what my hands have handled of the Word of Life, what hath been inwardly manifested to me of the things of God.[3]

A more contemporary Friend, Rufus Jones, discusses a Quaker approach to ministry and pastoral care this way:

> Our religion begins with life, not with theory or report. The life is mightier than the book that reports it. The most important thing in the world is to get our faith out of the book and out of a creed and into living experience and deed of life.[4]

A central task for me, as a chaplain, is to continue to integrate my own grief experience with my faith, my identity, and with my ministry as a chaplain to others who are grieving. New losses require new work on my part. This past winter, as chaplain, I dealt with death from weather-related automobile accidents. In three different incidents an eight-year-old, two teens, and a local pastor/volunteer chaplain died. I had to find ways to process those deaths. As I do that important work for myself, I am aware of my own grief process. As I am more self-aware I am a more effective chaplain, a clearer channel of God's healing.

The next section describes an afternoon of my ministry as a hospital chaplain. I witness a death and participate in a process of waiting. The names and other identifying information have been changed. There are ways this death stirs memories of my own father's death. I then reflect upon this experience in another section of "Gleanings," exploring Quaker concepts of waiting and leading.

Waiting

It's Friday afternoon; my week is almost gone. I can't believe it's 2:30 already. I have to be out of here by 4:30. I can't pull off my usual flurry of visiting through the supper hour tonight. Two hours left and there is so much remaining to be done. I haven't yet seen the new admissions that Dorothy, my chaplain assistant, talked to this morning. There is a list of "yes's" sitting on my desk, representing patients waiting to see the chaplain. I haven't called Deedee about the grant proposal; the fundraising letters are piled on my floor; and the letter to my volunteer chaplains is still in my head. I haven't revised the salary schedule, claimed the reimbursements I need or even started to call the heart walk leaders I'm supposed to recruit. I've got to set up that certification committee meeting and the volunteer chaplains' training is supposed to occur in the spring. It's already June. So much work waiting.

My pager starts to beep. Thank goodness! I may be saved from this paralysis of undone administrative tasks. It's Debi on the medical floor.

"Worth, we have a patient, Mr. Underwood in 236, who is going fast. We just admitted him this afternoon. His blood pressure is dropping rapidly. It would be good if you could be here. We've called his family but they are not here yet."

"I'll be right up," I reply.

All the while I am thinking: "OK, Worth. You need to let go of this stuff on your desk. Don't delay. Don't procrastinate. Don't try to squeeze in one more task before you go. This is Debi who just called you. She's on your board, she's your friend, and she doesn't often call you. Move, jump, and respond, you're already late. People in need are waiting."

I work in a 125-bed community hospital. It's a short trip upstairs to the medical floor. I'm there in a minute. Debi ushers me into the room. Mr. Jesse Underwood is in the bed by the door. He's got short-cropped hair, the stubble of a beard on his face. The white sheet is pulled up close to his chin. His head is tilted back—mouth open—his breathing slow and labored. His eyes are glazed over and distant. It's a familiar pose to me, the look of cancer ready to take another life, waiting for the last resistance to go.

The nursing staff does not want Jesse to die alone. Sharon, a nursing aide, is holding his right hand and Debi has moved to his left side. I pull up a chair to the foot of his bed and take my place in what has become a circle of concern. Debi checks Jesse's blood pressure and listens to his heartbeat. It's falling quickly. I recall Mr. Underwood's son being paged to return to his father's room right before my beeper went off. Now the staff, and maybe Jesse, are waiting for family, waiting for this circle of concern to widen.

Where is Jesse's family? Will loved ones surround him as he moves from this life to the next? I've been through many hospital death bed scenes. I've seen patients covered with love, comfort, stories, tears, and prayers. I have also seen patients die alone—

families alienated, distant, estranged, absent, or reluctantly present. I know which way I want to go out.

Jesse is going to have some very caring nurses and a chaplain with him, but I always feel like a substitute, a fill-in, a representative of who ought to be here—family. So what is the story? Are Jesse's family temporarily worn out and taking a little break? Maybe something about Jesse's life or personality alienated his family. I know so little about this man, this life that is passing before me. I am called to be a witness to this most important passage from life to death to eternal life. Yet I know so little about Jesse's life on earth or his life to come. I'm waiting for answers, waiting for "Thy kingdom come, Thy will be done."

I'm not sure when his family will come, and Jesse is close to death. I can say a prayer as Debi watches over him. Sharon has moved on to other duties.

"Let's say a prayer." Debi and I join hands over Jesse.

God, we ask your care and blessings for Jesse. You know his heart. We know You are a loving, forgiving, compassionate God ready to receive Jesse into Your everlasting arms. Be close to him. Watch over him in this time of transition. May Jesse lean on You, trust in You, and rest in You as his rock and salvation. God, we thank you for Debi and Sharon and all those caring for Jesse today. Use their skills and wisdom for care and healing. May they know themselves as channels of Your love and comfort. God, we ask your support and comfort for Jesse's family today and in the days ahead. Give them strength, faith and hope in You. We pray in Jesus' name who is our friend, our healer, the One in whom we know resurrection and life eternal. Amen.

It's good to pray with Debi. I want Debi and other staff members to know and hear my prayers for them. I feel better, as if I've done something besides waiting.

Oh look, here come some family. Debi introduces me to Jesse's son. With him is a neighbor.

"Hello, I'm Worth Hartman, the chaplain. The nurses called me saying your dad wasn't doing so well. I've been with him a while and we said a prayer. I'm glad you are here."

"Yeah, we were out in the parking lot."

"So they just brought your dad in today?"

"Yeah, we've been taking care of him at home but he got real bad today so we brought him in."

The son settles in, caring for his dad. He takes his place by the head of the bed and the friend sits at Jesse's right side. This son is present and involved emotionally in his dad's death. He has assumed his place as family. I know I feel a sense of relief. I'm not waiting alone. Things are as they should be.

The son is stroking his father's head, talking to him.

"You rest now, Daddy. You're tired. You need your rest. You go ahead and rest. It's OK. Daddy, you've worked so hard. You can rest now. We're right here, Daddy."

This was the son's recurring refrain: "The struggle is over. You have tried your best. Rest now. Rest in peace." The friend is quiet but very attentive, emotion-filled. Both men are tense, somewhat choked and baggy-eyed, with sobs and tears inside, waiting to come out.

We're all watching Jesse, focused on each breath. Every heave of the chest is labored and seems so intentional. He can't last long like this. After one breath there is an unusually long pause. Jesse's son asks, " Is he gone?"

Debi leans over Jesse, her stethoscope hanging to his chest. She listens intently and we all listen with her.

"He still has a heart beat."

Yes, I can hear and see the rasp and rattle of another breath, the upper chest lifting slightly. We all wait for succeeding breaths. Jesse must be willing each one. His son hovers, arranging his pillow, caressing his head.

"You go to sleep now, Daddy, you rest. You're tired. You can rest now. You need your rest. You've fought so hard. You can take it easy now. You just rest now, Daddy."

The son takes his father's hands. Their hands look so much alike. It is hard to tell which hand belongs to which man. These hands are speckled and brown, wrinkled, not gnarled but long and expressive. It hits me how much this father and son look alike. They both are tall, lean, with short dark hair and dark complexion.

"You look a lot like your dad. Your hands there are so alike."

"People say that, I guess I do look like him."

I'm also struck with the emotional connection this son has with his father. There is a tenderness and sense of caretaking with this son that expands upon his brief explanation earlier, "We've been taking care of him at home." I'm thinking back over five years of attending deaths and I can't remember a son as involved physically and emotionally in his father's death. It is usually the daughter, wife, or mother who leaves other duties and comes to wait at the hospital. She waits for word, waits for a change, waits for hope, and waits for death. I am thankful for a son who will be here, will show he cares, will utter soft reassurances to his dying father, words I didn't get to say to my father who died suddenly and unexpectedly eleven years ago.

I tell the son, " I'm really glad you are here and care about your dad so much. He's got a great family. I bet he feels your love and presence right now."

"Yeah, he's been a good dad to me. I want to be with him." The son is quiet. This isn't the sort of deathwatch where the family starts telling me all about the dying one. I'm not hearing great stories or receiving testimonies to this father's goodness. There is just quiet service and attention, which speaks just as loudly of family love and a well-lived life.

Oh, it looks like he's stopped breathing again. Debi checks. No, he is still with us. I just noticed a major blood vessel heading up Jesse's neck. I can see it throbbing, pulsing in and out. I will watch that spot. The pulse will go on after the breathing. I'll try not to get fooled again. I've learned death isn't as clear and precise as I thought it would be. Jesse has no machines or life support prolonging or confusing his death and it is still elusive. There is something of a cat and mouse quality to this watching and waiting, a subtle humor to being fooled, thinking we know or control the moment when death comes.

This can't go on much longer. Jesse's breaths are further and further apart. I want to mark this passing with a prayer. I don't have much of a clue about Jesse and his family's faith, but I feel lots of love and concern between son and father that spoken prayer could voice. I want to give something to this family. I want to consecrate this waiting as something we do in God's watch. I want to acknowledge this family's love and this father's life as gifts from a loving Creator.

"Would it be okay if I said a prayer?" The son nods with permission and relief. I stand by Jesse's head and place a hand on his shoulder. Jesse's son and friend gather around standing in respect and attention. Debi is at her place across from me at Jesse's head.

> "Dear God, we thank you for Jesse. We are thankful for his life, for the love he has shared, for the lives he has touched. Bless his family and friends who are gathered around him now in this circle of love. Comfort them. Help them now and in the days ahead. God, we thank you for the doctors and nurses, all who are caring for Jesse. We know sometimes all we try to do falls short. We can't do enough. We have to rely on your eternal love and care. God receive Jesse in your loving arms. Give him rest and peace in you. Grant him freedom from this earthly struggle. Guide him to you, Lord, and to your kingdom in heaven. God, we pray in Jesus name in whom we know hope and resurrection and life eternal. Amen.

We sit down again; it seems our prayers have hastened Jesse's death. He takes one more breath and it is not repeated. This interval is the longest yet. The throbbing blood vessel in his neck is stilled. Debi listens once more to his chest.

"He's gone." There is a certainty and finality in her voice. It is over. Our vigil is complete. Our waiting finished. I see no additional outpouring of emotion from Jesse's son. He looks relieved and is telling his father, "You can rest now, Daddy. It's all over. You're at peace now. No more pain and struggle. You rest now, you sleep. You were so tired. You can sleep now."

Debi asks the usual questions about organ donation, personal effects, funeral home, and I say some words of support, wrapping up, and departure. Sounds like the son will do some additional waiting for more family to arrive, announcing his dad's death as family come into the room, sharing this event of loss. I look at the clock. It's 3:30 PM. I have only been in this room one hour and yet it seemed so much longer.

Gleanings

My experience the last hour has been one of waiting; waiting for family, waiting for death, waiting for what I need to say or do in this situation. Waiting doesn't come easy. There were times in this hour I felt like shouting, "Family, hurry up and get here, I don't want to do this alone!" "Jesse, hurry up and die!" "God, hurry up and take him, this is getting hard on everybody." Hospitals are places of waiting, waiting for a doctor's visit, waiting for a test result, waiting for a diagnosis, an answer to what is wrong and how this will come out. Patients are waiting for a meal, waiting to go home, waiting for the next shot, treatment, surgery, waiting for the pain to end, waiting to die. "Hurry up and wait," is a phrase I hear patients and family laughingly repeat.

As a Quaker, waiting is something I know about, something we claim as central to worship. Waiting is an important pathway to knowing God. Robert Barclay, an early Quaker theologian, wrote in 1676:

When we meet together our purpose and form of worship
is to watch and wait for God to draw us inward and away
from all visible things . . . when the desire to wait upon
him is truly present, the Lord shows compassion . . . when
the conscious mind sinks down it waits for the appearance
of life. . . . [5]

Robert Barclay was describing a new and powerful form of worship that was sweeping across England in the mid 1600s. Small
groups of Christians, dissatisfied with the formal, shallow worship
of the state church, were seeking God's immediate, empowering,
renewing, discerning Spirit. They would gather in silence and wait
expectantly for God's spirit to be felt among them. The Spirit was
present and worshipers might share words, spoken ministry, cry,
quake (thus the "Quakers") or just find a deep feeling of peace,
clarity, joy, or renewal. This corporate ministry and seeking of
God's will is also relied upon for decision-making.

The process of putting aside talk and action, coming quietly
before God, waiting expectantly for God's spirit and will to be
felt, are central to Quaker worship and Quaker pastoral care. It is
a regular movement of consciously turning over one's own motions, will, agenda, and plans to the openness of God's affirmation
or redirection. In stillness and waiting we make room in our spirits to feel God's healing and see God's light.

Waiting for Jesse to die took me to a place of worshipful
watching and waiting, which helped me center and focus. All the
busyness and undone work of the week dropped away. I was drawn
inward to the mysteries of life, death, fathers, and sons. So my
waiting was not only restless and uncertain but as Barclay describes,
deep, inward, compassionate, and full of life.

The psalmists experienced waiting as a way to know God's truth
and salvation. "Lead me to your truth and teach me, for you are the
God of my salvation, for you I wait all day long" (25:5). In waiting
we can know God's strength: "Wait for the Lord; be strong and let
your heart take courage; wait for the Lord" (27:14). In waiting we

know God hears our questions and listens to our cries and pains: "But it is for you, O Lord, that I wait: it is you, O Lord my God, who will answer" (38:15). In waiting we find forgiveness and hope:

> I wait for the Lord, my soul waits, and in his word I hope; my soul waits for the Lord more than those who watch for the morning, more than those who watch for the morning. (130:5,6).

The hour of waiting with Jesse, that gathered hour of prayer, reflection, and silence had the qualities of "waiting upon the Lord." Being called to watch someone die throws me upon God's mercy. I don't think I could bear it without these promised gifts of learning, answering, strength, courage, forgiveness, and hope. In a sacred sense of waiting, God is present, caring for me. God waits with me. God works through me to wait compassionately with others. So even through the impatience, judging, mental wandering, and ineffectual times of waiting, God is working. I can trust God's light will come to the darkness just as the watcher trusts the coming of dawn's light.

Howard Macy, a contemporary Quaker, describes waiting:

> When we wait, we yield up our expectations of what God should do, our precious hoards of ritual and doctrine, our social awareness, and our self-concepts. Waiting is totally submitting to God and inviting God to move in our hearts with complete freedom.[6]

In waiting with Jesse and his family I am submitting to God's timing. In silence I put aside what I think to say and let words flow from what arises in the moment. In waiting I let God strip away my control and management as I realize a larger drama is being acted out here.

My hope and prayer is to continue to be attentive to waiting in my spiritual and professional life. May God strip away my busyness, reshuffle my piles of work, and draw me into the spiritual disciplines of quiet, silence, and waiting. I trust that in that place of openness and yielding God will use me, teach me, and help me minister to others. With the psalmist we may all pray, "O Lord be gracious to us; we wait for you" (33:2).

Conclusion

Tasks, demands and calls for attention and response flood me as I move through the day. Hundreds of people surround me with needs, concerns, even gifts to offer me when I walk through the door of my hospital. Both of my stories begin with me, beleaguered with urgent tasks, feeling behind and overwhelmed. In both stories I'm drawn from that scene to very intense and focused experiences that are central to my identity and ministry. These experiences take on more meaning as I reflect on them and let them illuminate my spirit.

My most common prayer as I go through the day is "Lord of all the people here and all the tasks before me, show me whom to see, what to do, when to come and when to go." As this prayer is answered I'm guided to a set of people and experiences where I'm to listen and learn and care.

Quakers have used the term "leading" to describe the way God guides us, directs us, and brings us to the right place at the right time. God provides an internal compass that helps us navigate the choppy waters of multiple channels, choices and directions. This sense of leading involves discerning how God forms us— identity; what God has given us—gifts; whom God sends us— companions; where God directs us—destination. A leading can be confirmed in everyday visits, tasks and encounters. It may need the discernment of a group to confirm the divine source and the practical living out of our leading.

I know I need to create spaces in my day and life to submit my tugs and pulls, choices, my deeper leadings, to God. I may need to gather a group for discernment, to seek clarity about God's guidance and direction for my workday and work life. Through my day, I can pray, wait, grieve, sit in silence, or sing. I can go next door to the chapel, kneel in a hospital room, eat with a friend, or counsel with my chaplaincy board. During my chaplaincy training I helped structure the daily morning staff meeting to include some open, silent time out of which I could center, pray, feel, seek discernment about the day's tasks and relationships, and clarify leadings.

As I continue to minister as a Quaker chaplain I seek openness to God's presence and instruction in my experiences, even in my painful ones. I pray for guidance in my stewardship of time and responsiveness to a multitude of concerns. I desire to wait upon the Lord, wait hopefully with others as I practice pastoral care.

The Quaker poet John Greenleaf Whitter, using the language of his day, expresses this practice and prayer in his hymn, "Dear Lord and Father of Mankind."

> Dear Lord and Father of man-kind, Forgive our foolish ways;
> Reclothe us in our rightful mind; In purer lives thy service find, in
> deeper reverence, praise.
>
> In simple trust like theirs who heard, Beside the Syrian Sea,
> The gracious calling of the Lord, Let us, like them without a word,
> Rise up and follow Thee.
>
> O Sabbath rest by Galilee! O calm of hills above!
> Where Jesus knelt to share with Thee the silence of eternity,
> Interpreted by love.
>
> Drop thy still dews of quietness, till all our strivings cease;
> Take from our souls the strain and stress, And let our ordered lives
> confess The beauty of thy peace.
>
> Breathe through the heats of our desire Thy coolness and thy balm;
> Let sense be dumb, let flesh retire; Speak through the earth-quake,
> wind and fire, O still small voice of calm!

As a person of faith and as a Quaker hospital chaplain, I have
gleaned two stories and accompanying reflections from a rich crop
of experience. These bits and pieces help me understand how God
is working in my life and ministry. I have found my spiritual and
vocational home among Friends. I filter my experiences and understand my particular call through the lens of Quaker tradition
and spirituality. My Quaker chaplaincy style is an intuitive one
that reflection and writing help make more conscious.

In Friend's tradition I have focussed on my experiences. As
chaplain, I become a sign of God's presence in the hospital. I trust
God can become visible and felt in the places I minister. I help
others understand the ways God is present and transforming their
lives. I help people listen for God in their own grief, pain, strength,
and hope. I help people "wait upon the Lord," trusting God is
there to hear, hold, carry, and lead them. My hope and prayer is
that my words, my story, and my ministry as a chaplain will speak
clearly of God's closeness, God's responsiveness, and God's leading.

Notes

1. John L. Nickalls, ed., *The Journal of George Fox* (Philadelphia, PA:
   Philadelphia Yearly Meeting, 1997), 11.

2. *Christian Faith and practice in the experience of the Society of Friends*,
   London Yearly Meeting of the Religious Society of Friends, 1960
   (Richmond, Indiana, Friends United Press, 1973), No. 20.

3. Robert Barclay, *Apology* (Philadelphia, PA: n.p., 1859), 9, 10.

4. *Friends Journal*, November 1, 1963, Cover Quote.

5. Dean Freiday, ed., *Barclay's Apology in Modern English* (Alburtis,
   PA: Hemlock Press, 1967), 255.

6. Howard R. Macy, *Rhythms of the Inner Life* (Old Tappan, NJ: Fleming
   H. Revell Company, 1988), 42.

XV. Through the (Shattered) Looking Glass: A View of the Kingdom

Mickey Edgerton

STORIES ABOUT PERSONS WITH BROKEN LIVES provide us with a view of the Kingdom of God. The lives of Jim and Gloria, Denise, Maggie, and Harry are shattered because of terminal illness, and, like broken mirrors, reflect the light off those silvered shards in many surprising and colorful directions. The very brokenness of the mirror reveals new perspectives of literal reality, allowing aspects of truth to be revealed that an unrefracted reflection does not contain. Just as in Lewis Carrol's *Through the Looking Glass*, everything is upside down and backwards; so it is in the Kingdom of God.

What follows is an account of how Jim and Gloria, Denise, Maggie, and Harry reflected back rays of new light, a sharpening view of the Kingdom. These stories come from my ministry as a pastoral counselor with a Catholic hospice program.

Jim and Gloria

During my first year at Holy Redeemer Hospice I met Jim and Gloria. Jim was terminally ill with prostatic cancer. When I first visited them in their home, they invited me in and made me welcome. They were both in their late sixties, had been married to one another for forty-plus years, and were deeply devoted to one another. Jim was still ambulatory at that point, but tired easily. He was not nearly as talkative as Gloria, perhaps because of his debilitating illness, but more likely as a mark of a long-standing pattern in their life together. Gloria tended to speak for Jim; while he was reflecting on what had just been said to him, Gloria often jumped right in and provided an answer. Jim did not seem to mind that; perhaps he had long ago made peace with this practice of hers, and did not even notice it any more.

As is my usual approach on an initial visit, I asked them about their church affiliation and faith history. I learned that Gloria had been brought up Lutheran, Jim was baptized Roman Catholic and had attended Catholic schools. When they married, he agreed to attend Lutheran church with her, and their children were also raised in that denomination. Jim had not attended a Catholic Church for many years. Gloria volunteered "Jim would not want you to call a priest for him," although I had not asked that question.

On subsequent visits I learned that Jim's sister, Flo, lived just three blocks away. The children in both families had grown up together and they had all been very close until eleven years ago when Jim and Flo's mother died. Something took place then in the settlement of her estate that caused a rift between Jim and Flo, and they had been estranged ever since. None of the members of either of the two households had spoken to one another or visited one another's homes in the ensuing eleven years. As far as Jim and Gloria knew, Flo had not been told that her brother was terminally ill.

As the weeks went on, Jim's condition worsened, and he became confined to bed. Finally, as I always do when the patient was born and raised Catholic, I asked him if he would like to see a priest.

Before Jim could answer, Gloria spoke for him, saying "Oh no, Jim has never wanted that, do you honey?"

"No, I guess not," Jim replied.

Gloria added, "Goodness, I wouldn't want some priest in here hollering at me for taking Jim away from the church."

I said, "I'm not sure that would happen," but she was obdurate.

Actually, since I didn't yet know any of the priests in the parish that served their neighborhood, I couldn't be sure that wouldn't happen. But since Gloria seemed so certain that Jim didn't want that and he wasn't saying much at all, I let it drop.

I let it drop, but Gloria did not. On the next three visits, Gloria initiated the subject again and again, explaining that she just couldn't bear the thought of being blamed and scolded by a priest for taking Jim away from his church. Finally, on a day when he was not only confined to bed but barely speaking, and then only in a barely audible whisper, and Gloria was once again "explaining" why it would not be good to call a priest, I "got" it.

"Gloria, I think we ought to ask Jim what he wants. If he says he does want to see a priest, and perhaps he does not, but if he does, I promise I'll personally tell the priest he's not allowed to yell at you!"

We approached the bed and I said "Jim, how are you doing?"

He whispered weakly, "Not so good."

I said, "Jim, remember I asked you a couple of months ago if you wanted to see a priest and you said no. Well, I just wondered if you've changed your mind about that since then. Would you like me to call a priest to come and see you?"

Jim looked up at me and whispered "Yes."

Gloria, at my elbow, looked alarmed, took his hand and said "Jim, honey, maybe you didn't understand what Mickey said. She asked if you want to see a priest. You don't, do you honey?"

Jim looked at both of us, and then said, louder this time. "Yes, yes, I do want to see a priest."

Gloria burst into tears, and I turned and hugged her and said, "Gloria, it's okay, it will be okay—I'll make sure the priest doesn't yell at you. But if it's what Jim wants, it's important to give him that. You've done everything else for him that you could, you've taken wonderful care of him—he needs you to say yes to this too."

Gloria consented.

When I got back to the agency, I called the rectory of the local parish and spoke to Father Steve Katziner. I'm using his real name here (with his permission) for I want this record to show, to bear witness to the true vocational faithfulness this man gives not only to his own parishioners but to anyone who needs his help. Later I got to know Father Steve Katziner well and to depend on his help, but on this first meeting on the phone, I didn't know what to expect. I laid out to him all the facts as I knew them—Jim's having been baptized and raised as a Catholic, married a Lutheran woman and helping to raise their children in the Lutheran church. I reported that he had not been in a Catholic church for many years. I told Father Steve that Jim would probably not live much longer and he had expressed a desire to see a priest. I also told him of Gloria's fear of being yelled at and scolded for taking Jim away from his church, and that I had promised her that the priest would not do that. Father Katziner chuckled as he responded: "I would be glad to go to see them, and no, I won't yell at them."

That was a Thursday. Father Steve went to see Jim and Gloria on Friday, spoke with both of them together for a time, then saw Jim by himself, heard his confession and anointed him with the Sacrament of the Sick (what used to be known as "last rites" or "extreme unction"). Afterward, he contrived to leave his prayer book behind at their home, so had to return on Saturday to retrieve it, and spent more time with Jim and Gloria, praying with them.

When I returned to work the next Tuesday, I called Gloria to see how things were going. (I have learned when one works in a hospice, and has been off for several days, one does not ask on the phone how the patient is. Instead, one asks how things are going, for it may be that the patient has died in the meantime.) Gloria brought me up to date about Father Katziner's visits, that they went well, and that no, he hadn't yelled at them. She also told me about the events of the weekend. Late Saturday night, about 10:30 p.m. (after the priest's second visit), Jim roused from a near-coma and called Gloria over to his bed. He whispered something that she could not quite hear, and when she asked him to repeat, he said "I want to see my sister." Gloria could not believe her ears. "You want what, do you mean Flo?" He nodded. She said "But Jim, it's 10:30 at night!" Jim mustered all his strength and said, quite plainly, "I want to see Flo." Full of trepidation, but not willing to go against what might turn out to be his last wish, she dashed out into the night and up the street three blocks to fetch the woman neither of them had spoken to in over eleven years.

Flo accompanied Gloria back to Jim's bedside, and there was a joyful tear-filled reunion. Flo returned the next day, Sunday, and spent the day. Early Monday morning, Jim died peacefully in his sleep. When Gloria and I spoke on the phone on Tuesday, she told me that Flo was helping with the funeral plans and had promised to help with the food when friends and relatives returned to Gloria's home after the funeral. There was no more talk of the matter that had caused the long estrangement. Gloria's sorrow for Jim's death was mixed with joy and relief at the peace he showed during his last hours and at the renewed relationship with her sister-in-law.

At our next twice-yearly Hospice Memorial Service at our agency, Father Steve led the service. Gloria was there, and afterwards during the refreshment period, she, still a good Lutheran, embraced Father Steve, and he hugged her back—brother and sister in Christ.

Jim and Gloria's life as they knew it was shattered by Jim's terminal illness. And yet, in the process of his dying, amazing healing took place in the form of reconciliation both with his church and within his family. His death brought renewed life.

Denise

When I first met her, Denise was a thirty-five-year-old Roman Catholic divorced mother of two daughters and one son, a nurse with terminal ovarian cancer. She had been raised in a devout Catholic family, educated in Catholic schools, married young, had her children and was divorced while they were still young. After that she left the church for quite a time. A few years ago she had returned, and at the time I met her, she identified herself as a charismatic Catholic. She was very active in a local prayer group and was one of the members of that group who was sought out for spiritual encouragement and direction.

As a nurse, she knew every detail of her medical situation. Having endured the rigors of chemotherapy and radiation to little avail, she embarked on an alternative medicine route— macrobiotic diet, shark cartilage, restorative teas, etc. She also attended frequent healing prayer sessions, and she knew that her own prayer group prayed for her "early and often."

On my first visit to her, I took a middle-aged pastoral care student with me. He was a second career seminarian who had been a successful "right to life" lawyer before receiving the vocational call to enter the priesthood. As a second year student in seminary, he was assigned for his one-day-a-week field ministry to our hospice Pastoral Care Department. This was his first visit to a terminally ill patient. As such, I conducted this first interview; Earl listened and observed. The plan was that after this first visit, he would take over as the primary pastoral care giver, and report back to me regularly for supervision. This was explained to Denise on this first visit, and she readily assented.

This first visit found our patient to be highly intelligent, self-aware, articulate, sophisticated, humorous, and very, very sad. She readily shared the information detailed above. Denise spoke easily of her faith story, and expressed much gratitude for the loving presence of God in her life, and for the support she was receiving from her prayer group.

When I asked how her present situation (meaning her terminal condition) influenced or was influenced by her religious faith, she said that she felt very fearful. I made the assumption, based on her status as a nurse and her knowledge about what she would likely have to endure physically as she approached death, that she was afraid of the physical suffering involved. When I asked her what in particular she was afraid of about dying, she said quickly, "Oh, it's not dying I'm afraid of, it's purgatory I'm afraid of."

I had no response. At that time I did not know very much about purgatory theology. My off-the-top-of-my-head opinion was that it was just a scary theory the Church had made up to frighten its members into righteous living. So, I wound up the visit soon after, promising that Earl would visit her again the following week.

Soon after that, I attended the monthly luncheon for eight to ten of the hospice pastoral counselors/chaplains in this metropolitan area. This is a very precious time together when we chat, laugh, cry, blow off steam, and do occasional informal case conferencing. At one point, I called us all to (more or less) order and said, "OK, I have a problem," told them about Denise and asked them what they thought would be a useful pastoral intervention. It seemed that the issue of her divorce had not kept her from returning to the Church; in fact she had told us that the priest offered her private instruction and re-baptized her into the church on her return. So why would she still be fearful of purgatory? After much helpful discussion, one of the pastoral counselors suggested that perhaps she had had an abortion at sometime during her hiatus from the church and did not feel forgiven for that. They also suggested that I find out a bit more about what purgatory means to practicing Catholics. It certainly did not seem to anyone, including myself, that it would be particularly useful to enter into a discussion with her from the point of view that it is a silly superstition.

Keeping in mind the seminarian's history of activism in the right-to-life movement, I was not sure that he was the best person to explore the possibility of abortion-based guilt with Denise. (And, as it turned out, he was extremely helpful in ways that astonished both of us!) I arranged to visit her before Earl returned for his second field day the following Thursday. This time, I picked up where we left off at the end of our last session, asking her to tell me a bit more about her fear of purgatory; what was that all about? She launched into an account of a long love affair she engaged in after her marriage ended. It was with someone she loved but did not wish to marry, and, sure enough, she became pregnant and ended the pregnancy with an abortion.

"Have you confessed and received absolution," I asked.

"Yes," she replied, "but I still felt guilty somehow. The thing I felt worst about, even more than about the abortion itself, was that my lover was black. I cannot be absolutely sure the real reason I chose to abort was because the baby might be black." She then added, " I am haunted by the possibility that racism was what impelled me into that decision, and that makes it even more sinful for me."

I asked her what would be her response to a woman in that same situation who came to her seeking her spiritual advice, as women often did, in fact, in various anxiety-producing situations. She smiled and said "Of course, I'd tell them that God is endlessly loving and forgiving and, if she were truly penitent, then it is as if it never happened." She went on to say, very soberly, "But don't you see, in my own case it feels very different, and despite all I know of God's love and forgiveness, I cannot stop believing that I will have to experience purgatory after I die-—and I am so frightened." Before I left, we prayed together. I prayed that she would continue to experience God's love and forgiveness and I asked God to comfort her.

When Earl returned to my office the following Thursday, his face was aglow. He walked into my cubicle, holding a book aloft triumphantly. "Look what I found," he said. "I'm supposed to write a paper on a fourteenth or fifteenth century saint. By the time I got to the library (late!), all the Saints I knew anything about were gone, so I picked this one—St. Catherine of Genoa—and look, the whole second half of the book is her teachings on purgatory. Let's give this to Denise." "Oh great," I thought to myself, "Just what she needs to reinforce her fears." To Earl, I said, "Well, let me look at it and see if I think it will be useful to her."

That afternoon I started reading about St. Catherine's life, how she came to be canonized, and what she had to say about purgatory. Very simply put, her thesis is that every person of faith wants, more than anything else, to be fully united with God. After death, the soul has no memory of any of the transgressions that were committed during life, hence no guilt, no remorse, no fear, nothing except a total all-consuming desire to be fully united with God. The fires of purgatory were designed to burn away all impurities or imperfections that would interfere with fully merging with God—rather like a smelter producing steel by burning away all impurities in the fuel. The desire to be fully united with God was all the soul in purgatory experienced, and the process whereby that occurs is incorporated into that desire.

I know from experience that "burning desire" to have my will perfectly aligned with God's will, and although purgatory isn't my story, it clearly was Denise's. I knew that she too experienced a burning desire to be completely united with God when she died.

Since Earl needed the book to do his paper, I photocopied the section on purgatory and took it to Denise. She accepted it with gratitude, and promised to read it. When I visited her again in a few days, her condition was very altered. Whereas she had been ambulatory, though quite weak, by now she was bed-bound and drifting in and out of consciousness. She woke briefly, thanked me for the article and said she'd loaned it to a friend in her prayer group who then loaned it to someone else. Her demeanor was very changed, and it wasn't just the medications. In fact, she needed very little pain medication during those last few days, according to her care-giving daughter. Her anxiety was gone; she was at peace. She opened her eyes again and said "It's OK; I'm ready; I'm not afraid." I prayed with her once more, thanking God for giving her peace and comfort and asking God to give her safe passage on her journey to Him. She squeezed my hand, said goodbye, and two days later, she died peacefully.

When Earl returned the next Thursday, I told him about Denise's last days and her peaceful death. He was ecstatic. He was so thrilled that even though he had not been her primary pastoral care giver, he had found the book that seemed to have helped Denise through that last dreaded time for her. He said, "You know, I don't think finding that book was just a coincidence, do you?"

"Well, Earl, I think it's got the Holy Spirit's fingerprints all over it!" I said.

"And to think of it," he said. "If I'd started my paper when I should have, I'd have probably picked a whole different Saint!"

Maggie

Maggie was a fifty-six-year-old, obese female with terminal breast cancer and with metastasis to the liver. Her already ample frame was additionally swollen by retained fluid in her belly. By the time I met her, she was still ambulatory but had a great deal of difficulty getting around. She lived in a tiny apartment in the rear of a dilapidated old apartment house in a very economically depressed section of the city. At the end of a long hall, the door to the apartment opened into a small living room. To the right was a tiny bathroom, a small bedroom, and to the left a tiny kitchen. Sharing her home was a long-time friend, Bill, who cared tenderly for her. He was close to her age, and his health was nearly as precarious as hers. His huge belly contained an aortic aneurysm which, in his words, "could blow any minute!"

Every article of furniture was decorated with, or covered by, something crocheted. To the left of the door from the hallway was a small shrine, with statuary of the Blessed Mother, a crucifix, and an electric candle, which was always lit. Pictures of Jesus, the Blessed Mother, and various saints occupied prominent spots on the walls of all the rooms. The double bed was covered with a crocheted spread. In the upper left-hand corner of the bedroom was a knick-knack shelf holding a statue of the boy Jesus, clad in a blue crocheted robe. All this crochet work was from the busy fingers of Maggie herself. As long as she was able she was crocheting on one project or another, whenever I visited her.

Given all the religious paraphernalia around, I was surprised when Maggie denied any membership in a parish, and did not even know the name of the parish in which she resided. She said she had been born into a Catholic family and had sent her own children to Catholic schools. When I asked her if she would like to have the Eucharist brought to her every week from the local parish, she declined briskly and changed the subject.

It was clear from her present circumstances and the gradually shared details of her life that she had had a very hard life. She was divorced from an abusive alcoholic husband, and three of her four grown children were estranged from her. Yet she was delighted for me to pray with her, and spoke easily of her faith in God and the saints. She looked forward with enthusiasm to our visits together, and promised to crochet a doll for me, an offer she made and kept to me as well as to all the other hospice personnel involved in her care.

Maggie went through periodic episodes of depression, during which she was weepy and morose. I assumed these were normal symptoms of dealing with terminal illness, and never probed as to what else was underneath. She weakened so that even an occasional foray out on the Avenue in her wheelchair pushed by her faithful Bill, to the local K-Mart (her favorite outing), was no longer feasible. She then seemed to be depressed more of the time. We all knew and it had been discussed, that the time would come when she would be bed-bound and Bill would no longer be able to manage her care. The hospice social worker was trying to help her consent to go to a nursing home, and I made the assumption that this also accounted for her low spirits. Once again, I broached the subject of contacting the parish for a visit from the priest or at least weekly Eucharist ministry. This time, after a long silent pause, Maggie blurted out, "Well, I guess by now I can trust you," and her story came pouring out.

"I can't take communion, I was never baptized!" At this, there were great wrenching sobs, and she went on with many tears and groans to tell me more about her early life. Way back when she was in parochial school and it was time for her confirmation class, she was told to bring in her baptismal certificate. But there was no certificate. Maggie was the last of fourteen children and by then her mother was too tired, too dispirited, disorganized, or perhaps, all of the above, and just never got around to getting little Maggie baptized. As an adolescent it is not surprising but very regrettable that she internalized the guilt/shame around this omission and so she had never told but one other person about it in all these years. "I'm so ashamed," she said, over and over. She continued to attend Mass regularly for many years, but she always sat way in the back and never once went up to take communion. Finally she stopped attending altogether after her divorce, believing that the Church wouldn't want her anymore. Once, she told me, in recent years a friend of hers, who was a charismatic Catholic, talked her into attending Mass with her and taking communion, assuring her that God wouldn't mind and the priest didn't have to know that she'd never been baptized. Maggie did take communion that one time, but felt enormously guilty afterwards, believing that it was just one more sin for which she would probably never be forgiven.

There was more. Remember when I mentioned that Maggie's life had been hard? It wasn't until that day that I had any idea of how hard her life was. When Maggie was very young, her alcoholic father began an incestuous relationship with her that lasted until she was a teenager. She became pregnant by him and ran away from home. She did find someone who was willing to marry her and help her raise her baby girl. Unfortunately, as so often happens, this man was also alcoholic and abusive, and finally after another daughter and a son were born she found the courage to leave him. All these breaches of "moral theology"—no baptism, incest, illegitimate baby, divorcing her lawful wedded husband— built an impenetrable wall to ever receiving the sacraments, or so she thought.

I asked, "Do you really want to take communion?"

She looked at me with shocked eyes. "Of course I do, more than anything, but it would be wrong since I wasn't baptized."

"So, would you like to be baptized?"

"But Mickey, I can't, it's too late; and I'm divorced and all. . . ." Her voice trailed away, in tears again.

I said, "Look Maggie, as you already know, I'm not Catholic, but I really think it is possible. Let me find out about it, would that be okay? If I can arrange it do you want me to?"

So I found out which parish she resided in, called the priest, told him some of her story and asked if he or someone could baptize her. I told him she might not have the requisite six weeks, which is usually the time it takes to receive all the instruction before baptism. He agreed to go see her.

When I saw Maggie again next week, she looked transformed. Yes, she was still obese, still too weak to walk by herself, but she glowed! Her eyes sparkled, her face radiated a joy I had never seen on her before. Father Murphy had visited her the Friday before, heard her story, took her confession, and returned the next Wednesday, baptized her and gave her the Eucharist. Only the second Holy Communion she had ever taken and this one was legal! To her, at last she could truly experience a full measure of worship of her Lord who meant so very much to her, whom she loved so much and in her own words, "now I can really show Jesus how much I love him."

Soon after that, Maggie did go into a wonderful nursing home, run by the nuns of the Sacred Heart. They are old-order nuns, who still wear the starched white habits, complete with wimple and long skirts. Maggie thought she was in heaven, and the several times I visited her there, I could understand why. She was in a large sunny room with five other women; the whole southern exposure window wall was filled with flowering plants; there were cages of canaries; the bedspreads and sheets and pillow cases were lovely floral designs. Maggie had her own TV and VCR, and the nuns made sure she had plenty of her beloved Shirley Temple movie videotapes. They also supplied her with several different brightly flowered muumuus to wear. Her loyal friend Bill took public transportation every day to visit her, and soon began visiting other patients there as well, and continued on as a volunteer after Maggie's death. In her last days, she was surrounded by people who enjoyed and pampered her. The other patients in her room were mostly unresponsive, so the nuns were delighted to have someone so funny and feisty as Maggie to interact with. Best of all, she could, and did receive communion every day!

I was able to identify completely with Maggie's yearning to receive communion. Just as her "brokenness" had shut off her access to that powerful connection with God's Presence, so have I experienced my own brokenness acting to distract or even turn me away from worshipful silent worship. Yet, the very brokenness itself creates such a yearning for wholeness, for spiritual healing that the reconciliation is doubly precious. I know experientially that deep longing to experience God's presence.

Maggie's terminal illness was not the first shattering event in her life by any means, but the broken pieces of her life surely did reflect back a new view of the possibilities of reconciliation and paradoxically new life while she was preparing to die. Her last days, when she knew she was dying, were filled with a joy she had never experienced even when she was still "well." She fervently believed that her "life after life" would unite her completely with her beloved Lord, a hope that had been nearly extinguished before she knew she was dying. Upside down and backwards, indeed!

Harry

Harry was an eighty- four-year-old man with terminal bladder cancer. He had been in poor health for several years, was widowered, and therefore lived with his middle-aged son and daughter-in-law. Both householders worked full time, and were away from home from 6:00 a.m. to 6:00 p.m. on week days. Their home is in an affluent suburb north of the city.

Harry had been raised Roman Catholic, and had been quite devout, regularly attending Mass several times a week. Before he retired, he was a truck driver, and he claimed that whenever his route took him past a Catholic church, if his schedule permitted, he would stop and enter the church, light candles for his loved ones and pray. At some point several years ago, however, his young niece, age twenty-one, died of leukemia, and, he reported that event caused him to "lose his faith." When I questioned him as to what exactly happened, he said "I just couldn't believe any longer in a God that would let that happen." After that, he stopped attending church, no longer received communion, and disclaimed belief in any religion.

Harry often spoke of his loneliness. The long days alone in the house depressed him; he could not get interested in television or radio or even reading very much. He was convinced that his daughter-in-law disliked him and did not really want him to be there. She was very strict in her rules about what he could do while they were away. From the street, the house always looked as if the occupants were away on extended vacation. All the windows were shuttered with heavy drapes, which were not under any circumstances to be opened. The reason given to him for that was because the sun would fade the rugs and furniture. But even on cloudy days he was not to open those drapes, and he was fearful of her ire if he questioned the logic of this. His bedroom was very tiny with just a chest of drawers, a bed, and a small nightstand. Although he was permitted to stay in a sort of family room near the kitchen during the day, the shades were not to be opened and none of his personal gear was to be in evidence. The lighting, even when all the lamps were turned on, was very dim—must have been all 40-watt bulbs. Many days when I visited he did not even have the lights turned on; he was truly depressed.

When I first met him shortly after the doctor declared him terminal, he was somewhat cheered by the new people that hospice bought into his life. He could get around the house with some difficulty, with a cane and/or a walker; the three steps up into the kitchen were a barely surmountable problem. During the entire eight years he had lived with his son and daughter-in-law he was expected to provide and prepare his own food, never invited to the family table. Even though his condition had changed radically, the rules did not. His brother visited him twice a week and brought groceries and a sandwich for lunch on the days he came. By the time we hospice folk were seeing him, food preparation was just too hard for him so he would often make the arduous trip to the kitchen only once per day. The home health aide came every day, Monday through Friday, to bathe and dress him. Sometimes she could take the time to make him some soup. Because of his indwelling catheter the nurse visited three times a week; in addition a volunteer came for two hours once a week, and I visited once a week.

Harry was a gregarious man and looked forward to all of our visits. Even though he had announced to me on my first visit that he was not a believer, that he had no religious faith at all, he often asked me about my faith; what did I think God was like? How was it that I knew I had a faith? Then he would often say, "Gee, I wish I had a faith like yours." In the beginning, I was careful not to steer the conversation in that direction, being respectful of his non-faith claims. Instead, I would encourage him to talk of his life, his marriage, his wife's death some years ago, his work, the places he'd lived, etc. He wanted to hear about my life too, was fascinated by the different places I've lived, the different careers

I've had, and why it is I like to do hospice work. He was delighted to hear that most of my adult life I, too, had been a disbeliever, and then how that came to change. And then once again he would say, wistfully, "I wish I had a faith like yours." Finally, I "heard" him when he said that and said, "OK, let's talk about that." I was very much the counselor, not wanting to push my faith onto him until finally, when he pressed me for more details about how I experience God, I realized that in my concern with not being inappropriately evangelistic, I was ignoring some real spiritual hunger on Harry's part. Then I told him about my experience of knowing that I and everyone else are beloved children of God. Because of that experience, I had made a promise to God that I would spend the rest of my life exploring what that means. He said, "Well, that seems to make you pretty happy." I admitted that it did indeed, especially because it meant that I was no longer constantly searching for love in a lot of inappropriate places and from inappropriate people. He got a twinkle in his eye, and said, "Gee, Mickey, I'm sorry I didn't meet you twenty years ago!" I replied that he'd better be glad he hadn't, that I was doing him a lot more good now than I could have then! It was fun, a bit of harmless flirtation, very retrospective for both of us. Although I was probably much more content to be in present time than he was, and for good reason.

And then something wonderful happened. Harry had reached the point where it really wasn't safe for him to be alone all day, even with us hospice folk dropping in now and then. Because he was not eating properly, and certainly not regularly, sometimes his medication caused him to be confused. One cold day the home health aide found him out in the front yard in his bathrobe, hanging on to a small tree (it was windy out!) calling for help. He felt too weak to walk back into the house and could not remember why he had gone outside in the first place. So, the decision was made: he had to have someone present with him all day every day. That meant a paid companion, and fortunately his son was willing to spring for that. Someone was hired to be with him for eight of the twelve hours he was alone each week day.

Enter Evelyn, a nurse's aide who worked for an agency that supplied paid companions for patients who could no longer care adequately for themselves. Evelyn is a middle-aged black Baptist woman who loves the Lord and doesn't care who knows it! No, I said that wrong; she cares very much that everyone know it. She and her husband have had many foster children in their home over the years and they have managed to acquire another property to provide housing for homeless young people too old to be placed in foster care. She loves the work she does now, much as I do. It provides her with the avenue of ministry she feels called to—lonely people whom she can serve even as she serves her Lord.

She and I liked one another immediately. As soon as she knew I was the pastoral counselor, she stepped right into the role of colleague, and we shared a gratitude for one another's support in ministering to Harry. On her part, she saw to it that he was properly fed. After the first week there, she informed Harry's son, who had hired her to be there from 7 a.m. to 4 p.m. that she would be staying until 6 p.m. instead so that Harry would be sure to get his supper; the flabbergasted son agreed. She also opened the drapes in the family room and the kitchen, saying that Harry was free to sit in the dark all day if he liked but she wasn't about to! Harry warned her that his daughter-in-law wouldn't like it and "there'd be hell to pay." Evelyn said "Well, we'll see about that." As far as I know, the daughter-in-law never raised the issue. Evelyn had the sort of cheerful, no-nonsense authority that cut through unreasonable edicts. We hospice folk had been seduced into the drama of Harry's view of the unreasonableness of his daughter-in-law, had tiptoed around her "rules," heeding his pleas not to rock the boat. We were caught in the apparent bind between supporting patient autonomy and risking making things worse for him. Evelyn did not trouble herself with all that; she just knew that a little light needed to be brought into that situation. And so it was!

She also set about to bring some light into Harry's soul. Whenever I would visit, she would say, "OK now, Harry, there's two of us in here who know that God loves us, how about making it an even three?" She would turn to me and say, "Now Harry told me all about you and how you found out that everyone is God's beloved; now there are two of us to help him to know that about himself too." Then, turning to him, she'd say, "Now Harry, you know all you have to do is take Jesus Christ into your heart as your saviour and then you will know that he loves you just like Mickey and I do! Isn't that right, Mickey?" Harry caught my eye above Evelyn's earnest head and raised his eyebrows as if to say "Listen to that girl go on!" But he looked pleased too, as if he were delighted at the efforts of these two wonderful women trying to get him saved! I was nervous; this was neither my language nor my theology of salvation. I was still in the process of figuring out how my relationship with Jesus figured into my relationship with God, and I had not used the "Jesus Christ as my personal Savior" formula since I was a child. But when Evelyn looked to me for confirmation of her fervent admonition, I found myself nodding my head in agreement and said, "That's right, Harry."

Variations of this scenario played themselves out over the next couple of weeks; then I missed my weekly visit. I heard at the next hospice team meeting that Harry had suddenly declined to the point of being bed-bound. An unexpected sick day prevented me from visiting that week either, and at the next team meeting, I learned that Harry had died on the previous Sunday.

Almost always, when we hear that one of our patients has finally died, we are relieved and grateful that he/she has finally been released from the life that was surely running out. But this time, I burst into tears. I knew that Harry had dreaded dying on a weekend, for he would be more alone then than when his son and wife were away all day. On weekends, his son spent most of the time at the racetrack, and his daughter-in-law stayed away from him. Hospice staff and Evelyn were not there either for those two days. Harry used to beg me to promise to be with him when he died, and of course I could promise no such thing. So, when I heard that he died on Sunday, I was certain that he had died alone and afraid.

I called the agency which had sent Evelyn to us and asked them to have her call me back. I knew she'd be sad also about his dying alone. When she returned my call, her voice sounded strong and cheerful.

She said "Mickey, are you sitting down?"

"No, but I will if I should," I replied.

"Well," she said, "The most wonderful thing has happened!"

I interrupted her, "Evelyn, you do know that Harry died on Sunday, don't you?"

She replied, "Oh yes! Thank God, the poor man is finally at peace. Let me tell you what happened last Wednesday. He called me over to his bed and said, 'Well Evelyn, I've finally decided that you and Mickey are right. I do want to ask Jesus to come into my heart, and to forgive me for all the things I shouldn't have done.'"

Evelyn responded, "Well bless your heart. He already has, you know—forgiven you I mean. . . . So then we just prayed together and he just changed right before my eyes; he just got so peaceful and that wrinkled up old brow of his just smoothed out and his eyes didn't look scared any more."

He said, "It's just like you and Mickey said, I really can feel that God loves me."

"Well Mickey, I s'pose you can guess that we were both crying by then and I was saying 'thank you Jesus', and he was just smiling in that real peaceful way people do when they know they've got Jesus in their hearts at last."

"And Mickey, here's the other thing I want to tell you. I think that God sent both of us to Harry on purpose, you know, so we could help each other help him out. You know, maybe not everybody would have loved that funny old man, but I did and I could tell you did too. And I think that's what helped him to know that God loved him too. So that's what he needed to know so he could die without being afraid. And even though I wasn't there when he died, I just know that's how it happened."

I agree with Evelyn. The way I described my experience of God in my life was not the same as the way she described her experience, but both of us were genuine in the expressions of God's love coursing through us for dear Harry, and the words we used were genuine descriptions of God acting through us. I may or may not ever come to use the "Christ Jesus as my personal Savior" language. But as for now, I'm so grateful that Evelyn and I were able to collaborate in bringing this man to the Inward Teacher and leaving him there, as some Quakers would describe it. Her story, my story, Harry's story, they are all Sacred Stories.

Reflections

My understanding of the Kingdom of God,[1] as Jesus referred to it throughout the Gospels, is that it is a way of living that is fully demonstrative of alignment with God's will for us; a way of love, of mercy, of justice, of compassion. We live in the Realm of God when we live the Truth of who and Whose we humans are, beloved children of God, and therefore members one of the other. I know that my own deepest heart's desire is to realize that in my own life, and that perceived and real differences in matters of religious faith often throw up road blocks to experiencing deeply our common heritage as beloved children of God. The people and their situations in these stories, what happened between us, and the Spirit's gracious presence projected new visions of what Kingdom living could be like on the screen of this broken world.

As a Quaker doing my ministry in a Roman Catholic agency, I necessarily deal with patients, families, and colleagues with different theological beliefs and practices from my own. This is a welcome exercise for me as it expands my understanding of how different individuals, and communities of faith experience and think about God. A core Quaker belief attests that some measure of God's Spirit resides in every human being. People have constructed many different stories to describe how it is that we are related to the Divine One, and how we are called to live out that relationship. My experience of Quaker spirituality is more akin to Catholic spirituality than to that of many Protestants. Experiencing the Divine Presence is central to both Friends and Catholics; our liturgical practices for evoking that Presence are different. Catholics use the sacrament of the Eucharist; Friends use silent waiting on the Lord in worship with their faith community. The desired result is the same.

Broken relationship is the common theme in the stories of these patients and their loved ones. Jim's estrangement from his sister and his church; Denise still feeling separated from full forgiveness; Maggie estranged from her church; Harry estranged from God.

The word "religion" derives from the Latin root *religio*, meaning "to bind together." Here we see paradox operating. Misunderstandings about the rules of their religion abound in each of their stories, and serve to "loose" these persons from their religious home. Jim and his wife Gloria assumed that their relationship with Jim's Catholic religion was broken by his marrying outside the faith. Denise feared that one of her past sins was unforgivable, thus she had lost her place in God's kingdom. Maggie thought the "religious rules" barred her from being "bound together" with the rest of her church's communicants. Harry misunderstood the true covenant between himself and God, and thus experienced being cast out of the community of faith. And yet, paradoxically, (through the looking glass!) the very same religion that seemed to cast these people out was in the end the means to their healing and reconciliation. Their very brokenness created the occasion for the Spirit to enter in to bind them together once more.

Notes

1. Realm of God, for those folk for whom the term "kingdom" is troubling or off-putting.

Concluding Reflections

Bill Ratliff

Gifts upon Gifts

FIFTEEN OF US WHO BELONG TO THE RELIGIOUS SOCIETY OF FRIENDS have shared insights and stories out of our experience. Our struggles and joys are also here. The process of writing and revising, reading other chapters and making comments, have aided in the clarity of our own thinking. What was inchoate and intuited has become more conscious and thereby more available to us in our ongoing ministry.

At a recent gathering of *Quakers in Pastoral Care and Counseling*, a panel composed of a number of the writers of these chapters shared what the process of writing had meant to them. While the stories differed, we all had benefited from this project. Marthajane Robinson, for example, reflected on how the process of contemplating and writing her chapter confirmed for her what she knew intuitively concerning the connection between her Quaker faith and her healing work. After a recent difficult work situation, she observed that "Writing the chapter was instrumental in restoring my sense of competency and re-confirmed the value of the work I do."

Two persons had such powerful experiences as a result of writing that they agreed to share their experiences. The first is Jane Brown, who wrote "Where Two or Three Are Gathered . . . "

> The day that I sent the full draft of my chapter was the same day that I found out that my heart was beating too

slowly to keep me alive (a pacemaker has remedied that situation—I am in good health now). That afternoon, when the doctor told me that my heart was in trouble, I did a quick review of my life to see if I had completed that which I had been created to do. I was surprised to find that this writing was almost at the top of the list. This book provided a means of sharing, in words that would outlive me, the most basic of my beliefs about the Spirit and its gracious and powerful work within and among us. I hope that these words might be a piece of the continuing of that work.

The second is Carolyn Treadway, who wrote "The Journey Home."

Little did I know, when I wrote the pages of my chapter, how important they were going to be . . . I spent a very intensive weekend writing and re-writing the main draft of my chapter. It was time to get the chapter in to the book's editor, but more than that I felt strangely impelled, absolutely impelled, to get the chapter *done*. I could not rest until it was all finished. It did not come easily. From Friday afternoon almost straight through to Sunday night I delved into my clients' lives and their processes of therapy, and wrestled with what I wanted to say about all of it. Even while sleeping those nights, I continued to labor with the material in my dreams. Only in retrospect could I possibly see that one of those dreams, about a double hearse, was a premonition or at least a preparation for things soon to come.

Mary, the client described at length in my chapter, had been doing quite well for some months. There were some minor ups and downs, but on the whole she had levelled out enormously. The very day after I wrote the chapter, she came in for her regular session in a very dark mood, reminiscent of old ways. She told me she had taken some pills that day, and had more pills with her. She took the pill bottle out of her purse. I thought she was going to give me the bottle for safekeeping, but instead, to my shock and horror, she dumped the entire bottle into her hand and then down her throat, without a drop of water!! It was an incredible moment.

I accompanied Mary to the emergency room, and stayed with her after her stomach was pumped and while arrangements were being made for her admission to the psychiatric intensive care unit. This took nearly two hours. During this time, on the other side of the cloth curtain in the ER room, we could hear a woman moaning in pain. Mary said the other woman was dying, and she wished it could be *her*, instead. I was intensely involved with Mary, and paid no attention to what was happening on the other side of the curtain. At one point, Mary told me she would *not* leave the hospital alive. She would find some way to kill herself for sure. The look in her eyes when she said this was cold and deadly. There had been several suicidal episodes before, but this one was different. I knew she was determined, and I started to cry. It was my spontaneous, instantaneous response. This person I cared deeply about was going to die, and I was grieving. Truly I did not believe I would see her again.

With tears flowing down my cheeks, I engaged deeply with Mary about her life, her death, her choices, our relationship, and others who loved her. It was a time of "theology in the trenches"—and it was some of the most profound work I have ever done. It came "*through* me," and was not "*of* me." I utilized every *single* thing I had remembered, thought, and felt about Mary's entire life all weekend long as I had reviewed her entire history and every aspect of our theraputic process together in order to write my chapter. *Just in time*, I was given all the information I would need to have available in ways I never would have imagined. Immersing myself all weekend long in Mary's process of therapy also illuminated for me the depth of that process and the strength of our bond. That bond and that strength (along with the love of God) allowed me to remain right with her, in the depths of her agony. If she *was* going to die, I would *not* abandon her (nor would I choose for her); I was going to love her and believe in her as best I knew how, right up until the very end. Writing the chapter, each word of which I needed to have in my mind and heart and on the tip of my tongue, was an incredible gift *just in time*.

As soon as Mary left the ER to be admitted, a man whom I did not know came to me from the other part of the room, and asked me to come with him behind the curtain. His wife was lying on the other bed, looking terrible. To my shock and horror, I discovered that the woman we had heard moaning in great pain was another person I knew and loved, a former client. All the time I had been talking with Mary, this other woman had recognized and heard my voice, and I had been ministering to her as well. I learned she was having crushing chest pains; later I learned that she had been having an heart attack all this time. A few hours later, after I finally went home from being with her as well, she almost died.

The next morning, as I opened my newspaper, again to my shock and horror, I learned that at the *exact* time I had been in the ER ministering to these two clients, a third client of mine who had been sick for some time actually died. I wondered if, in ways far beyond my knowing, I had also been ministering to him in his passing as well. I did with the two women what I would have done with him, if I had known he was dying. Only later did I remember my dream about the hearse. Only this third client actually needed a hearse. But my dream was about my ministry in life and death. That fateful evening I stood on the bridge between the two, as two women I cared deeply about hovered between life and death in different ways. They both survived, and are both now doing well.

That evening in the ER remains forever indelible in my memory. The whole evening might have turned out differently, if I had not just written the book chapter and received its incredible gifts *just in time*. I'll never know how different it could have been, only how it was. But I'll always believe that the timing of writing that chapter was *no* accident.

Pastoral care deals with life and death issues, though not always as dramatically as in the above two instances. The well of our faith needs to be deep, in order to deal with the severity of the issues which confront us, in our personal lives as well as in the persons for whom we care. The ministry of pastoral care is certainly a divine calling.

Theological Reflection

The theology present in these pages is "theology on the hoof," as Wayne Oates was fond of saying in my graduate school days. This is true, *practical* theology. These people in the trenches have come up long enough to reflect and write from their lived experience. Their lives are based on principles and beliefs that are grounded in their identity as Quakers. Quakers have never been very concerned with codified theology or with being theologically consistent. The lived beliefs reflected in this book can be summarized, however, in three theological statements, which emerged from a brief conversation with Dan Snyder, one of the chapter contributors:

First, these chapters reflect *a palpable sense of the Divine Spirit.* "From the beginning the Society of Friends has been a movement of the Holy Spirit,"[1] and that remains true today. Living deeply in the life of the Spirit makes possible caring for others. The Spirit also refreshes us in our ministry and makes possible good self-care.

Living in the Spirit also entails a vulnerability to others and to unseen directions to one's own life. Carolyn's openness with her client who took the pills goes beyond detached professionalism! After the incident, she saw the Spirit's preparation of her for what was to occur.

Second, good Quaker pastoral care as described in this book, *incarnates the presence of God.* Mickey Edgerton's wonderful stories of ministry with hospice patients demonstrate how she brought God's presence into lives that were broken and alienated. With her gentleness and caring, these patients were enabled, with God's help, to die more whole than they had been living. Mickey's presence in some way embodied God's presence.

Third, good Quaker pastoral care *incarnates grace.* "Grace in Christian theology refers to the unconditional, comprehensive, empowering love of God for the world."[3] The incarnation of grace is the way the presence of God comes to us. The second and third statements are aspects of the one reality of God's presence in our midst. While the second assertion deals with the *fact* of God's presence in the pastoral care relationship, the third assertion describes the *way* in which God's presence is primarily experienced in the relationship.

The way in which the pastoral care giver listens and responds, profoundly respects the other person, and faithfully follows through in the relationship, embodies the love of God to that person. Particularly striking is how many writers talk explicitly about love. Maureen Graham states forthrightly that "Pastoral care is about loving. . . ."[3] Modern pastoral care literature generally does not speak about love. Our Quaker faith seems to draw such a response from us. This loving response also draws us beyond professionalism, while remaining aware of boundaries and roles.

This grace is mutual, since we care givers often find ourselves being given to, in ways that the other person may not even be aware. We find again and again that we are loved by a Source greater than ourselves and that we are enabled to embody that love to others in helpful ways. Grace happens.

Notes

1. Wilmer Cooper, *A Living Faith: An Historical Study of Quaker Beliefs* (Richmond, IN: Friend United Press, 1990), 17.

2. R.J. Hunter, "Grace and Pastoral Care," in *Dictionary of Pastoral Care and Counseling,* Rodney J. Hunter, General Editor (Nashville, TN: Abingdon Press, 1990), 468.

3. Maureen Graham, "Quaker Ministry and Pastoral Care: Centered Presence, Relational Engagement, Prophetic Witness," *Out of the Silence* (Wallingford, PA: Pendle Hill Publications, 2001), 7.

Select, Annotated Bibliography

1. Addictions and Friends Ministry

Al-Anon. *Courage to Be Me*. Virginia Beach, VA: Al-Anon
Family Group Headquarters, Inc., 1996.

> *Courage to Be Me* reaches out to teenagers living in alcoholic fami-
> lies and introduces them to Ala-teen. The Steps and Traditions are
> explained in detail and personal stories are included. Questions and
> exercises give the reader an opportunity to explore how their lives
> are affected by family alcoholism.

Alcoholics Anonymous. *The Big Book*, Third Edition. New
York, NY: Alcoholics Anonymous World Services, Inc.,1976.

> This basic text for Alcoholics Anonymous, originally published in
> 1939, remains unchanged. The book explains how AA works, dis-
> cusses alcoholism, and recounts 44 personal stories.

Alcoholics Anonymous. *Twelve Steps and Twelve Traditions*. New
York, NY: Alcoholics Anonymous World Services, Inc., 1991.

> The contents include in-depth definitions of the twelve steps and
> twelve traditions of Alcoholics Anonymous.

Dorris, Michael. *The Broken Cord*. New York: Harper and Row,
1989.

> Michael Dorris was a Native American scholar who adopted a child
> suffering from FAS - fetal alcohol syndrome. FAS causes permanent
> developmental problems in children. This was the first book written
> for the general reader that describes the devastation of this prevent-
> able syndrome.

House Made of Dawn, produced and directed by Richardson
    Morse based on the pulitzer prize novel "House Made of
    Dawn" by Scott Momaday, New Line Home Video, 1996.

> Abel, a young Native American man, struggles to find his way in Los
> Angeles. Alcohol, marijuana, and ritual combine in his attempt to
> find himself in the world of the White man. A contemporary story,
> it exemplifies the difficulty of leaving one's culture and the strong
> role that ritual and spiritual practice play in psychological well-
> being and healing.

Jorns, Auguste. *The Quakers as Pioneers in Social Work* (studien
    uber die Sozialpolitik der Quaker). Translated by Thomas
    Kite Brown. New York: Macmillan, 1931.

> "The Battle Against Alcoholism," chapter three of this out-of-print
> book, is well worth hunting down in a used book store or Friends
> Library. Its eleven pages provide an overview of Friends efforts against
> alcoholism in England and the United States. Other chapters may
> be interesting to readers curious about Friends' reform efforts.

Kurtz, Ernest. *Not God: A History of Alcoholics Anonymous.*
    Center City, MN: Hazelden, 1979 (expanded edition, 1991).
    436 pp. Call 1-800-328-9000 to order.

> This stands out as the best overall account of the history of Alcoholics
> Anonymous. This volume assembles a wealth of resources and presents
> them in a highly readable style. The title is a restatement of
> "First of all we had to quit playing God," from Alcoholics Anonymous.

Levering, Robert. *Friends and Alcohol: Recovering a Forgotten
    Testimony.* Pendle Hill Pamphlet # 313. Wallingford, PA:
    Pendle Hill Publications, 1994. 40 pp. Call 1-800-742-3150
    to order this one or subscribe to the series.

> In addition to reviewing the history of Friends' testimonies and
> efforts regarding alcohol, Friend Levering poses timely questions about
> the subtitle. He makes a convincing case for restoring the traditional
> Friends' testimony against alcohol, for the example it provides.

May, Gerald. *Addiction and Grace*. New York: Harper and Row, 1988.

May believes addiction is a maladaptive attempt to have control over our lives. Real recovery comes when we surrender to grace and learn to come to terms with ourselves and the world.

Milam, James R. and Ketcham, Katherine. *Under the Influence, a Guide to the Myths and Realities of Alcoholism*. New York: Bantam Books, 1988.

First written in 1981, *Under the Influence* has been credited with being the most important breakthrough in the field of alcoholism since AA. Stressing the physiological susceptibility to the disease of addiction, the stigma of psychological weakness is removed. The recovery process is thus supported by removing the disease from the arena of moral weakness and guilt. A treatment program is outlined.

Orr, Judith L., "Hard Work, Hard Lovin', Hard Times, Hardly Worth It: Care of Working-class Men" in *The Care of Men*, ed. Christie Cozad Neuger and James Newton Poling. Nashville, TN: Abingdon Press, 1997.

Orr discusses the use of alcohol among working-class men as a symbol of personal freedom and as a means of experiencing inexpensive celebration. Substances may also numb the pain of working-class men who are not quite making it or feeling man enough in today's society.

Quaker Life issue, "A Different Spirit," June, 1997 (Series XXXVIII, #5). To order, contact Quaker Life, 101 Quaker Hill Drive, Richmond, IN 47374-1980, 765-962-7573, or e-mail at QuakerLife@xc.org.

This issue of the Friends United Meeting magazine focuses on drugs and alcohol, providing seven articles ranging from a "Report on Alcohol Abuse Worldwide" to "Nairobi Street Children." For a historical overview, Sabrina Reynolds Newton's "Quakers on Alcohol" covers some fascinating worldwide high points.

West, James W. *The Betty Ford Center Book of Answers*. New York: Pocket Books. 1997

West presents a series of commonly asked questions and answers them. Questions relate to the physiological and psychological affects of alcoholism and addictive chemicals. Dual disorders, early signs of addiction, intervention, and new treatments are addressed in a simple, straightforward manner.

II. Care Giving: Foundations

Kelsey, Morton T. *The Other side of Silence*. New York: Paulist Press, 1976.

A warm but practical manual for meditation from a Christian perspective. Invites the reader/seeker into a loving relationship with Christ.

Kornfeld, Margaret. *Cultivating Wholeness: A Guide to Care and Counseling in Faith Communities*. New York: Continuum, 1998.

Using the image of the garden, this book lays out a holistic approach to pastoral care that is deeply grounded in the Spirit while providing concrete guidance and the latest information in the field. The centrality of the faith community lies at the heart of this book. The author is a sojourning member of a Quaker Meeting, where her husband is a member.

Nouwen, Henri. *Reaching Out*. New York: Doubleday & Co. Inc., 1975.

A book born out of Nouwen's search for authentic Christian spirituality. The results of the journey are not easy answers but painful awarenesses that paradoxically give hopeful signs of meaning.

III. Children and Pastoral Care

Boulding, Elise. *Children and Solitude*. Pendle Hill Pamphlet 125, Wallingford, PA: Pendle Hill Publications, 1983.

This is a brief, scholarly, and easy-to-read reflection by a professional sociologist who is sympathetic to and knowledgeable about children in Quaker Meetings.

Capps, Donald. *The Child's Song: The Religious Abuse of Children*. Louisville, KY: Westminster John Knox Press, 1995.

In an age when we tend to use the word "abuse" to refer to sexual deviancy, we often forget that the roots of such behavior can be found in teachings that foster shame and discomfort in children and adults with regard to their bodies. A healthy spirituality fosters a more en-riching sense of being embodied spirits.

Jones, Rufus. *Finding the Trail of Life*. N.Y.: The MacMillan Company, 1926.

Rufus Jones continues to be one of the best-loved philosophers of Quaker spirituality, as he adapted traditional modes of spiritual growth to the demands of a modern, busier, and more secular age.

Loukes, Harold. *Friends and their Children*. London: George G. Harrap & Co. Ltd., 1958.

Loukes was a very erudite Quaker writer of his time, and this book deserves to be reissued. The context of his theories may be a bit dated, but his commitment to traditional resources for spiritual growth is inspiring.

IV. Family Therapy and Spirituality

Doherty, William. *Soul Searching; Why Psychotherapy Must Promote Moral Responsibility*. New York: Perseus Books, 1995.

This short and clearly written book explores the ground between and morality, and it calls for the inclusion of moral discourse in the practice of psychotherapy and the cultivation in therapists of the virtues and skills needed to be moral consultants to their clients in a pluralistic and morally opaque world.

Jordan, Merle R. *Reclaiming Your Story: Family History and Spiritual Growth*. Louisville, KY: Westminster John Knox Press, 1999.

Jordan examines the negative god-images that sometimes form in our families of origin and suggests ways that we can free ourselves so that spiritual growth is possible. Includes practical exercises.

Pipher, Mary. *The Shelter of Each Other; Rebuilding our Families*. New York: Random House, 1996.

A thought-provoking and affirming book with a strong integration of clinical and spiritual values. Pipher charges family therapists with looking at the whole family and all its needs, including building good character, controlling consumption, violence and addictions, diffusing anxiety and coping with stress.

Walsh, Froma, ed. *Spiritual Resources in Family Therapy* New York: Guilford Press, 1999.

A ground-breaking book that provides legitimacy for the place of spirituality in clinical practice of family therapy, these chapters examine the topic from a variety of perspectives. A pastoral counselor/educator has written one chapter.

V. Healing

Capra, Fritjof. *The Tao of Physics*. Boston: Shambhala, 1991.

Explores the relationship between modern physics and spirituality.

Hodges, David. *George Fox and the Healing Ministry*. Surrey, England: Friends Fellowship of Healing, 1995.

Accounts of George Fox's healing experiences of himself and others.

Moyers, Bill. *Healing and the Mind*. New York: Doubleday, 1995.

The companion volume to Moyers' PBS television series by the same name. Moyers speaks with a number of practitioners of different complementary therapies and draws conclusions about how the mind works with the body to facilitate healing.

Ken Wilbur, *No Boundary: Eastern and Western Approaches to Personal Growth*. Boston: New Science Library, 1979.

A look at combining western and eastern approaches to psychology and how they can be used together.

VI. *"Opportunity" And Pastoral Care*

Drayton, Brian. "On Opportunities," *Friends Journal*. September 1990: 8.

A good description of the historical background and contemporary possibilities of the opportunity.

Rushby, William. "Cyrus Cooper's Memorial and the Free Gospel Ministry," *Quaker History* 89 (Spring 200):35-36.

This entire article, which begins on page 28, describes the classic style of Quaker ministry that survived among Conservative Friends into the twentieth century. The specific reference cited above gives examples of the opportunity during the twentieth century. Almost any Quaker journal written during the eighteenth or nineteenth centuries will have at least some references to this once common Quaker practice.

Taber, William. "The Opportunity as Ministry," *Quaker Life*. October 1988: 29.

A description of how one contemporary Friend uses the opportunity in ministry today.

VII. Pastoral Care Across Cultures

Augsburger, David. *Pastoral Counseling Across Cultures*.
   Philadelphia: Westminster Press, 1986.

> This classic book is the result of the author's experience in over a
> dozen different countries of the world. Solidly grounded in theology,
> Augsburger includes a multitude of insights and studies from wide-
> ranging disciplines. While not a quick read, it is the starting place
> for any serious work on this topic.

van Beek, Aart M. *Cross-Cultural Counseling*. *Creative Pastoral
   Care and Counseling Series*. Minneapolis: Fortress Press, 1996.

> This small paperback is a more practical guide for care givers in cross-
> cultural situations. Written from the author's experience in the south-
> western United States and in Southeast Asia, the book offers ways
> to combine specific skills into one's own theology and view of the
> world.

Culbertson, Philip, ed. *Counseling Issues & South Pacific Communities*. Auckland, New Zealand: Accent Publications, 1997.

> This edited book includes chapters on the way pastoral care and coun-
> seling is done by indigenous people in various island countries in the
> South Pacific. The introduction is an excellent overview of cross-
> cultural issues in pastoral care.

VIII. Quakerism and Pastoral Care

Pastoral Care Newsletter. Published quarterly by the Care and
   Counsel and Meetings and Members of Philadelphia Yearly
   Meeting, 1515 Cherry Street, Philadelphia, PA 19102
   (To subscribe, contact Steve Gulick, 215-241-7068 or
   HYPERLINK "mailto:steveg@pym.org" steveg@pym.org).

This newsletter is designed for persons who provide pastoral care in unprogrammed Friends Meetings. Each issue has a theme, with an article on the theme and a list of further readings. Can also be helpful for persons who are interested in learning more about the Quaker context and shape of pastoral care in unprogrammed Meetings.

White, Zoe. *A Quaker Theology of Pastoral Care*. Wallingford, PA: Pendle Hill Publications, 1988.

A small booklet written by the author following her experience in Clinical Pastoral Education, it reflects theologically and experientially on a Quaker way of doing pastoral care.

9. Quakerism Introduction

Cooper, Wilmer A. *A Living Faith: An Historical Study of Quaker Beliefs*. Richmond, IN: Friends United Press, 1990.

An excellent introduction to what Quakers believe, including a short history of the Religious Society of Friends.

Punshon, John. *Encounter with Silence: Reflections from the Quaker Tradition*. Richmond, IN: Friends United Press, 1987.

This book looks at the use of silence among Quakers, and includes some practical help with those who are new to sitting in worship for an hour with no programmed activities.

10. Worship and Pastoral Care

Anderson, Herbert and Foley, Edward. *Mighty Stories, Dangerous Rituals: Weaving Together the Human and the Divine*. San Francisco: Jossey-Bass Publishers, 1998.

Pastoral care givers, ministers, and worship leaders are challenged to use storytelling in a worship service or ritual setting to bring meaning to our lives and draw us closer to God and one another. The authors, a Roman Catholic and a Lutheran, specifically look at how life events such as weddings, funerals, leaving home, miscarriage, adoption, divorce, withdrawing life support, and Sunday morning worship can be made more meaningful through storytelling. The book itself is woven together with life-stories allowing the authors' theories to come alive.

Willimon, William H. *Worship as Pastoral Care*. Nashville, TN: Abingdon, 1979).

Written from a mainline Protestant perspective, Willimon suggests that all church services (even Friends) have a "liturgy" of sorts. This liturgy is strengthened and the worship community deepened when worship leaders are intentional about the variety of ways in which Christian worship and pastoral care support one another. Willimon illustrates this by providing an in-depth look at four acts of Protestant worship: the funeral, the wedding, baptism, and the Lord's Supper.

Out of the Silence

was composed on a Power Macintosh 7600 computer using
Adobe Pagemake 6.5 and Adobe Type Faces: Goudy for text
and Adobe Caslon Ornaments for incidentals.

The book was printed in the United States of America by
Thomson-Shore Inc., Dexter, Michigan. 60# Gladfelter
Recycled paper was used for this printing of 1,500 copies.

History of the Type Faces

Goudy has to be one of the most beautiful typefaces ever
designed, truly achieving the quality of elegance. Flaring
graceful serifs invite the eye to follow along forever. In 1915,
Frederic W. Goudy designed Goudy Old Style, his twenty-
fifth typeface, and his first for American Type Founders. Flexible enough for both text and display, it's one of the most
popular typefaces ever produced, frequently used for pack-
aging and advertising. Its recognizable features include the
diamond-shaped dots on i, j, and on punctuation marks; the
upturned ear of the g, and the base of E and L. Several years
later Lanston Monotype commissioned Frederic Goudy to
design heavy versions of Goudy Old Style—Goudy
Heavyface and Goudy Heavyface Italic were released in 1925.
The huge success of Goudy's typefaces led to the addition of
several weights to many of his typefaces.

Book Design by
Eva Fernandez Beehler and Rebecca Kratz Mays